Read This Only
to Yourself

Read This Only to Yourself

THE PRIVATE WRITINGS
OF MIDWESTERN WOMEN,
1880–1910

Elizabeth Hampsten

Indiana University Press / *Bloomington*

To the brave women in this book,
and to Florence Clifford

Library of Congress Cataloging in Publication Data

Hampsten, Elizabeth, 1932-
    Read this only to yourself.

    Includes index
    1. Rural women—Middle West—History.
2. American prose literature—Middle West—Women
authors. I. Title.
HQ1438.A14H35   1981   305.4'2'0977   81-47008
ISBN 0-253-34836-6   AACR2
    2 3 4 5 86 85 84

Contents

PREFACE
Pen in Hand

Although there is a strong tradition in American letters of working class men as authors (James Baldwin, Arthur Miller, Theodore Roethke—the list would be long), among women, Tillie Olsen's name is one of the few that come to mind. Willa Cather, Emily Dickinson, and Mary McCarthy all grew up in families of the upper middle or professional classes, and they were better educated than their contemporaries, men or women. Our idea of the writing style of the late nineteenth and early twentieth centuries is the style of men or of privileged women; we hardly know how working class women have written. Even recent historical studies based on women's private writings, like *The Bonds of Womanhood* by Nancy F. Cott or Carroll Smith-Rosenberg's essay on friendships, are based largely on writings by women of the upper middle class. And May Pinzer, of *The Mamie Papers*, although formerly a prostitute, wrote that she wanted to return to her first profession as a journalist.[1] The literature of working class women is the literature of a class of women who have been silent, and it bears few resemblances either to public literature of the period or to the private writing of men or of upper class women. To reach it, one must read letters and diaries, for the thoughts of working women are recorded nowhere else.

For that matter, *no* women's everyday writings—letters to friends and relations, jottings in a copybook—have been well read or systematically kept. Most heirs and archivists worry first about manuscripts' "historical value," as they put it. If memorable events or notable persons are referred to, or if the writer participated in a public drama, then her papers will pass for history. Few manuscripts

by women have survived in this way, not only because women participated less than men in public affairs, but also because they put so
little emphasis on those events when they did take part. For all
practical purposes, private writings of all women, regardless of their
station in life, have effectively been obscured.

Studies using private writing typically have been organized around
the life of a notable person or of a group (women who corresponded
with George Bernard Shaw, records of the Oneida Society), or
around an important event (the Civil War, the Gold Rush), and these
studies have sought out from historical archives only those parts of
private writings that apply to the topic, omitting the rest. My own
effort is the reverse. I have wanted to read entire collections and to
stay in one place, reading whatever I came across no matter what its
subject. My reading falls in the fifty-year period from 1860 to 1910,
most examples dating from 1880–1900. Although these years coincide with major settlement of the Northern Plains, I have not particularly sought out descriptions of that experience; in fact many
writings reflect quite other ways of living. Staying in one spot, as it
were, and reading all that was available by any given writer, I sought
to learn what women were saying about their lives at the turn of the
twentieth century.

If nothing else were to persuade me that reading private writings
by ordinary women is not a whimsical exercise, it would be the
seriousness with which these women took their own writing. Along
with exchanging photographs and scraps of dress material, writing
enabled women to keep in touch with one another. It was important
to write well in order to sustain one's audience, so it would continue
to nourish such creative expressions. "You spoke about your letters
not being very interesting. Now Mamie I think you write a nice letter
and I am always pleased to hear from you. In regard to your writing
you write all right"—encouragements from Gwendoline Kinkaid in
Palmyra, Wisconsin to Mamie Goodwater in Grand Forks, North
Dakota (9–4–95). These were cousins who wrote back and forth for
many years;[2] their letters, like so many, were clearly a substitute for
conversation—"How I would like to see you. I could talk better than
write" (Gwendoline to Mamie, 6–29–98)—and of course they were
read aloud, and passed on to other households to be read aloud
again. Always privacy was a difficult achievement in the full households women describe, and yet letter writing allowed a certain sur-
reptitious privacy, and scattered throughout Gwendoline's letters are

such phrases as "Read this only to yourself," "Don't read aloud." "Keep these things to yourself," and sometimes requests for a separate, secret reply in addition to the main letter.

Sometimes writing was virtually the only activity women could call their own, and they describe writing after the rest of the household have gone to bed or before anyone was up in the morning. Small children could transform writing a letter into an athletic event: "If I make many blunders don't wonder for Lelah is playing and talking to her dolly, she comes up to me every four minutes and wants to write too. O she is a little witch if there is one she learns very quick and has got good memory" (Jane Freeland to Eliza Keyes, 3–23–60).[3] Addie Coss in Wasioja, Minnesota, and Mamie Goodwater were cousins who began corresponding when Mamie was sixteen years old, evidently before they had met. Letters, pictures, even bits of hair were important rituals in a growing intimacy which included these letters from Addie to Mamie and continued for a lifetime.

> I have looked for your picture but haven't seen it yet but want to. I am going to have mine before long and if you will send me yours I will send mine. But you won't see anything very pretty. We all have red hair but the baby his is dark and black eyes. Edie has dark brown eyes and auburn hair. I am the lightest one, both us girls' hair is curly, but I don't like red hair, have scolded more about it than anything else. What color is your hair and eyes. Both of Sam's children have red hair and Sumner's little girl has white hair. (Addie to Mamie, 8–1–87)

> Well it is getting late and I have got another letter to write so I must close for this time. I hope I may hear from you often and I wish I could see you. I know I should like you by your letters. I will send you a piece of my *Bangs* and when you write send me a piece of your hair Good night from Addie. Write soon. (Addie to Mamie, 2–13–88)

> You wanted me to send my picture. I had to give them to folks that had give me theirs but I am agoing to have some more finished and will send you one sure. I wanted to send you one when I had them but everybody was on hand and I had to give them up or make them mad. I had two kinds taken, one with my hair on top of my head and one with my hair down (side view). I have nice hair if it wasn't red. I would give anything if it was the color of yours. My hair is 40 inches long, how long is yours. (Addie to Mamie, 3–18–88)[4]

Photographs of the kind Addie mentioned were printed on sturdy postcard-size cardboard, with the photographer's name prominently printed at the bottom. Exchanging photographs had its etiquette, as Gwendoline Kinkaid, another cousin, reminded Mamie Goodwater:

"I don't know what makes people so queer not to write when any one sends them a picture. You know we always write right back when any of you send us a picture" (9–4–85). There is an appropriate ring of resolution to the cliché phrase "I now take pen in hand."

These writings happen to be "in" North Dakota; that is, they were mailed from elsewhere to people residing in that state, or exchanged among residents. All the writers seem to be representative of women and men living in rural parts of the United States at the turn of the twentieth century. None writes as though she thought she were peculiarly different from kin and acquaintances, or that North Dakota was an eccentric place to live. Because these writers did not appear to see anything remarkable about themselves, their manners, or their place of living, I see no reason to either, and therefore offer the documents described in these pages as representative of late nineteenth century America.

In some respects, however, these writings may reflect special qualities for having been located in North Dakota. For one thing, I have not yet detected in North Dakota an urgent sense of regional history. Abandoned implements lie scattered about farm yards and fallow fields, and immigrant wagons can be discovered in overgrown shrubbery. I know of no comprehensive public collection of agricultural implements, machinery, and transport vehicles, although, since the 1976 centennial, a number of towns have expanded their historical societies and model villages. But so far North Dakota has not been aggressive about preserving and reconstructing its past, and for some purposes, that modesty may be all to the good: a certain casualness prevails.[5]

Time also has been advantageous to my desire to read private writings in North Dakota. Because settlement occurred barely a hundred years ago, some infants of those first arrivals are still alive (longevity being characteristic of continuous North Dakota residence). Furthermore, although half of the original immigrants to the state moved on, many of those who remained have tended to stay put on or near the family farm or town, a stability that favors people keeping things. And many have. Collections of letters and diaries spanning many years are to be found both in state archives and in private hands, with more, one hopes, to come. Some of these collections are notable for not having been tampered with and still include items that people who worry about family propriety would likely have got rid of. I think that the circumstances by which one acquires manuscripts may be more crucial to their trustworthiness than some readers of private writings so far have considered.

This acquisition is fraught, I am increasingly convinced, with special problems for women. For one thing, as I have said, because it is generally assumed that what is worth keeping is what has historical value, and because historical value is measured by accounts of discrete events (boundaries laid, lands bought and sold), which men are more likely than women to participate in and to describe, the writings of men are likely to be kept and to find their way to permanent archives. How many times has someone said that writings of a particular woman had no historical value because they were merely about daily events?

The writings of men also are likely to be favored for keeping over those of women because of what one might call a principle of derring-do. It is considered admirable in a man to write, as he speaks, with strong feeling, to show off his antipathies as well as his enthusiasms. He is permitted to swear, to attack people, to revel in obscenity, and generally to use language in an aggressive manner. Women are not; should their writing exhibit such characteristics, it is likely to be suppressed, or not taken seriously. I suspect also that the more prestigious the source (book, scholarly journal, deposit in manuscript library) the more likely that any given document will conform to the popular notion of historical worth: that it will primarily be by or about men, that it will refer as little as possible to personal or emotional events, and that it will not be focused on a woman's consciousness of herself. If it is women one wants to know, traditional tools of scholarship are not necessarily prepared to help.

In spite of such detractions, I am inclined to think that those of us now wanting to know women well are being especially favored, and that our allies are growing stronger. Although few archivists away from national centers specializing in women's collections have done well either in acquiring women's writings or in making available what they may indeed have (letters from women to notable men are likely to be filed under "miscellaneous"), individual women informally cooperating with archivists are increasingly able to find collections and to persuade women to share them, a phenomenon that in itself may be a scholarly "discovery" worth taking note of. In addition, there is the recent popularity of amateur history—the publishing of county, town, and family chronicles, the sometimes elaborate obsessions with genealogies, the proliferation of oral histories—these efforts, which vary widely in quality, have generally been disregarded by academic scholars. Many efforts admittedly are hortatory and unreliable, but not all of them are, and at the very least we can sometimes find through them directions to first-hand writings. (Though not always, as when I was told I could not read the diary of a certain immigrant because it was too "personal," and in the same breath that it was being used for a family history. The unrevealed silence in that family I fear will continue, and I mourn it.)

Because the writings to which I am referring are not accessible as published works would be, I have allowed quotations sometimes to be fairly long, so that others can see for themselves what this writing is like. Punctuation I have modified only when that seemed necessary to avoid confusion, because I think that the general arrangement of a sentence closely reflects a person's manner of thinking. Spelling is another matter. No one I know, children included, would spell in an unconventional way if she or he could help it. Spelling does not reflect thinking; it merely shows whether or not someone remembers arbitrary arrangements of letters in a system accepted, since the eighteenth century, for the convenience of printers. Transposing any writing from hand lettering to print is a drastic change that exaggerates irregular spelling, making it look "worse"—meaning foolish, ignorant, quaint, none of which are attributes of any writer referred to in these pages. Therefore I have normalized spelling except where I thought it was more important to indicate what looked like special pronunciations, as "prevenative" for "preventive."

Our culture's habit of belittling private writing by women is meeting increasingly strong resistance now by men and women who keep and do not destroy papers, even though some apologize, saying their predecessors were not known by anyone but family and friends. My being able to comment at all on those writings which were too compelling to throw away owes everything to women and men who valued what they had enough to keep it, and then generously let others read. As many as possible are named in the notes describing the collections for which they have been responsible.

State archivists also have made available their manuscripts and photographs: Larry Remele, Tod Strand, and Frank Vyzralek at the State Historical Society of North Dakota, Bismarck; John Bye at the Institute for Regional Studies, North Dakota State University, Fargo; and Ed Oetting (since University Archivist, SUNY Albany), Colleen

Oihus, and Dan Rylance at the Chester Fritz Library, University of North Dakota, Grand Forks. Translating and copying of some manuscripts has been supported by Faculty Research grants at the University of North Dakota.

I am also indebted to colleagues who read and criticized the manuscript: Hardin Aasand, Thomas Clifford, Richard Hampsten, Annette Kolodny, Charles M. Linkletter, Elwyn Robinson, Sheryl O'Donnell, and Jean Lee.

I

Introduction:
"This Is Christmas Eve and I Am in Tintah"

Fortunately, it is by now a commonplace that women have been badly served in the writing of history. Patriarchy in Europe and America not only has excluded women from centers of power in politics, commerce, arts, and the professions, but it has virtually deleted us from the records as well. Even men agree, and Henry Adams speaks for them:

> The study of history is useful to the historian by teaching him his ignorance of women; and the mass of this ignorance crushes one who is familiar enough with what are called historical sources to realize how few women have ever been known. The woman who is known only through a man is known wrong, and excepting one or two like Mme. de Sevigné, no woman has pictured herself. The American woman of the nineteenth century will live only as the man saw her; probably she will be less known than the woman of the eighteenth; none of the female descendants of Abigail Adams can ever be nearly so familiar as her letters have made her; and all this is pure loss to history, for the American woman of the nineteenth century was much better company than the American man; she was probably much better company than her grandmothers.[1]

This neglect is changing slowly with new scholarship dedicated to retrieving what records women have left of themselves. We are picturing ourselves, catching up on the knowledge of our past, and simultaneously tightening our hold on the present, as public policies increasingly purport to include women in the work force. The millennium is far from accomplished when women can claim full cultural citizenry, but the days of women "pioneers" in this or that hitherto unlikely work may mercifully be closing.

1

It is also generally true, however, that the record of women's endeavors continues to be even more highly selective than men's has been. Women are noticed for *not* being like other women. For if one of the criteria of "true womanhood" is to be supportive of others (men and children) and inconspicuous oneself, then it is not likely that one will be remarked upon as a maker of history. History has traditionally recorded those discrete events that manifest change and progress: battles, the rise and fall of kingdoms and governments, the conquests of warriors or of railroad moguls. But the lives of women, so seldom being given to mobility or progress, have scarcely appeared in traditional history. Nor in the arts. Art is judged by how long it lasts, whereas the most common artistry of women is occasional and impermanent: food cooked, clothes sewn, letters written. These are consumed, worn out, thrown away, and they go out of style or out of date if kept too long. So it is understandable that the usual focus of history upon chronology and change should leave women out, for it is difficult to write about events that do not happen, or about conditions of living that hardly change. Women, by their own account, do all they can to keep stable the lives of others in their care; they work so hard to see that as little as possible "happens" that their writing obliges us to look deeper, to the very repetitive daily-ness that both literature and history have schooled us away from.

With some exceptions (folk art and music, popular culture, debates about "Black English"), cultural history also continues to favor exceptional over ordinary persons, a preference even more strictly applied to women than to men. There are more sociological studies of sex-role behavior in bars than in laundromats, beauty parlors, or supermarkets.[2] The "common man" has long been a patriotic folk hero, but calling a woman common is a way of sneering at her sexuality.

The problem of knowing women at all (let alone correctly, in Henry Adams's meaning) is complicated, and not to be solved by a surfeit of data. Of course critical knowledge will require more quantitative information, like studies of laundromats to set beside those of bars, but there is a fallacy in supposing that "discoveries" about women's lives will burst upon us the way we typically expect new knowledge to do. When Columbus discovered America, or Madame Curie isolated radium, or, should it happen, someone devises a cure for cancer, the event will have come belatedly, for the substances

always were there, the discovery occurring in the eye of the behold-
er. Furthermore, discoveries invariably turn the new into the image
of the old as soon as possible, its meaning and value judged by
connections to the past. The new-found land mass west of Europe
was made desirable by naming it for the old, beginning with the
name of the continent itself. As women become "discovered," part of
the new information will make the hidden known. For instance, the
realization that women habitually have sustained themselves by
friendships with other women in spite of scorn from both women
and men—that "fact" may be new to some observers who now, at
long last, are being persuaded by the sheer quantity of information
made public to that effect. There is a store of knowledge that women
have always "known" about themselves, obvious to them, but not said
aloud. Now to speak of discoveries gives public credence to these old
truths.

   In addition to increased information, it is going to take a strenuous change of mind, public and private, for women to be known,
and what makes the study of women's lives even more complex is
that those lives change in the process of knowing. Scientists are fond
of quoting Pasteur's remark that Nature favors a prepared mind.
The preparation we shall need really to know women, ourselves, is
first of all going to have to include the realization that women do
have individual lives, an idea that apparently gives considerable
difficulty to some people. It has been especially difficult for women,
so important was it to disguise the amount of room we take up.
Successful deceptions have come perilously close to making some of
us disappear, even to ourselves. Yet we need to know that we are
indeed central to ourselves in spite of efforts to pretend otherwise,
and in spite also of the damage those efforts have done to our sense
of presence.

   Western culture for centuries has encouraged men to think that
each is primarily responsible for himself—the I-am-the-captain-of-
my-soul school of thought—which is not to say that service, public
and private, is not an important good also; public good is not
understood to be in irreconcilable conflict with a strong sense of self.
But few men have made that assumption about women, whom they
think of as a class placed aside from the center of collective human
effort, meaning the special society of men. Men typically assume of
other men that each is central to himself, but they assume that
women are satellite to those male centers.

Since it is not taken for granted that women are as palpably real to themselves as men are, that their reality is confirmed largely in their relationship to a man (father, husband, brother, employer, priest, depending on her circumstances), this partial life attributed to women has wide consequences. In the writing of history it has meant that while we read of what "the" government, army, revolution, team of explorers, or whatever group one cares to mention has accomplished, we wonder what women were doing, or how they were affected by the realization that they were not "doing" anything. Literature, freed of the constraints of quantitative analysis, focuses on the qualities of individual lives, and to be sure has had much to say about women, but persists even so in presenting women as exotics, nearly incomprehensible, a limitation that feminist criticism and art increasingly are addressing. Finally, private writings of women ask of us, if we wish to read them knowingly, a special inventive patience. We must interpret what is not written as well as what is, and, rather than dismiss repetitions, value them especially. "Nothing happened" asks that we wonder what, in the context of a particular woman's stream of days, she means by something happening.

Such realizations are becoming more frequent as works of scholarship increasingly avail themselves of private writings of ordinary people, including women. If these books did nothing else, the sheer lengths of their bibliographies of printed and manuscript sources prove that unknown people were not silent after all. These studies have accomplished much in organizing and synthesizing the varied and scattered reportings, but, at least in regard to women's understandings, they have not shown as much curiosity as I think they might. Even those which concentrate on women have tended to present evidence in much the same manner as it always has been done in accounts of men's affairs. A center on women's consciousness still eludes this quantitative approach (miles traveled, diseases suffered, meals cooked).

The Plains Across by John D. Unruh[3] contains much information, based on personal writings at the time as well as on later reminiscences and newspaper reports: public reactions to the westward trek; plans and provisions; how people got along with each other enroute; what help or hindrance they received from scouts, Indians, Mormon settlements, shopkeepers and other entrepreneurs along the way; the hazards of weather, bad health, exhaustion, malnutrition, starvation; dangerous river crossings. Unruh emphasizes constantly changing conditions from year to year in an effort to dispel misconceptions that overland travel was always the same. "Change through time" is his thematic focus.

But where were the women? John Unruh describes crossing the plains as men knew the experience, even though he emphasizes that all migrations except the ones to California in 1849–50 were family journeys. There were thousands of people on these trails, so many that members of the same party could lose each other. There is a fascinating chapter on the importance of physicians and their generosity in volunteering services and even medicines, but, for all the descriptions of diseases and injuries, not a word about childbirth. Unruh has much to say about the economic value to later travelers and to settlers, particularly to Mormons, of the extra baggage that emigrants discarded along the way, but he is silent about the inconvenience and heartbreak for women in giving up stoves, cooking utensils, clothing, to say nothing of pianos and other luxuries. The perceptions of women go virtually unmentioned.

The word "family" in *The Plains Across* means that women are present. A photograph (p. 384) shows two wagons, and, grouped in front of them, three women, four children (a boy and three young girls), and one man. The man, with the two youngest children near him, sprawls across the foreground, the women and girls sit farther back. Unruh's caption reads: "The rigors of the trail are evident on the faces of this family, posing for the camera at the end of a long day." Everyone but the children looks glum. Unless the photographer is a male who was also part of the group, "family" in this case means three adult females, three young females, one male child, and a single adult male, and while that male is placed most conspicuously in the photograph, the family's journey cannot have been unaffected by the presence of the women, at least one of whom would have been obliged to drive the second wagon.

When Unruh does mention women specifically, the effect can be quite astonishing. Thus, in describing people who turned back because of cholera: "Ezra Meeker later recalled meeting a train of eleven returning wagons in 1852, all driven by women. Not a single male remained alive in the entire train" (124). Or, in the chapter entitled "Emigrant Interaction": "On occasion ladies functioned as nurses among the sick in other trains. And, as proof that the amenities of civilized life were not neglected on the plains, Charlotte

Pengra reported in 1853 that she gave her sunbonnet pattern to another lady who had admired it while passing by. Sunbonnets were peripheral, of course. . . ." (143). Or this: "Along the Humboldt River in 1850, after traveling with his goods on his back for a day, Hugh Skinner secured accommodations in an Illinois wagon, thanks to a lady whose kindness led Skinner to remark, 'I have uniformly found the women on the road more alive to the sufferings of their fellow creatures than the men'" (145). It was easier for Hugh Skinner than for John Unruh to think that women were themselves rather than "ladies."

It is one thing, it seems to me, to emphasize the collective nature of the experience of overland travel (or of any other historical phenomenon) but quite another to blur distinctions among people to such an extent that the collective actually becomes the account of only one part of the group, the men. Another anecdote illustrates dimensions of the overland venture that Unruh has overlooked:

> Examples further illustrating the collective nature of the emigrating experience abound, but few are more persuasive than the experience related by Margaret Windsor, a young girl traveling overland in 1852. During the last 500 miles of the journey Margaret cared for a baby whose mother had died en route. At each campground Margaret would seek out a woman to nurse the infant. She was, she later recalled, never once refused. (390)

That child's survival depended on strategies at least as complicated as the behaviors leading to hunting and even organizing the journey, yet John Unruh's book hardly begins to show curiosity about the deeper lives of children and women.

The year 1979 was a banner year for books about westward travel based on personal accounts, and some of these focused on women's writing. *Women and Men on the Overland Trail* by John Mack Faragher describes the eight-month journey that started in the Mississippi River towns of Council Bluffs, Iowa and St. Joseph and Independence, Missouri, traversed the Rocky Mountains in the region of the Great Salt Lake, then branched either to the Snake and Columbia Rivers leading to Oregon, or along the Humboldt River into the Sacramento Valley of California.[4] This desperate enterprise was a family affair, Faragher says, and many journals written during the experience by both women and men, as well as their letters home and later reminiscences, attest to people keeping intact patterns of behavior that were as like their usual habits as possible. That is, people preserved conventional sex roles both in the way work continued to be divided according to what had always been thought suitable for men and for women, and they preserved values that conformed to sex-segregated and patriarchal ways of living common to rural midwestern America in the mid-nineteenth century. Thus men made the primary decision about when and under what conditions to move, sometimes abruptly announcing their intentions without consulting their wives. Women tried to take along as many housewares as they could, but when loads had to be lightened over the mountain passes, pianos and cookstoves invariably were the first items to go, making women's work for the rest of the journey that much more difficult. While traveling, men decided which routes to take, and when they moved in groups, devised ways of organizing themselves into quasi-governmental units which nevertheless did not last long. They walked or rode horseback and almost never rode in the wagons. At the end of a day, they gathered to smoke and talk. For recreation they hunted, a wasteful sport because they could not hope to butcher, much less carry, all the game they shot. Women, meanwhile, sometimes rode with their children in the wagons. They took part in very little social activity, but got up before anyone else to cook breakfast and set to work cooking and making camp as soon as the wagons stopped for the night. Women enjoyed no recreation comparable to hunting. Faragher more than Unruh interprets travelers' reportings for evidence of sex role divisions in activities, social and personal relationships, and private matters generally, paying less attention to such interests of Unruh's as travelers' associations with settlers and Indians, economic factors, logistics. To what extent the emphasis of each author might be attributable to sources (most of them women in Faragher's book, men in Unruh's) is not a question raised by either.

In order to "test the thematic concerns of diarists in a systematic way," Faragher says he used a modification of the anthropological method of content analysis. He scored twenty-two men's and twenty-eight women's diaries on the basis of fifty-three "values," and summarized totals in a percentage table. He found in this manner that men and women wrote with about equal frequency about "practical," "psychological," and "aesthetic" values, and in proportions of nearly two to óne, respectively, in "aggressive" and "amiable" categories. Faragher tabulated and ranked by frequency of occurrence each diary for every value because, he says, he "wanted to consider and study the diaries as whole documents." But this method does not describe the intensity of writing in any single diary on any tabulated value, nor does it observe the interrelatedness of values.

Faragher does not demonstrate how the sum of a column of "values" indeed adds up to knowledge of "whole documents." His tabulations ignore relationships among parts of diaries. He says nothing of length of entries, their frequency, style, diction, language, repetitions, or other criteria usually considered in an analysis of literature. He has not even wondered, apparently, about the credibility of what he has read. Judging from his bibliography, it would appear that most manuscripts have either been published in separate volumes or in periodicals like the *Oregon Historical Quarterly*. Most of his unpublished sources are deposited at the Huntington Library or the Beinecke Library at Yale University. Faragher apparently has not taken into account in his application of content analysis a question that I have found vital to any critical examination of writing that was not intended for publication: how complete is what we have?

People cherish tender feelings toward immediate family history, a fact that obliges any reader of private writing to consider its lineage: the reason for its being written in the first place, the confidence demonstrated between writer and intended reader, the age of both, the obvious omissions. One wants to know in whose keeping each document has been, and under what conditions. And, crucially, is there reason to suppose that parts have been changed or thrown away? The very prestige as well as the acquisition policies of manuscript libraries may affect a collection—does an institution's mere presence preselect relics? People's motives are never simple, and in the case of manuscript donors, vanity and shame may well conflict. The trustworthiness of such materials in printed form may be even more problematical, especially if their publication was undertaken by friends and relations intent on memorializing the writer.

John Faragher discusses none of these issues, an inattention that may account for his strange observation that

> these historical sources allow not even a glimpse at sexuality; this was one of those human concerns too dangerous to commit to paper. . . .
> Indeed, nearly all the evidence one can marshal concerning the relations of midwestern men and women suggests that the notion of companionate marriage was foreign to the thoughts and feelings of ordinary farm folks. (147–48)

Referring to newspapers and folk songs, Faragher finds deep anxiety about marriage and other sexual human relationships, but not, he says, in people's writing: "For all the romance of the trip itself, there was little time for interpersonal involvements between men and women on the trail. People were just too busy for that" (148). It seems to me that either Faragher has lighted on something quite extraordinary about the peculiar exigencies of the overland trail experience, or that all of his sources have been radically and systematically excised, or that content analysis has not spotted a fifty-fourth value. I am astonished at this omission because sexuality is consistently present in the North Dakota-based writings I have seen. Some people write about sex easily, with humor; for others it is a difficult matter; but the signs of "companionate" marriages are not hard to find. John Unruh does not allude to sexuality as such, but he does include a single arresting quotation on the subject when he describes the larger-than-life aspect of reminiscences about the trip: "John Lewis, who thought the sun to be hotter on the plains than anywhere else, suggested that in the West even sexual intercourse took on a new dimension: ' . . . love is hotter here than anywhere that I have seen when they love here they love with all thare mite & some times a little harder'" (397).

Frontier Women: The Trans-Mississippi West 1840–1880 by Julie Roy Jeffrey retraces those combinations of event and myth that Americans have come to think of as "western expansion," this time from the point of view of ordinary women who took part in those ventures.[5] Not surprisingly, both fact and fancy are due some readjustment. If the move west—whether to California gold fields, to ranching, farming, logging, to boom towns, or later to homesteading on the plains between the Rocky Mountains and the great dividing line that the Mississippi River had become—if all this meant the lure of fortune and adventure for men, Jeffrey's large supply of evidence speaks to rather differing perceptions on the part of most women. Reactionary, conservative, backward-looking—the unflattering words (not hers) describe the effect of the many quotations from women's letters and diaries: how reluctant many women were to set off in the first place; how what they were leaving behind was stronger in their imaginings than what they might come upon at the end of the journey; how much effort they put into making personal connections with other women along the way and what a loss it was to part again; how the trip itself was marked in losses of energy and

self-regard because of sunburn, worry, exhaustion, dirt, illness, starvation, as well as prized belongings jettisoned along the way.

Frontier Women revises those general conditions of western living in
the later part of the nineteenth century that do not always substan-
tiate the myths. Even after the initial trek, many people continued to
move several times during their lives, making it seem all the more
remarkable that the few who stayed put in the early founding of
communities were able to give such distinctive character to western
towns. From the beginning more people settled in towns than on
farms and ranches, replicating settlement patterns in the eastern
part of the country.

Westerners also followed national contemporary preferences for
small families and late marriages. The west differed from the east,
however, in showing less interest in religion and in education. Mis-
sionaries and teachers, many of them women, were hard put to earn
a living by founding either churches or schools. Protestant denomi-
nations found it especially difficult to gain a foothold among sparse
settlements, and free public education came late. For most women,
the move west did not come from a desire for drastic change; on the
contrary, Jeffrey affirms, what women wanted was to replicate as
quickly as possible the manner of living they had known before the
trip: "The reality of the frontier, far from rejecting the civilizing
mission, reaffirmed it" (106).

The focus of *Frontier Women* is more sharply on the women themselves than on women as members of family units or as persons
accompanying men. Not surprisingly, Jeffrey finds and quotes wom-
en's writings about sexuality, childbirth, children, and the conjugal
relationships that Faragher said people had no time for ("I dreamed
of seeing you last night and I thought I had a pair of twins'" [68]).
Like the other studies, however, *Frontier Women* presents its sources
quantitatively; we are not privy to the entire body of writing of any
single correspondent. Some quotations suggest that, if we were, we
might see even finer complexities of women's experiences. An
example:

> Some diaries poignantly describe the tears shed by men and women
> alike as they set out. Others have terse, yet equally revealing, entries
> like the one written by Amelia Knight, "STARTED FROM HOME."
> The very brevity conveys the emotion of the scene. (36)

> No wonder a deep sense of loss pervades the records. In her journal,
> Lodisa Frizell asked herself, "Who is there that does not recollect their

first night when started on a long journey, the wellknown voices of our friends still ring in our ears, the parting kiss feels still warm upon our lips, and that last separating word *Farewell*! sinks deeply into the heart. It may be the last we ever hear from some or all of them, and to those who start . . . there can be no more solemn scene of parting only at death." That women so often compared leave-taking to death was at once a realistic assessment that it was "not at all probable that we will meet again on this side of the dark river," as well as a symbolic recognition that the emotional void was like death itself. (37)

I would like to know whether "STARTED FROM HOME" is typical of Amelia Knight's entries; whether all her writing is stark and laconic or whether in general it was as prolix as Lodisa Frizell's, in which case the three capitalized words must astonishingly contrast to the rest. Knowing more about her writing would not detract from the poignancy Jeffrey attributes to the entry, and it might help us to know more precisely what Amelia Knight's feelings were on that occasion. I would like to know more about Lodisa Frizell's writing habits in order to judge how literarily self-conscious she is. Her passage moves one less to recollect experience than literature—the romantic stories of tearful leave-takings, even that famous silent farewell of Christian's in *Pilgrim's Progress*, who flees wife and little children with fingers in his ears so as not to hear their crying. From a consideration of all of her writing that is available, I would hope for an idea of the extent to which Lodisa Frizell shaped her perceptions according to literary models.

Some women who were left behind by their husbands joined them later when both realized that what had begun as a short venture would turn to change for a lifetime.

As Augusta Knapp told her husband, "Do not imagine that I want to come, for I do not, and think that you will be a real goose to stay, for all the gold in the mines; but if you do stay, I am coming, or else I will get a divorce. . . . And whatever you do, Gid, do not *imagine* even that you can live without me, for you cannot and shall not." Gid eventually came home, but other men did not, and their wives went west to maintain their marriages. Many seem to have shared the expectation, however, that the sojourn in the West would be temporary and left their children behind. (119)

Of course this passage does provide an illustrative example of the connection between marriage and gold mining, but by itself it is tantalizingly inexplicit about Knapp familial habits. Are there enough of Augusta Knapp's letters for us to tell whether she is teasing her husband, whether she is given to witticism or is in the habit of feeling slightly superior to him? From so few lines it is hard to judge the probable degree of intimacy revealed, yet they suggest rather emphatically that there is more being addressed than the question of domicile.

Most other studies of private chronicles of unfamous people have, like those by Unruh, Faragher, and Jeffrey, chiefly selected from them quantitative evidence to support one or another observation, paying relatively little attention to journal or letter writers as writers. Carroll Smith-Rosenberg's analysis of letters between women friends in the nineteenth century supports her contention that intimate relationships between women constitute normal, not deviant, behavior. Although she cites many specific letters and diaries among collections of thirty-five families, she does not dwell upon the style of any single writer, or upon the entire body of a correspondence as a literary work. Her concentration is on the one topic: intense writing about love and friendship among women.[6]

The Bonds of Womanhood: "Woman's Sphere" in New England, 1780–1834, by Nancy F. Cott, describes work, domesticity, education, religion, and sisterhood of that period on the basis of women's private writings.[7] While her study, like the others I have mentioned, uses private writings quantitatively, Cott also considers the writers:

> These sources themselves indicate that the study will not investigate the condition of the whole female sex but will be limited to the literate (and, perhaps, writing-prone) portion of it, particularly those whose lives conformed to the ruling norms of American life. The women to whom I will refer throughout this work when I speak of "women" were, with few exceptions, white, middle-class or wealthier, American-born, resident on farms, in rural towns, and cities. These were the women who supplied scholars for female academies and members for evangelical churches, religious voluntary associations, reform movements, and eventually feminist meetings; the kind who read ladies' magazines, who became schoolteachers, who spend their adult lives as mothers of families. (9)

She takes into account also the fact that a high proportion of diary writers were single women, at a time when 90 percent of women married, an apparent distortion until one realizes the upward shift in age of population during the nineteenth century. Most diaries are by very young women, who presumably had more time to write than older married women, although many also regularly continued to write all of their lives. Some diary writing was religiously inspired, an exercise in self-examination and self-improvement. Writers varied in their habits, the length and frequency of their entries. Nancy Cott has been especially sensitive to the complexity of the genre of private writing, its incompleteness and idiosyncrasy, noticing that these works do not "lend themselves to efficient weighting and ordering. One might want to say that women who left diaries were more self-conscious than those who were their peers in other respects and did not do so, but even that element is imponderable because other variables, such as a family tradition of diary-keeping, or particular religious scruples, might have exerted equal influence" (16). She comments interestingly also about the writings of ordinary women in comparison with the two other kinds of sources on women, didactic literature and published works by women authors: "It is worth pointing out that the more historians have relied on women's personal documents the more positively they have evaluated woman's sphere" (197).

Annette Kolodny's book, *The Lay of the Land* (1975),[8] demonstrates the convergence of images of women and images of the landscape in men's fantasies about America, both ripe for settlement and conquest. Her later article, "'To Render Home a Paradise': Women on the New World Landscape" (1978),[9] examines the figurative language of women's private writings. As women confronted the frontier, Kolodny finds, they admired the wilderness, and sometimes feared it, but invariably attempted as quickly as possible to domesticate the terrain into cultivated gardens. Their writings about landscape, not surprisingly, Kolodny finds different from men's. For, she says, whereas "the transformation of the American wilderness implied a projection of masculine mastery over a quintessentially feminine realm . . . the women appear rather consistently to inhabit a gender-neutral landscape, whose garden is neither virginal nor maternal" (40). She cites two diaries in particular, one of a journey from Philadelphia to Louisiana in 1783–84, the other of life on a North Carolina plantation in the first half of the nineteenth century, whose writers "express a kind of frustration at being trapped within landscapes upon which they can make no significant imprint" (42). These writers are literate, educated women, to whom a sometimes artificially poetic language comes naturally even for private expression, and Kolodny is surprised, she says, at "the ease with which the women let go the images upon which the men still struggled" (42). There was Sarah Lloyd, in her teens, living near New Haven, who wrote a letter in 1772 to Rebecca Woolsey that is a pastiche of pastoral clichés, including a verse about a "kind Muse" and an "ambitious Maid." Toward the end: "I fear I must bid adieu to my retirement before I close, a Sprinkling bids me hasten to a Shelter ... I Promise to wait on you in the pretty flowery Islands but company prevented & now it is dark. I think it as well to Stay at home & write" (43). Sarah Lloyd's writing illustrates "the disparate elements of these women's rejection of certain popular image patterns, their sense of discomfort in both the wilderness and the plantation garden, and their consistent attention to the small garden plots of their own cultivation" (43). I admire Annette Kolodny's arguments that all the writers felt as alien from the landscape as her excerpts suggest, but Sarah Lloyd's exuberance—and her capitalization and ampersands—trouble me: might she be joking, showing off in the way of teenagers? Although playfulness does not discount seriousness, I should like to know more about the rest of her letters (admittedly difficult in a single article); perhaps she habitually tried her hand at mannered styles on subjects other than her garden bower.

These growing numbers of studies based on private writings of unknown people are heartening, and my wanting even more from them is not for lack of appreciation for what they have already given. In fact, in hazarding reservations at all, I am awed that so much has been read, knowing how impenetrable private writings can be, beginning with their illegibility and faded ink or pencil. More baffling still can be the manner of writing itself, so disciplined by the self-limiting conventions of modesty, silence, service to others that most women have adhered to. Such reading is by no means an easy or immediately rewarding venture, a perhaps self-evident observation that nevertheless merits brief mention.

What is it we are reading? It is one thing to want to be able to read as many documents as, with the knowledgeable generosity of current families, can be made available. But it is another matter to know what value to give to writings at hand. In extreme and rare instances one stumbles onto passages that are too raw to be read—about pitiful quarrels, for instance. But usually the quest is for a sense of presence. In journals and diaries, letters and scraps, we hear the voices of our predecessors speaking for themselves. We read because we want to know what was on their minds. Historians and philosophers, and certainly poets, have spoken more memorably about the human condition, but often a remark meant for no one in particular can bring us up short. Private chronicles can corroborate public ones; historians record and interpret, novelists imaginatively re-create, and diary writers show us what they meant. We read private chronicles in the expectation that they will be true to life, though we do not expect them to be consistently true to fact or even to be always interesting. Inaccuracy and boredom are true to much of life.

Nor are we necessarily looking for depths of self-knowledge or assuming that what people have to say for themselves will be more accurate than the evaluation of a historian or biographer. In fact, wanting to know what people have had on their minds may lead us to the discovery that some have had very little. The effort to find whatever it is that these voices out of the past can truly tell us is, I think, urgently worth making if we are to retrieve a genuine history of people who so far have largely been unaccounted for. The effort can also, I think, illuminate again the sources of writing itself.

How do people manage to say what is on their minds? What strategies do they use, what ruses even, to overcome inarticulateness—their own or inhibitions they sense from others? Let me apply some general principles of critical reading to one of several copybook volumes of daily entries by Amy Sylvia Cory for the years 1909 and early 1910, when she was living in a small town in southern Illinois, was married to Alfred Cory, a Methodist clergyman, and cared for several small children.[10] Her journals are examples of spare writing—about keeping house, looking after children, occasional short trips by train, making and receiving a great many calls in the line of a clergyman's duty. The entry for 6–24–09 is typical, though slightly longer than most: "Charles B brought butter milk. Went out calling. Thunimans, Corys, Shumans, McPheeters. Robert and Philip went to see the little pups. Philip fell about noon cutting gash in his head. Alfred went to Methodist meeting in evening."

What Amy Sylvia Cory does not write about is also important. She seldom mentions money, but does note supplemental gifts like this day's buttermilk. She names callers without saying what their conversations were about. Occasionally she tallies: "Feb. 15th to March 1st made 150 calls, received 125 calls." Her husband was away a good deal, and she records his departures more often than what he did when he was near by. What she omits from her journal—family finances, information about other people, religious reflections, statements of opinion, her relationship with her husband—also leaves herself out, as do the topics on which she did report: names of callers and people called upon; a few purchases, like an occasional blouse or hat for herself, clothing for the children, food, furnishings for the house; Alfred's meetings and journeyings; her attendance at church or Sunday school or her nonattendance. The one place where she gives herself a little more scope is in writing about the two little boys, Robert and Philip, when she reveals as much as she does anywhere what has been on her mind:

> Children lots of trouble. . . . Robert ran a splinter in his foot. Philip pulled tub of water off the stool. . . . Alfred sick. Philip spilled milk, stewed raisins and broke dish. . . . Philip spilled talcum. . . . Philip smeared the cold cream. . . . Philip cranky. . . . Philip spilled ink, pearline and water. . . . Philip got his finger hurt. . . . Philip fell and nicked his teeth. . . . Philip helped with cleaning by pouring the camphor into the sink. . . . Robert broke window shortly after dinner.

> Philip was so glad that papa was going to let him out of doors to play, that he said, "Papa oor nice boy." . . . Philip very good. After drinking almost a cup full of milk, he said, "I believe I don't like it." Used curling iron for a gun. Philip sang "My fodder had a mule." Robert pretended there was a policeman in the study. Shot him so he would not get Philip. . . . Philip went to Sunday School for the first time. Said "Mr. Powers tell me everything." Robert got himself and Philip ready for bed. . . . Philip saw parade and said they were "marching as to war." . . . While eating dinner Robert was talking about what would happen in case of fire. He said very thoughtfully "Well we would have to get Mamma's hats out."

These remarks present themselves as reflections of what she herself is close to thinking and feeling. There are no theological statements, nothing about her religious opinions, only "Philip, 'Jesus God Almighty.' . . . Philip shot God with his revolver." She does not generalize about being a parent, but she notes the manner in which the children's affections toward herself ebb and flow: "Philip started to run off and when I called him he said, 'Keep still now Mama.' . . . Philip wanted to play with Densil. I told him he could not go, and he said, 'I wun off Mamma. I will' . . . Philip said, 'I love oo Mamma.'" She never writes a complaint against her husband, but the children's remarks focus also on considerable tension regarding their father. Writing down what little children say is permitted to a fond parent:

"Washday. Alfred went fishing with Dr. Butler. Took 9:30m train for Mattoon on way to Nevego. Philip said, 'I get Mamma affer you papa.' . . . Philip said, 'I tell policeman on you papa.' . . . Philip said, 'Want papa go to Guiney, way off.'" Whether *she* wanted him to go or not, Amy Sylvia Cory certainly does not say, but what she chose to write about her children's speeches appears to have been a way for her to express what she did not feel was permitted otherwise.

What I have been looking for are passages that tell me what it is the writers have had on their minds, and the quest has been difficult. So much of the writing gives the appearance of information (dates and times of departures and arrivals, weather conditions, crop prices) without leaving a residue of something said. One misses more often than not a sense of presence, of the event being felt in someone's mind. I do not want to know what happened, I want to know what it was like, and then I will know what happened. Here, from the WPA's Historical Data Project of the 1930s, is an instance of someone who affirms her presence, though she does not reflect. Emma Frances Enger retells her mother's story of a prairie fire:

> She said she took my tiny sister Margaret in her arms wrapped a blanket around her to keep the smoke from smothering the baby, then took me by the hand and followed the men who were fighting with backfires. She said that when she went out of the shack she did not expect to go back to it and find it still there, but it was saved and she was very glad of it as she was tired when she did get back.(HDP)[11]

Tired? No novelist or historian would let it go at that, but this frightened woman does. She cannot afford to think what she is doing in that shack. Her evasions are true to the life of survival, though not adequate to history or fiction.

But sometimes private records miss the presence. One Historical Data Project interview tells of a very young woman who answered an advertisement in a Stockholm newspaper for a housekeeper. She traveled by ship and train to Devils Lake, where she was met by her employer who escorted her, walking, the five miles to his farm, where he was living alone because his wife had left him. The housekeeper had been at work only a few days when the wife returned in high dudgeon and told her to leave. The young woman not surprisingly asked to be sent home, but the farmer could not afford the price of the return journey. His brother George, however, lived down the road and might be persuaded to take a housekeeper. He was. The young woman removed her belongings to George's house, married him, and brought up fourteen or so children. Those, roughly, are the "facts" of a life. But what sort of a person was she to undertake such a venture? What possessed her? I don't know.

As often as not, the facts *are* the life. In the 1890s Mary Larson lived near Elliott, North Dakota, and hauled water for the oxen that her husband drove at the plough.

> She hitched one horse to a wagon on which she had three 60-gallon barrels. She filled the barrels at the well near the Northern Pacific Railroad Section house near Englevale. She had to draw the water from the well by hand by means of a rope and buckets. The rope went over a flanged pulley which was fastened to a frame overhead and an oaken bucket was attached to either end of the rope. She poured the water into a tub and then dipped it from this with a pail and poured the water into the barrels on the wagon. This was a daily job. The distance to where Mr. Larson was plowing was over 6 miles from the well in Englevale. (HDP)

It does not matter, I think, that Mary Larson was talking to an interviewer who wrote down something close to her words. What women wrote on their own behalf primarily captured conversation, and at the same time took careful shape. Here, the name of the town, Englevale, frames Mary Larson's exhausting chore. It comes early and is the last word of the passage. Four sentences begin with the word *she* before a verb. Sentences accumulate lightly subordinated and rhythmical phrases: "The rope went / over a flanged pulley / which was fastened / to a frame overhead / and an oaken bucket was attached / to either end / of the rope." The appalling distance she had to carry this water by horse and wagon, six miles doubled, over and over, appears, in the last sentence, as a different category of information from the rest; it breaks the spell, as it were, and gives distance to the intense close focus of the rest.

Often the oral quality of such writing obscures connections among sentence parts; passages that may puzzle the eye become clear enough to the ear.

> There was a girl named Mary Spencer who used to go to school in the district, who was a very good singer. She used to go out in the coulees and sing, and people said that the birds would come and sit on the ground near her to listen, and that the snakes would do the same. She died suddenly, and no one seems to know the cause of her death, about

1907. . . . Her brother, Tommy, used to play the violin by ear. He learned by stretching strings across the backs of chairs. (Jane Duhamel, HDP)

Or this:

> While the war was in the South. One day his father's sister had fixed dinner the table all set for herself and two daughters, she stepped out when she got back two soldiers were there had gobbled up all the dinner they dident harm any one but helped themselves to everything took the butter which melted in their hands but dident seem to do much harm. She was afraid she would loose her Jewelry so put them in a large neck bottle dug the jar in the garden and placed a cabbage plant over it. (Rosetha Knox, HDP)

Jane Duhamel conveyed a child's eerie mysteriousness in rhythms and repetitions that take precedence over strict sentence parsing: "There was a girl / named Mary Spencer / who used to go to school / in the district, / who was a very good singer." *Named, used,* and *was* give the appearance of parallelism, but are not so, nor are the two *who*'s, the first seemingly more restrictive than the second. "There was a girl who used to go to school in the district named Mary Spencer, who was a very good singer": that cumbersome corrected arrangement loses singing cadences. Order rests on muted and repeated verbs: "used to" again in the second sentence, "would come," "would be," the many *and*'s. "About 1907," like the six miles between Mr. Larson's plowing and the well at Englevale, stands as a coda, a way of releasing the intense description to a more general and less concentratedly emotional context. The improbable cabbage plant performs that service in Rosetha Knox's paragraph, which also has added more and more material details that culminate in melting butter. A Historical Data Project supervisor in the Bismarck office wanted to know in red pencil whether the soldiers were Yankee or Southern, and why did they hold butter in their hands? He was right, of course, this is not the stuff of history, but it is true to the rush and jumble people hold in their memories.

We know that such passages as these are special because they are longer than other parts of the rapid biographical narratives they come from, and they record rare moments among scattered leavings when the sound of a voice seems recoverable. The facts—incredible, bizarre, romantic, embarrassing—are not in dispute, but the voices, collective and anonymous, mumble. Yet now and then, virtually by

accident, someone can be heard although we may not always be sure
to what effect.

The most effective private chronicles I have been reading do not
make a habit of decorative language; they do not play with words or
tell jokes or even make metaphorical comparisons, at least not when
they are intently having their say. A blanket and a shack; barrels, a
pail, a flanged pulley; butter, jewelry, a cabbage plant—these ac-
tualities define lives and dictate a language fit to account for them.
The language is literal, immediate, the grammar scarcely subordinated. It is rare to find any other that rings true, certainly not the
bathetic though arresting opening line of a poetic "Tribute to the
Tongue River": "Flow on babbling Tongue, flow on." It is the unor-
namented language that seems so stunted in parts of Larry
Woiwode's *Beyond the Bedroom Wall,* especially the section called "Burial," or in such a story of inarticulateness as Willa Cather's
"Canuck." It is a habit of language that finds much reflective generalization very difficult.

> She is quite religious and when her twins were born and her mother
> placed them beside her in the bed, she said, "Oh, Mother! How can I
> take care of them both?" and her mother answered, "God will never lay
> a greater burden on you than you can bear." So she took heart. And
> examining the babies found one had been born without a right hand.
> With her mother's motto in mind she carried on. (HDP)

In fiction and poetry of professional writers we take for granted
that heightened language signals heightened feeling, the bursts into
simile and metaphor. Figures of speech extend ordinary speech
beyond itself when that alone no longer suffices. "The Lord is my
shepherd, I shall not want." "Do not go gentle into that good night."
We are used to seeing longing for consolation or anger against death
particularized in metaphorical language, at least in the literature of
high culture. Nor does popular culture differ essentially in this
respect. Advertising imagery harps on transformations. Perfect husbands materialize at the thresholds of golden waxy floors, and beautiful maidens on the hoods of automobiles. Whatever the audience,
most public literature assumes that if the speaker is moved, or
enthusiastic, or worth paying attention to, language will signal that
importance in metaphor, if no more than the Zoom, Bam, Zowie of
comic strips.

There are few such signals in the writings of working women that

I have been reading, almost no metaphors or adjectives even, and few reflective pauses. There are virtually no figures of speech, speech remaining constant in the material. But this is not to say that women's writing lacks strong feeling, only that metaphor does not extend ordinary expression to another magnitude. This writing signals intensity of experience by quantity. It tells us more and more of the same, without comparisons. Literal, factual details, added one after another, take on the force that, in public literature, would fall to metaphor.

Such shying away from figurative language may help to explain why private writings of working women are so devoid of religious language. The years at the turn of the twentieth century in America are remembered as a time of religious devotion, when women were allied with the clergy in "feminizing" American culture, as Ann Douglas has argued.[12] Although churches along with schools, hospitals, and other institutions came relatively slowly to the plains and western frontier, they did arrive to dot the rural landscape of farm states. Indeed, in letters and diaries women often wrote of attending church and prayer meetings, but they did not use the language of religious devotion, not even Amy Sylvia Cory, who was married to a Methodist clergyman. But this absence of words usually associated with devotional habits ought not be taken as a gauge of women's piety or of their interest in religious matters. They say they went to church. They certainly built the churches and supported active congregations. I would connect the absence in their writings of religious sentiments to the absence also of virtually any metaphorical language, and note that only in metaphor can religious sentiment be expressed.

The three passages (p. 27) from Historical Data Project interviews illustrate the manner in which concentratedly nonmetaphorical and material language of working women describes intense experience quantitatively, by accelerated detail. The selections show care for shape and rhythm, even though they evolved by two hands, the person being interviewed and the interviewer who wrote down what was said.

But how complex a life can be revealed, how strong a presence can be felt in a strict adherence to the unmetaphorical style, I should like to illustrate in a longer example, from a journal by Louisa Wanner, who began writing and working at the hotel in Tintah, Minnesota, on December 23, 1903.[13] "This was the day before Christmas eve.

And not a soul was here today. . . . This morning the first thing when I came down stairs the clerk took me and threw me outdoors for getting up a little too late." Not an auspicious beginning. December 24: "This is Christmas eve and I am in Tintah, and the greenest people I ever saw in my life was in church." Though persuaded to join the Christmas program, she was "homesick or rather lonesome for Willie." Louisa Wanner wrote in pencil in a tall, narrow, lined ledger book, the rest of which is filled with monthly accounts, in a finer hand, by William Siebert, who became her husband. (Her references to Willie illustrate what I have said about these writers' willingness to express themselves on sexual subjects.)

In Tintah, on the Saturday after Christmas, she did her chamber, scrubbed, ironed, unpacked her trunk and hung some pictures in her room "so it would look more like home," and she "was over to Dr. Mucklo's after the milk." On Sunday Louisa washed, went to church in the evening, made another trip for milk, and wrote four letters. "I got a hard knock on my left hand today from the dining room door. And a headache I had again the whole day. My cough came back again but not as bad as it was." Monday's account is torn. "Tuesday my ironing day and a lot to Iron I had. It was a cold day too but I kept warm with a hot iron in front of me and the hot stove back of me." There was a large crowd for supper, "and Leo had to wipe the dishes for me, he got mad at me because I did not want to do it alone. . . . I must go to bed now for I am so tired and my feet ache all over pretty near."

That was the first week. The next began with more ironing, bread baking, four letters and "no time to comb my hair today, busy all day long." The next evening she was writing after eleven: "This is the latest I ever went to bed since I am in Tintah. . . . I always go to bed early so I would not be so lonesome. I wrote a letter to Will this evening." On New Year's: "I was awful lonesome for Will that I cried as I was in bed." The next Monday she "had a great big long letter from Will. They did tease me awful about it." A letter from Will arrived every two or three days. "Today was a long lonesome day but this evening I got a letter from Will then I wasn't so lonesome no more."

Two months at the Tintah hotel continued in this vein. She was very tired at night, often cold, had colds and headaches.

> I am awful tired and sleepy tonight. If this keeps up that I have to work so awful hard I will soon be sick again.

I had a letter from Will today I also had time to comb my hair and change my dress today. But I am tired just the same.

Lizzie fine combed my hair this evening. I can not wash my hair because I catch cold so easy and we have no soft water.

Thursday I didn't do not anything I was sick in bed all day. I wrote a letter to Willie while I was in bed.

I got chilblains so bad I couldn't have on my shoes this evening.

This was a cold Saturday and I had on overshoes all day to keep my feet warm in the kitchen.

She found pleasure, too. She bought some material and sewed herself a Mother Hubbard; she visited Annie on her trips to Dr. Mucklo's for milk; she went uptown. "I got my goods for a waist and a new game that is called pit." She and Susie played smear. She went with Vellma to her brother's place "and had a pretty good time," and two days later, "I was over to the farmers after sour milk and we played cards there we had a fine time. The first time I had a good time since I am in Tintah."

Job opportunities expanded somewhat on February 11: "Today I was here ten weeks. I am waiting on the table now, but I don't like that work for there are too many strange men around and I don't like to speak to them." A week later: "Today I had the show troop to wait on again and in the afternoon I polished the silverware and ironed some napkins. I have a bad cold again." Leo, who had begrudged helping wipe dishes the first week, continued cheeky: "Today was a dead day and I didn't do much but ironed and I took my time at that. I wrote a letter to Will tonight. Leo would not let me alone while I was writing as I went out in the kitchen and then he always came and teased me, till I cried so mad I was at him. I wouldn't care if I wasn't writing." But Leo got his comeuppance ten days later: "This evening Leo was setting on the kitchen table so I rubbed my dirty dish rag in his face just because he was acting so smart. He got mad at me that he didn't speak to me no more."

At the end of February she went home. "This was my first day since I came home, and in the morning soon after I got up Will came in. I was awful glad to see him, he stayed all day Sunday. We didn't go to bed till half past three in the morning." The next day: "Will went away again. I could hardly keep my tears back as he left." She rallied, made two waists, skated, went to Renville ("the first time I was in Renville for three months"). The week home is measured in chores. "Today I melted ice to wash my black skirt, and I made my white woolen waist today too. This evening I copied a dialogue for Eddie & afterwards I wrote two letters one to Lizzie and the other one to Will." On Monday she left home again for a job at Saathoff's farm. On March 8 "in the evening Will came over. I was glad to see him." He came over the next three evenings as well, and on the 13th: "Sunday I got the meals & washed the kids after supper, Will came and he stayed till 3 o'clock."

There had been entries every day from her arrival at Tintah on December 23, 1903, through this last on March 13, 1904, but then there is a gap to May 18, when she wrote: "Today I came to Johnsons' to start work. I wrote a letter to Will, but did not mail it yet. Will and I slept in the same room last night and towards morning Will came to bed with me." The next day, May 19: "This morning I got up and helped to get breakfast then I washed the dishes and afterwards I started to take up the carpet, and then clean the pantry. I had the nose bleed bad after dinner. This afternoon I pounded the carpet and afterwards I ground some horse radish. Then I washed dishes and it was 10 o'clock when I got done." This strenuous activity at Johnsons', after the comparative lassitude at Saathoffs', lasted for two more entries. The second reads: "This morning I got breakfast, washed the dishes, ground sausage, then dinner, after fried down meat then mopped, cleaned pig feet, then got supper, washed dishes again, and then sat in the door, and wrote a letter to Eddie. I had the nose bleed again today." And then there is no more, but the renewed energy of these last entries, details piled on details, speak for her feelings after the few hours in bed with Will. Verbs are more energetic than usual: "pounded the carpet," "ground horse radish." Pig feet had not been mentioned before.

Here is a young woman who was employed as chambermaid and waitress at a hotel in Tintah, Minnesota. She left after two months, visited her farm home for a week, and went into service in the households of one and then another farm family, all the while in love (though not using the word) with one "dear Willie." Her writing is laconic, yet she has made us know her and her situation rather well. How has she done it? Largely, I think, by her focus on the moment and on herself within it: *I* and *today* pepper her pages. There is no sense of duty about the entries, none are taken up with what she thinks she ought to be writing about. There is no mention of parents or employers, nothing of what is in all the letters she wrote and received, no description of Will. She never mentions wages. Theodore Roosevelt was elected president in 1904, but, as so often is the way of private writing, public life does not appear. Louisa Wanner is recording at very close range, and all observations begin with her presence. She is herself entirely *there* in everything she writes, even to her bemusing superior sense of herself: "the greenest people I ever saw in my life was in Church," or "I was over to the depot to hear a Graphone, the first time I was where anything was going on."

Why is it Louisa Wanner has succeeded in writing a short diary that is worth reading still? One reason may be fortuitous. Robert A. Fothergill, in *Private Chronicles: A Study of English Diaries,*[14] says that people are more apt to write interesting diaries when their lives are in a period of change. Louisa Wanner had left her parents' home and not yet established her own (which she did after her marriage to William Siebert in November 1904 when she moved to Bottineau and then to a tarpaper shack on a homestead near Greene in Renville County, North Dakota). Although she wrote daily calendar entries for the rest of her life—expenditures and income, weather, letters sent and received, daily activities—there is in them, at least for the two years in the mid-thirties I have also read, much less of the concentrated presence that informs the Tintah journal.

Fothergill also maintains that "diary writing was a habit to which the dissenting bourgeois mentality was particularly drawn," and he illustrates the trend to self-examination by quoting Samuel Johnson: "My general resolution to which I humbly implore the help of God is to methodise my life; to resist sloth and combat scruples. I hope from this time to keep a journal" (25). Although Louisa Wanner does not speak of self-improvement, for introspection is not her style, she implies a manner intent upon an accounting of herself. Her diary is also shaped by its emotional rhythms. It begins with tension between work, friends, and amusements in Tintah and her countervailing colds, homesickness, and fatigue; then moves with some impatience through a visit home and two similar jobs. After the quiet and arresting information that "towards morning Will came to bed with me," the diary ends in a short and energetic spurt of entries longer and more graphic than any previous ones.

Louisa Wanner has composed her diary in consistent and satisfactory language. Her vocabulary refers to objects, to work and physical activity; it accounts for time (the last, the first time something happened). It is only minimally descriptive; it seldom generalizes and then wryly ("the greenest people"). If we read private chronicles such as hers to find out what was on people's minds, we must allow that this Louisa Wanner does not tell us in so many words. Yet she affirms a presence that is so rooted in the concrete and particular that that *is* the state of mind, to which reflective abstractions do not apply. What this writing style accomplishes is to affirm: "This is Christmas eve and I am in Tintah," though so stolid a life, however well affirmed, is little enough to go on. In this style there is virtually no distancing, no reflection on possible meanings or consequences of events. It is the way working class women write; virtually all of them who write at all do so in the manner of Louisa Wanner, and nearly all such writing is likely to be by working women. Its interest is its concreteness; its limitations are the omissions, what the writers do not attempt. These writers of the stolid style tend, however, not to attempt what they cannot adequately write about, and seldom are there false efforts.

When the writing departs to something more abstract, literary and detached, the result can be bathos. Flora E. Baker, for instance, composing her autobiographical essay for the Historical Data Project, indicated that although she had taken part in the settlement experience as a person of working class beginnings, her later experiences had tried to soften them. She looked back through styles of language as well as over the years.

> It has been my privilege to witness the passing of the saloon as the territory of Dakota became a state in 1889, to see roads laid out on section lines instead of taking a star by night in the heavens for a guide and striking off over the prairie to our various destinations. Should it be necessary to make a night trip the winds wafted the howls of the timber wolves and coyotes to our ears, causing shivers to travel up and down our spines. Bravery was a cultivated virtue in every pioneer mother.

The privilege to witness, the star by night in the heavens, the winds wafting, the dangling subjunctive—her language has been displaced from one context to another. She imitates sentimental novels in allegiance to a class other than the one of persons who actually experienced the events she refers to. Louisa Wanner is central to the writing of her weeks in Tintah, but Flora Baker looks on, as though her earlier days had happened in literature, not in actuality. In the case of these writers, the fact of class is important.

Though I hesitate to use the term "class," imprecise as it is and easily given to misinterpretation, I can think of no other that suggests as well the social and cultural "home" of particular persons, their immediate locale in regard to aspirations. The distinction of class is worth making, I think, because it appears to be the one factor that separates some writings from others, that invites sorting them into categories, marked by the distance women describe around themselves, the degree of explanation (to an outsider) they allow. No other division that I can think of does so. Region does not: letters from one sister in Buffalo, New York, are more similar than not to those of a second sister in rural Dazey, North Dakota. Whether women were farming, teaching school, or keeping house in town, their occupation did not make much difference to their manner of writing. Nor did age, or conditions of health, their family situation, even the year. Only women's expectations of social position appear to be reflected strongly in their manner of writing, and it is on such understanding of class that I am finding it compelling to separate the documents I have been reading.

Upward mobility was a rallying cry at the turn of the twentieth century: "Educate and be educated," as Alonzo Choate put it to his Civil War comrade in the hope that both would achieve riches and happiness. Although education, income, and similar indicators affect women's expectations of social position as well as men's, it has seemed to me that their language identifies them as to class more than do other details, and to a more pronounced degree than it does men. Private writing of working class men—Ben Goodwater's letters we shall look at to his wife Mamie about wood-hauling, for example—are easier for a stranger to understand than similar writings of working class women; they allow wider context. One might expect there to be a particularly intimate connection between language and class among women because of women's relative lack of mobility. Men of working class origins have been assimilated into politics and the arts to a greater extent than have either working or upper middle class women, in spite of the latter's access to education. Yet, although all classes of women traditionally are excluded from public life, that bond does not hold to their writing. There are sharp differences: working women like Louisa Wanner write concretely but at a short range; more leisured women like Florence Baker remove themselves farther from the experience they describe, and neither appears to be strongly aware of region. Topography, occu-

pation, political association, the more obvious characteristics of "regionalism" that have been important in identifying many American
male writers, especially in nonurban settings, these do not appear to
affect most women one way or the other. They do not "place"
themselves ethnographically.

I want to explore how women do place themselves by reading
critically and in their entirety the private writings of ordinary persons. Their language bears scrutiny to begin with: for what it
omits—regional allegiances particularly—and for the strands it follows, identification by a social setting and preoccupations with the
near-at-hand, like health, personal relationships, sexuality and birth
control, the dailyness of living. These are the general principles we
can "discover," I think, in a limited informational way. Expanding
them to particular lives will test them out in complicated and interre-
lated particularities. Reading private writings will not in most instances yield satisfying biographies; sketches stop in mid-passage,
like a severed bridge. But large and vivid portions of lives are
available, thanks, often, to accident, or to the fortuitous care of a
family.

II

Little Houses on the Prairie: Class and Place in Women's Writings

Regional Perspectives

What women—the ordinary women whose casual writings I have been describing—have written least about is the one subject that our schooling in literature has taught us to expect writers to begin with: their place, locale, the landscape of wherever they are. These women's writings do not do that; their "place" is not where we had expected to find them. In much of this writing, for all its particularity, it is hard to tell (if the postmark is missing) where the writers are, for they do not bother to tell us in words we are used to. If there is something to be said for "regionalism" as a mode of literature, the term hardly applies, I find, to the private writings of ordinary women, and I think it is important to make a note of that when we describe their literature.

A regional perspective does, admittedly, speak to an insatiable human desire to order and arrange, and it would be convenient to think that mountain, river, state, and county boundaries always corresponded to social groupings, as they have determined political ones. History, topography, climate, and the like have, of course, had consequences for human nature. Pronunciation and word usages can be localized, as can some foods, games, jokes. But I do not think that these go as deeply into people's essential myths as proponents of regionalism think. As a principle in literary criticism, regionalism has largely misjudged and ignored the manners in which women have reported their sense of locale, and most of the time has imposed criteria that are alien to women's perceptions. These matters are worth exploring.

29

Interest in naming regional literature is a fairly recent event in literary history. An early document, *Southern Writers in the Modern World* (1957) by Donald Davies,[1] traces two sequential literary movements of the 1920s through the 1940s that centered among a group of writers and teachers at Vanderbilt University. This is Davies' summary description of "Fugitives" and "Agrarians":

> Our total purpose was to seek the image of the South which we could cherish with high conviction and to give it, wherever we could, the finality of art in those forms, fictional, poetical, or dramatic, that have the character of myth and, therefore, resting on belief, secure belief in others, and, unlike arguments, are unanswerable, are in themselves fulfilled and complete. . . . In the modern world there is no other way for the Southern writer to enjoy and use his rightful heritage, and still be in any true sense a Southern writer. (60)

Davies mentions, besides himself, John Crowe Ransom, Alan Tate, Robert Penn Warren, Caroline Gordon—all examples, he says of "the South against Leviathan, or in more positive terms, the South for the Southern tradition and our heritage of Western civilization" (60). Whether or not there exists a "Southern" writer, I do not want to argue here, but there are two details in the book about which I have reservations. 1) The unanswerable Southern myth Davies speaks of evolves with hardly a mention of the Black experience, and 2) the persons secured by these beliefs were Davies' faculty colleagues at Vanderbilt University. On the first, an image of the American South without Blacks does not convince me. On the second, it is true that the sharing of fruitful personal and professional relations ought to be cherished, but it has happened before without elevation to mythology: among the courtier writers who came to Mary Sidney's house parties at Pembroke in the 1680s; among the suffrage leaders in Syracuse, New York, in the 1880s; among Virginia and Vanessa Stephen's Thursday evenings in Bloomsbury in the 1900s, to name a few varied groups. Though American feminism deserves to be memorialized in Syracuse, no special character of that town has been attributed, that I know of, to the women's movement in America.

Another reservation leads me to observe that, to the extent that regional cultural characteristics may be valid, they are more applicable to men's activities than to women's. Depending on where he lives, a man can be a cattle raiser, a whaler, or a miner; what women do all day long is much the same from one place to another. The cowboy boot has come to symbolize a rather glamorous way of life; as an article of clothing it lessens the danger of one's being dragged by a horse. But men are the ones who ride fences and drive cattle, while back on the ranch women have always worn whatever was in fashion for all women. I object to applying regional criteria to women's experience because these have only reinforced women's already long and institutionalized disenfranchisement from culture, industry, and politics, and because no focus on regionalism takes into account women's observations as they have reported them.

To cite an example: *Northern Lights,* a film about the Non-Partisan League in North Dakota (1918–19), won a gold medal at the 1979 Cannes festival.[2] Partly filmed in Crosby, North Dakota, *Northern Lights* draws its story from a journal kept by one of the organizers of the League, Henry Martinson, who still lives in Fargo. Among a large cast, partly of Crosby citizens, only three women speak: the mother in the principal family who early on is removed to attend to a sick sister in Ohio; a young woman who expects to be married to the central male character; and an older woman, her counselor in patience and fortitude. *Northern Lights* ostensibly describes a brief and intense political movement in a remote region of the country (the attempt to organize grain farmers against the rapacity of railroads), an event which the film takes pains to describe from the participants' point of view, beginning with Martinson's diary. But this apparent focus on the personal underscores, I think, the degree to which women habitually are left out of art as out of politics. In scenes of farm foreclosures, the always-silent women wonder where they will bed and feed their children, and they are the ones who wait while husbands and lovers look for work or stump the countryside organizing, for what they never understand. In their brief appearances, women are usually in the way, and *Northern Lights* gives no lengthy consideration to their lives.

Regional literature characteristically makes much of the landscape: in *Northern Lights* are many brooding pictures of stubble fields sunk in snow. Annette Kolodny's book *The Lay of the Land* explores the association men have long made between women and the land, permitting themselves to conquer, rape, and pillage both.[3] The question remains, how do women see themselves in relation to land? Do they feel a special kinship with the earth, as men's dual exploitation might lead one to expect? My reading of both public and private

writing by women at the turn of the twentieth century tells me
otherwise, for I find women writing of the landscape neutrally if at
all, and working women especially, those living in the midst of what
we call "the land," hardly ever. The land is somewhere outside. No
one says of herself, "I am the grass."

To illustrate: in the summer of 1888, Lulah Cavileer, twenty-four
years old, traveled by carriage from her home in Pembina, now on
the Canadian border in North Dakota, to Walhalla, a distance of
about thirty miles.

> It was a lovely sunshiny morning and we arrived in Neche at noon,
> rested the horses, and from there passed through a lovely wheat coun-
> try. Never saw such immense and beautiful fields. The air was just
> strong enough to blow the numerous mosquitoes away from us. The
> wild flowers looked so pretty, and the birds sang so happily. Part way
> we went through the woods and passed over rustic looking bridges and
> ravines as we approached Walhalla. The sun and clouds cast shadows
> over the mountains, just after a shower, it looked very beautiful, and as
> we crossed the Pembina River again, we followed a wood road for two
> miles and a half on each side of the road belonging to John Everling.
> Walhalla nestles at the foot of the Mountains, looking very restful and
> quiet.[4]

Later a Mr. Miller "drove us up on the mountains, the drive is
beautiful, and the wheat fields were a perfect marvel to me." Hers is
a landscape of travelogues, picture postcards, romantic novels: a
nestling town, pretty flowers, happy singing birds, rustic bridges.
The lack of mosquitoes, the one detail she is precise about (as well
she might be, for other travelers have described very painful journeys) has to do with her immediate comfort. She does note someone's prodigious industry in woodcutting, but she might also have
mentioned the considerable stands of live oak that still cover the
Pembina escarpment. Wheat fields are aesthetic, outside the passing
carriage—lovely, immense, beautiful, a perfect marvel—and have
nothing to do with her. Earlier pages of the same diary describe a
journey by rail with her mother to Minneapolis and Chicago to visit
numerous relations, pay calls, go to tea parties and dinners, opera
and theater. All was social, personal, indoors, and the Walhalla trip
is no different. There she attended a meeting on Sunday school and
church affairs. Lulah Cavileer lived all her life in Pembina, where
her father, one of the initial settlers, was postmaster, but her consciousness was rooted in class and station, not in place, even though

a nearby county bears her family's name. For all of that, the countryside she viewed was benign, and she herself sufficiently content; nevertheless she thought of herself indoors looking out. Lulah had more to say on the encounter with Mr. Miller: "Mr. M. introduced Jennie as *Miss* Cavileer and me as Miss Lulah to some wealthy bachelor farmers living up there. We were conducted to such a lovely bedroom, rafts above our heads and curtains made of sheet and spreads as partitions between other beds." Her landscapes are never that precise.

As a middle class educated woman Lulah Cavileer resembles another whom people know better, Willa Cather. The depth of Willa Cather's regard for Nebraska settler families in *My Antonia*[5] is indistinguishable to me from the other woman's distant gaze over the landscape and inhabitants of North Dakota. Willa Cather wrote for a public audience and with finer skill, yet the novel is hardly less disoriented than the diaries. For all my struggle with her footnote on pronunciation, I cannot make *Antonia* sound like *Anthony*. Cather's gender fit is just as awkward. It is only because she frequently repeats Jim Burden's name that I remember that the narrator is male and the object of his mystification female. Jim Burden, like the women diary writers, is the accommodating but disengaged outsider, who, for all his snuggling in straw and tall grass, never truly engages himself in Nebraska prairie life, whereas Antonia, seen from a distance, appears to conquer all before her. Jim Burden moves among female characters as one of them, erotically empathetic but not sexual: "I took her hands and held them against my breast, feeling once more how strong and warm and good they were, those brown hands, and remembering how many kind things they had done for me. I held them now a long while, over my heart." (322)

Goodness and comforting strength are more the companionable virtues of sisters and mothers than of lovers. In fact, it surprises me when Burden says to one of Antonia's children, "I was very much in love with your mother once" (346). The book's nostalgic detachment begins in the "Introduction," where the author/editor explains receiving from Burden, on a train, the manuscript of his reminiscences, and how, "when we were crossing Iowa, our talk kept returning to a central figure, a Bohemian girl whom we had known long ago. More than any other person we remembered, this girl seemed to mean to us the country, the conditions, the whole adventure of our childhood." Out of this, as a pastime, came the book:

"'From time to time, I've been writing down what I remember about Antonia,' he told me. 'On my long trips across the country, I amuse myself like that, in my stateroom.'" For two urban and sometimes bored railway passengers, Antonia is the image of Nebraska they have cherished. But their imaginations do not probe hers, and we do not know, because no one ever asks, how Antonia views herself or her environment. What does their myth mean to her? To call *My Antonia* a regional novel, as most people do, is to close off that question, and to continue to diminish, I think, the value of experiences of women, as characters and as writers.

Though art and life may imitate each other, they are not of course the same, yet if an Antonia were to speak for herself, she might well sound like one Caroline who wrote from Devils Lake, North Dakota, on Whitsunday, June 9, 1889, to her cousin Christine in Norway.

Me and mother are well and lead a good life under the circumstances since there are fairly tough times now that the timber froze over large parts of this country. It was fairly difficult for many to get hold of wood last year and it was so expensive. And it doesn't look good this year either because it is so dry. Yes, if we get a bad year this year again, it will be best to leave Dakota.

You say aunt wonders whether I still own land. Well I have it mainly because as long as I keep it we have a home. Mother lives there mostly alone. I am at home in the winter time and gone in the summer. This summer I work just 4 miles away from home so I can often go there and mother comes here as often as she wants to. You can believe I have good days in the summer. Just one man to cook for, a tight American. I have sown 30 acres wheat on my land this year so if something comes out of that I will have something, if not, it is too bad because I owe for the sowing wheat since what I had last year froze. Well you see, I earn some in the summer but we have to have food and drink and wood through the winter and then there is not much left for someone who has to hire help for everything. You know I cannot take care of the land like a man. All I can do is to live there as much as I can and to plow what I can so that no one can take it away from me because I hope in time to sell and maybe get a couple of thousand dollars for it if we get railway over here. But that can last a few years yet, but when I get that then I can sell wheat for 2 or 300 dollars every year beside what I earn myself. So mother and me are OK. Yes I might say we have it very well.

Mother is fine and does things she likes. She came here today and stays until Tuesday and I have it as I want, no old lady to boss me around
. . . .

I wish you were here today so I could talk to you for a while. I am very lonely here as my work is not much. I crochet and knit and sew. Right now I am making a skirt for myself. Here you can see a sample of the material of it. It is simple, but good enough for the Dakota prairie because there isn't enough money for lots of fine dresses for me who is farming. But when I come to Norway again I am going to have a silk skirt I have been kind of thinking to myself.[6]

Caroline's letter reminds us that there were women who homesteaded on their own. She is knowledgeable, canny, thinks well of her resourceful independence ("no old lady to boss me around"), she admits to lonely moments, and amusingly thinks about presenting herself in Norway in a silk skirt. But there is nothing to indicate an emotional identification with the land; it is her livelihood and nothing else: "I have it mainly because as long as I keep it we have a home." She explains at some length her schemes for doing so, but describes nothing of topography, plants, or animals. Not a tourist like Lulah Cavileer, Caroline thinks of her land as a financial investment that demands physical exertion and careful management, but not emotional attachment—that she invests elsewhere, in friendship with Christine.

Letters of European immigrants to North Dakota differ in degree rather than in kind from letters of people from other states—the differences are between thousands and hundreds of miles, or between letters exchanged at intervals of years rather than weeks or months (Caroline: "You wait three years before you answer my letter"). She reports at too close a range to be found on a map, so to speak. I am persuaded by my reading to associate this short perspective with writings of working women. It is concrete, uneuphemistic, unmysterious, with little generalization and no irony. A public example is Tillie Olsen's novel *Yonnondio from the Thirties,*[7] where one is only incidentally aware that the settings include a Wyoming mining camp, a Dakota farm, and a packing-plant company town in Illinois: "Mazie lay under the hot Wyoming sun, between the outhouse and the garbage dump. There was no other place for Mazie to lie, for the one patch of green in the yard was between these two spots. From the ground arose a nauseating smell. Food had been rotting in the garbage piles for years" (12). Physical surroundings take their cue from a character's state of mind. The smells from the garbage dump are not describing Wyoming as a region, but Mazie's despair, as shack, suburbs and chickens describe

Mrs. Cole's well-being. In a passage of rare contentment, when Mazie's mother has taken the children foraging for dandelion greens in a vacant lot, the surroundings acquire her benign coloring: "River wind shimmered and burnished the bright grasses, her mother's hand stroked, stroked. Young catalpa leaves overhead quivered and glistened, bright reflected light flowed over, lumined their faces" (119). Hopeful interludes on the South Dakota farm are described through characters' awareness of surroundings. "Once, hungry, degraded, after a beating from Anna for some mischief, Mazie lay by the roadside, bedded in the clover, belly down, feeling the earth push back against her, feeling the patterns of clover smell twine into her nostrils till she was drugged with the scent. The soft plodding of a buggy gathered into her consciousness" (43). That buggy belongs to the single encouraging outsider in the book. Even descriptions at long range of what one thinks of as Dakota landscapes but cut to fit the landscape within characters' minds, a device which is common enough in literature, are nearly nonexistent. This is virtually the only one: "They reached the farm at midnight. Anna had awakened Mazie so she could see. There were flattened fields, low houses, some with towers her father softly pointed out as silos" (39). By contrast, Willa Cather attributed to Jim Burden, on his first glimpse of the Nebraska prairie from the straw bed in back of a cart, cosmic knowledge of his surroundings:

> There seemed to be nothing to see; no fences, no creeks or trees, no hills or fields. If there was a road, I could not make it out in the faint starlight. There was nothing but land: not a country at all, but the material out of which countries are made. . . . I had the feeling that the world was left behind, that we had got over the edge of it, and were outside man's jurisdiction. I had never before looked up at the sky when there was not a familiar mountain ridge against it. But this was the complete dome of heaven, all there was to it. . . . Between that earth and that sky I felt erased, blotted out. (8)

Cather has invested topography with the idea, and then adjusted character to it (never mind whether a tired and sleepy twelve-year-old would rouse himself to such reflections). In *Yonnondio* no one sees the complete dome of heaven, only tiny particles of green grass patches or patterns of field, house, and silo. Geographically, we hardly know where we are.

Housing and Indians

But if rural working women have given little attention to objective description of their geographical surroundings, they have taken note of how important shelter is to physical survival in a very difficult environment, and they have described what effect living in these huts and shanties had on people's emotional lives. Even so, women omit directions for getting to them. The "Little House" books that Laura Ingalls Wilder wrote for children are preoccupied a good deal with shelter, as people remember the places they lived in as children. Place and region in these books radiate from houses.

"'Can't you get it all in?'" Pa was looking over the mess of furniture Ma was trying to cram into the one-room tarpaper shanty he had constructed. During a single year, the family of parents and four daughters who are the characters in *By the Shores of Silver Lake* (1939)[8] lived in four dwellings in the course of moving from a farmstead in eastern South Dakota, in the 1880s, to a homestead claim farther west in the territory. The Plum Creek farmstead was considered "settled country"; there was no more game, and money was scarce, but Mrs. Ingalls was loath to leave her cow, chickens, garden, and neighbors. The family had started from the "Big Woods" in Wisconsin, where the grandparents at last prospered enough to live in a frame house.

On their move west, the Ingalls family stopped for the summer at a railroad camp where Pa ran the company store. "'This is another kind of little house with only half a roof and no window,' said Ma. 'But it's a tight roof, and we don't need a window, so much air and light come through the doorway.'" She had partitioned off sections between beds with yardage bought at the company store. The children visited a homesteader's claim shanty: "It was a tiny room, boarded up-and-down, and its roof sloped all one way, so that it looked like half of a little house." During the winter, when the camp was closed, the family occupied the one frame house in the community, owned by the surveyor. Laura approached it on foot: "It stood up in front of her suddenly. It was a big house, a real house with two stories, and glass windows. Its up-and-down boards were weathering from yellow to gray, and every crack was battened, as Pa had said. The door had a china knob." Laura is awed by the many rooms,

board floors, windows, the luxury of space and light. In early spring
the Ingalls moved into a crowded claim shanty.

> Laura thought of setting the little bedsteads together, tight in the
> corner, and putting the foot of the big bedstead against them, with its
> headboard against the other wall. "Then we'll hang a curtain around
> our beds," she said to Ma, "and another curtain across beside yours,
> and that leaves room for the rocking chair against your curtain." . . .
> Against the foot of Laura's and Mary's bed the table fitted under the
> window that Pa was sawing in that wall. Ma's rocking chair went in
> beside the table, and the whatnot fitted in that corner, behind the door.
> In the fourth corner stood the stove, with the dish cupboard made of a
> packing box behind it, and the trunk fitted between the stove and
> Mary's rocking chair. "There," said Ma. "And the boxes will go under
> the beds. It couldn't be better." At dinner Pa said, "Before night I'll
> finish this half of the house." And he did. He put in a window beside
> the stove, to the south. He hung in the doorway a door bought from
> the lumberyard in town. Then all over the outside of the shanty he put
> black tar paper, fastening it down with lath.

The well dug and covered, Pa drove his wagon to a lake for wood
and young trees to plant around the house, and in the evening built
smudge fires of wet grass to keep mosquitoes off the tethered cow
and horses. In this manner the "Little House" family set up housekeeping on a prairie homestead.

Certainly Laura Ingalls Wilder has the details right: the tight
spaces people lived in, their many moves, their ingenuity at circum-
venting inconvenience. But other effects of the "little house" way of
living are softer in her books than in most private accounts I have
read. Taken all together, the environment of the upper Great Plains
eighty years or so ago was one that is difficult to replicate in this day
and age. One was confined to very close and rather darkened quarters within doors, and found almost no object to rest the eye upon in
the glaring out-of-doors. Nearest neighbors were six miles, even
fifteen miles away, the writers tell us, nearest towns twenty-five or
more. Months could go by without company. Such unfocused, unlimited landscape partitioned only by the nearly miniature walls of a
house have resulted, I think, in environmental relationships that
were somewhat different from what they have been in more hilly,
wooded, and temperate sections of the country. It appears to me
that people even now who live in typical two-story frame houses in

the Dakotas are continuing the essentially adversarial relationship to the out-of-doors that the first settlers found thrust upon them. Both the early temporary and later permanent housing arrangements include almost no gradations between outdoors and indoors. The houses you see now along country roads were built, many of them, sixty or seventy years ago, straight sided two-story frame structures, some with an addition at the back when indoor bathrooms were installed and the kitchen remodeled. Typically, you can see all sides of the house as you drive by—it is set fairly close to the road, and there is nothing to obstruct the view, no walls or hedges or overhanging trees, no shrubbery or flower beds embroidering the foundations. Shelter belts on the north and east sides are set back. In summer, there is usually a large vegetable plot, and there may well be flowers, but these often magnificent stands of iris or peonies are in rows among the vegetables The overall effect of a farmstead setting suggests that people work out of doors, in the fields or gardens, then go indoors. They omit front porches and secluded garden spots inviting rest or play, or even safe enclosures for small children to play in. The shelter belts, crucially important for protection against the wind, are too overgrown with underbrush for walking through.

Women's letters tend to be filled with information about other people—illnesses, letters received, occasional visits, gossip and news—but except for mentioning the weather, they say very little about physical surroundings. To be sure, the northern plains are a hostile environment in every season, what with dangerous cold, snow, and wind in winter, and the likelihood of floods, fires, tornadoes, droughts, mosquitoes in the other months. Even so, women seldom mention going for walks, picnics, swimming, skating, sledding, horseback riding, or just sunning themselves. Presumably their fears of those expanses made it harder to think of venturing out, of extending their habitation to a chair beyond the outside door, with a floor beneath and screens on three sides, or of blocking by a hedge or low wall the view of that expanse. No wonder women were lonely, so lonely that some sickened and died or went mad. This loneliness, ostensibly attributed to their distance from family and friends, was exacerbated, I think, by their manner of building dwelling places, each (by law) by itself on its own property, each a fortification against the out-of doors.

Women, then, locate themselves in their immediate circumstances, and not in the kinds of unifying myths based on time and place that Davies has said legitimize the work of artists. Women describe where they are in relation to other people more than according to a spot on the map and its attendant history and economics. Often they even neglect to mention the name of a place. "Place" in these writings has other boundaries than topography: dangers, for one, the fearful elements that those who were poor and not conveniently and safely settled always had to worry about—fire, flood, cold, drought, disease, madness, and death. Indians, for instance, those indispensable furies in Western mythology, lose much seductive dreadfulness when settler women write about them in their usual neutral manner. Women emphasize what did *not* happen. Hannah Bell on her travels by wagon with her husband to the Black Hills remembered Indians matter-of-factly.

> Many Sioux Indians lived around us but they always seemed to be quite peaceable. . . . It was after we moved to Williston in 1889 that we had a real Indian scare, as many hundreds of Sioux Indians were on the war path. A large stockade was erected by the men of Williston and the government ordered soldiers from Fort Buford and conditions looked bad for the early settlers, but the affair did not prove to be serious after all.[9]

Margaret Fellman describes a fortification among caves and rocks on Moltzan Hill which went unused: "Later they were aware that only several Indians came causing no trouble what so ever. However they indicated by turning our cultivated soil over that the prairie was 'wrong side up.'"[10] Indians are one of the many anxieties in women's lives; the more precarious a woman's situation, the more afraid she is likely to say she is of Indians. Women who appear to feel relatively stable and safe write calmly about them. Here is one night in the life of a family who had come to New Rockford from Ontario by train in 1887. When Mrs. J. C. Smith uses the word *Indians,* she is thinking of a host of dreads in a generally precarious existence.

> The one dread of our lives was Indians. One evening late in the fall of 1888, father was away helping the neighbors to thresh. We had done the evening chores, carried in the wood from the scanty wood pile and the coal from the box beside the back door. The fire was low and we sat close to the stove. We heard teams around the house. A train of Indians had lost their way and they drove around in the yard—dogs, horses,

ponies and Indians and squaws—and out to the Indian trail which they had lost. This was the beginning of a restless night.

Soon we heard a team and a wagon drive up to the house—a knock at the one back door which we had crudely fastened with a stick between the step and the back shed door. We sat very still for we feared to open the door. Then tap, tap at the window pane and an ugly and whiskered face was pressed against the window. We were so frightened. Then Ole, that was his name, raised some papers over his head and we raised the window a few inches for him to hand them in to us. One of the attorneys had sent some papers to father.

Mother lay in bed with an umbrella over her head to keep the rain from leaking into her face. A baby girl had arrived at our house to claim her share of the already crowded space.

The night was cold, dark, and rainy and everything contributed to add to the loneliness of North Dakota prairies at that time. The neighbors were far away and it took time to travel by oxen. At that time our team of horses was the only team near by. We could hear the coyotes howling so we were already tense with fear, when we heard voices at the crossroads, at the corner as we called it. Mother lay very still and we children were fearful to add any further discomfort to her pitiful plight. The talking became louder, the wind blew the rain against the pane, the wolves howled, and we were practically alone. We whispered "Indians." We brought in the ax, the hatchet, the hammer and every available weapon of defense, drew the shades down tight and we sat in silent fear waiting for the worst. Everything sounded like Indians; although they had never molested us, we feared them intensely.

We older ones sat quietly each of us with a weapon in our hands when to our surprise in walked father. He had ridden home with a neighbor, and he was enjoying a friendly chat before coming into the house.[11]

A mother of several children in bed after childbirth in a cold room holds an umbrella over her head and waits for her husband to come home. No mention of other adults. Every noise she and the children hear they suppose comes from Indians. On such a night, who would not be afraid? For some women, fear is everything: "Mrs. Merry lived for years in a floorless log hut, cooking daily for a dozen or more hungry woodchoppers, never leaving the place or seeing another woman for months at a time; leading a lonely grueling existence, deathly afraid of the Indians, who came begging so often." But by no means were all women so paralyzed. There was Mrs. Gradin, who

was known to walk ten miles to a bachelor neighbor, Isaac Westman's whom she had known in Sweden, chop his wood to bake his bread and

cook for threshing crew; she also befriended the Indians, who were
frequent callers enroute to and from the Ft. Berthold reservation.
Among them was Sitting Bull, who often sat cross legged on her
kitchen floor, while she fed him.[12]

Typically, Indians were part of the landscape when women wrote
about it: "I can remember seeing the antelope running across the
prairies, also Indians coming over the hills like long trains."[13] "But
the affair did not prove to be serious after all": when women tell
their story of their contacts with native people, it is apt to be connected to their general well-being, and less sensational than most
people who are not native Americans have been led to suppose. Only
when their own lives were fearful because they had come to a
country for which they were unprepared, without enough money,
food, well-built shelter, or family and friends near them, then
women wrote about how afraid they were of Indians, along with
everything else.

Closely related to settlers' relationships to Indians was their dependence also upon buffalo, or, by the time the homesteaders tried
to settle and farm, upon what was left of the vast herds: their bones.
Hannah Bell has described how she and her husband prospered
from hunting, and then turned to cattle and horses when the buffalo
were gone. In the years since those hunts, Americans have mourned
the buffalo and have been astonished how quickly they disappeared.
Angus Neil, like Hannah Bell and her husband, owed his move
toward prosperity to the buffalo, and he knew it.

> Many of the early settlers arrived in the west with nothing but an old
> wagon, a worn out yoke of oxen, a brave wife, and a family of helpless
> children. Life was a struggle for them, as their funds were small and
> soon gave out, and they often had to suffer great hardships in order to
> live. But the great slaughter of buffalo on the prairies created an
> industry that was a blessing to the penniless newcomers.[14]

Another settler, Charles Rowe, describes this industry in detail.
Rowe was a cowboy who knew Theodore Roosevelt and worked
cattle near Wibeaux, Montana, where he had come as a boy in 1881.

> We had five buffalo hunters: Dave Brown, Burthold, Billy Underwood,
> Fred La Brash, and Victor Smith. Burthold was one of the best hunters.
> He had a 120 Sharps rifle with a telescopic sight, which was good for a
> mile or more, using bullets which he made himself. He held the record
> of killing buffalo, by dropping eighty from one stand. Victor Smith got

seventy-nine. Burthold told me that during the time that the buffalo were being killed off these western ranges, that there were 40,000 buffalo hides shipped from Miles City, Montana, 40,000 from Keith, Montana, and 90,000 from Sully Springs, North Dakota. (Burthold was a truthful man, and I had no occasion to doubt his word.) The buffalo were in herds of 10,000 up, and they were so many that they sometimes stopped trains and even steamboats on the Missouri River. The hides were piled up like cordwood and the bones of the dead animals were so thick on the prairies, where a killing was made, that you could step from bone to bone without stepping on the ground. These bones were hauled to Wibeaux, often as many as twenty-five or thirty wagon loads in a string. The bone hunters received $18.00 per ton for the bones delivered to the railway, and the bones were manufactured into fertilizer.[15]

"It was a curious sight to see hundreds of tons of buffalo bones piled up by the RR track," Angus Neil wrote. Neil was not a hunter, but one of the "penniless newcomers" he mentioned. "A settler who could not get work," he says, "could always make a living for himself and family as a bone picker," and he tells something of what that was like:

> The skinners would remove the hides, which were a source of immense profit [according to Hannah Bell, bull hides sold for $1.80 and cow hides for $2.50] and when this was done, and the choice portions of meat taken, thousands of carcasses were left on the prairies. Buzzards, coyotes, other animals and the weather would remove most of the meat that was stuck to the bones, and bone pickers would do the rest. They gathered the bones in fall, and piled them up, and when they had nothing else to do, they hauled them to the Rail Road and shipped them. The bones always commanded a good price. . . .

Angus Neil seemed amused by attitudes toward buffalo bone picking he had observed among people he knew. Some settlers, he wrote, "were proud to talk of their first work in the west," but others "would not own up to it." Charles Rowe, the cowboy, like Angus Neil, was writing the account of his pioneering experiences for a contest sponsored by the Mandan Creamery Company in 1933. Rowe comments on the long-term effect of the buffalo hunt which eventually led to prosperity for settlers, at the expense of a way of life for Native Americans: "When they killed off the buffalo, that's what tamed the Indians, and made way for the milk cows, and that's what made it possible for the creameries to get started."

Women's Mappings

On the evidence of their writing, the manner in which women
have "placed" themselves differs, I think from men's perspectives
that invented regions. Here is Charles Forbes, an ambitious young
doctor, newly arrived in Buxton, North Dakota, writing to his new
wife back in Michigan:

> You have no idea, Beulah, of what [the prairies] are like until you see
> them. For mile after mile there is not a sign of a tree or stone and just
> as level as the floor of your house. . . . Wheat never looked better and it
> is nothing but wheat. Just as far as a person can see on every side there
> is nothing but wheat, wheat, wheat. . . . Just around here the people are
> nearly all Norwegians but they are a steady, honest, industrious class of
> people. Nearly always square up all debts. . . . A doctor can always
> collect a debt. He can seize anything and everything that a man has got
> until the debt is paid, by the laws of Dakota. Fees are high too.
> (6–7–88)[16]

Forbes measured the lay of the land—topography, crop yield, ethnic
population, an entire interrelationship of facts that culminate in his
fee:

> Yesterday McIntyre went out and sewed up a little scalp wound on a
> girl 4 miles from town. He goes out again today and will probably go
> once or twice again. He will get about $20. I did just the same thing for
> a young fellow 3 miles from Wakelee and got $4. I set old Royal
> Cooper's leg and put $15 on the book against him and will never get a
> cent. Here it would be at least $50 sure pay. You see the difference.
> (6–10–88)

Hubbel Pierce arrived on his claim near Abbottsville, North Dakota,
in June of 1879 and wrote to his wife, also in Michigan, that she
could prepare for what he hoped would be better times.

> First the land is a black clay loam from two to three feet deep, the first
> plowing is rather hard after one crop it is as soft as can be, any team
> can work it. The water in the creek is soft and as clear as a crystal with a
> gravel bottom. The river is not so clear except in winter. The timber
> here is box elder, not very large, some oak and elm from one to two
> and some nearly four feet through but not very tall. (6–4–79)

And so on through yields of corn, wheat, and the price of land. Both

Pierce and Forbes size up opportunities with a long view.

But women measure their surroundings on a different scale. In the spring of 1900, Rosa Kately, age 25, moved from Utica, Minnesota, to Anamoose, North Dakota, where she took up a claim, farmed, built a sod house, taught school, and worked at other jobs. The variety of her activities, a mixture of rural and urban, "pioneer" and traditional, makes me think that we ought not to assume that people who broke sod were on new ground in all that they did. On July 19, 1901, Rosa Kately summarized her doings since the last entry in July of the year before:

> Fish .20, berries .25, bread .25, butter .05, eggs .13. Left the boys at Comstock about July 25. Went to Christine and heard of Mrs. V. Simons who needed a hired girl. Went to Wolverton and worked in the hotel for about two months. Came back taught school in District 15 School 1 from September 17 to November 9. Went to school No. 3 a week later and taught a two month term. Went to Minneapolis and stayed till April 2, worked four weeks at the Harlow House and one at Mr. T. Merrys.[17]

She was self-supporting, mobile, even restless, and undertook homesteading as one activity among several to support herself. This is what she says of her first look at the new land:

> April 18, 1900. Well here I am at Anamoose. Arrived here about midnight. There is a Dakota wind this morning. Everything is dry and dusty here. I saw the first "alkali surface" yesterday, it began in the Red River Valley and extends westward. Yesterday Mr. Williams gave me a box of fruit and a book entitled "Beyond the City." The day before he gave me "The Pirate."

> April 20, 1900. I went up to stay all night with Ida last night. Received examination questions today from Ida Herred, Casselman. I commenced work today noon. Ida came this evening.

> May 9, 1900. Came to the claim at 1 PM yesterday. Went to Erwin's in the afternoon. Went to Mrs. Johnson's after the milk and flour.

> June 12, 1900. Well today we will begin to build a house on my farm. Received letters from Stella, Ruby, Hannah and Pauline last Saturday. Mr. Johnson and ourselves went for a ride to the lakes last Sunday. Received paper from home in which was account of Edd T's death May 20, spinal trouble.

People's names occur more frequently in her pages than any other detail—people she sees, writes to, receives letters from, or hears about. Even when she ostensibly does describe physical surroundings, they could be anywhere. The boundaries of her map are formed by connections to people:

> July 28 I guess. Wolverton. Well I have been here since the evening of the 24. This is a small town 3 elevators, PO, restaurant, hotel, 2 stores, a very small depot. Several quite fine dwelling houses. A party in the woods today. 13 for dinner.

She engaged in prodigious activity, and yet reported it as if she were living on a smaller scale. Place, region, locale all are blotted out in names:

> October 7, 1901. Monday. Saturday I went over to Mrs. Larson's and dug 2 sacks of potatoes. Then I rode back to Mr. J. with Mrs. L. and walked home. Then I walked to Brushlate and back. Sunday, I went to Archie's looking for horses. Then home and washed and ironed. Monday. Ida came over about sunrise and took the colts home. Mr. P. Siements came while she was there to see about the flax. It is rainy today. 11 pupils.

Rosa was precise, confident, she knew what she was doing, but nothing she reports adds up to cultural particularity and nothing surprised her: "Ida was over this morning and brought me some meat. Only five pupils this morning. The wind blew the roof off my sod shanty this morning. Worked in my garden last night" (5–21–02), and a week later, "Have one more cow. My hens laid the first egg for me yesterday and Schnabel's yellow dog sucked it. A fine day. Went over to Mrs. Johnson." Only the section number of her claim tells where she lived. Charles Forbes saw "wheat, wheat, wheat," and a steady income in doctors' fees; Rosa Kately who was planting wheat, noted Ida's visits and that she had brought her meat.

Donald Davies laces a rationale for regionalism—"to seek an image of the South"—in myth-making phrases: "finality of art," "belief," "rightful heritage." In the minds of Vanderbilt University "Agrarians," weather, topography, and vegetation not only determined particular characteristics of the geographical place they found themselves, but these physical circumstances also suffused human lives with other meanings. What is so conspicuously missing from writings by women living in the midst of an as yet unurbanized countryside is any similar desire to mythologize. Even when they wrote much later about their first encounters with land and place, and might be expected in retrospect to transform some of that past to metaphor, they did not place those environs in a context of art, belief, or heritage. Women's written memories that I have read remain as consistently factual as their writings at the time, flattened, resisting myth-making when it would have been easy: "I remember . . . seeing a deer a short distance from the house and as I wanted to take my rifle and get the deer, and the grass was so high I did not dare to leave Oscar who was just at the toddling around age and would possibly follow and get lost, I tied him to a bed post with a rope while I shot and brought home the deer." It sounds as though Hannah Bell were still concerned lest someone think she had mistreated a small child.

To find an image, a mythology that expresses ordinary women thinking about themselves in relation to a past, we shall have to look elsewhere than at the topography, landscape, work, and politics usually associated with notions about region. Inside the two-story brick schoolhouse that the town of Minto, North Dakota, has converted to a museum, there hangs in a carved gilt frame a construction of many-colored flowers embroidered in wool on a cloth about eighteen inches square. In a clearing at the center of this riot of vegetation are two words in light blue thread: "ALL ALONE." The composition is the work of an eight-year-old who, I suppose, wanted it known that she made it herself. She has also, I think, hit upon an image that matches women's writing about new solitudes, no matter who else was there. Continually moving, from parents' family to marriage, from house to house or state to territory, women felt transplanted from so far away that, like embroidered flowers, they scarcely looked themselves. "All alone" was where they had to start again to reestablish ties that would restore them to themselves, with little help from those elements attributable to region (land, work, business, and government) that gave identities to men. Indeed, noticing how little women have had to say about such matters ought to make us pause in our latter-day enthusiasm for museum "heritage."

III

"Not to Use Correct and Elegant English Is to Plod": Class and Language in Women's Writings

School Grammar Books

Private writing by women a hundred years ago is strikingly different from the style of public literature, which is the style advocated by school textbooks on writing. Virtually all examples I have read, whether originating in New York, Michigan, Ohio, or Dakota Territory, disregard public writing, but the distance is most pronounced in the case of working women, whose letters and diaries do not sound like the newspaper account of, for instance, the death of Warren Coss in 1908: "He had just dictated a letter and seemed in the best of spirits when he arose to cross the room and fell back dead, death being the result of apoplexy."[1] Grammar texts presented writing as though it were a problem in construction, a page intended exclusively for a silent eye. Rhythms of sound or vibrations of emotional intensity carried by the dominating speaking voice that a letter, read aloud, would reproduce a second time—such spoken sound was absent from school books. Rather, these texts showed people how to lengthen the distance between experience and writing by inventing metaphorical comparisons, and by transposing the concrete and particular to generalizations, often formulas and clichés. They were also arbiters of etiquette and upward mobility, instructing students about what they ought to do and think and aspire to, as well as how they should write. Their teachings depended very much upon dissatisfied awareness of class distinctions.

The currency of the democratic myth of equal opportunity in a classless society makes it difficult to describe manifest class differences in America. Although the numbers of Americans truly believing that "anyone" can become president must be few, even to use the word *class* is to risk being called a snob or Marxist. Subtle complexities of our social structure also inhibit talk of class: occupation, language, income, ethnic background, education—these and other indicators mix in unpredictable ways. In her story "Revelation," Flannery O'Connor has dramatized our national ambivalence in the personage of Mrs. Turpin, a woman of complicated insecurities:

> Sometimes Mrs. Turpin occupied herself at night naming the classes of people. On the bottom of the heap were most colored people, not the kind she would have been if she had been one, but most of them; then next to them—not above, just away from—were the white-trash; then above them were the home-owners, and above them the home-and-land owners, to which she and Claud belonged. Above she and Claud were people with a lot of money and much bigger houses and much more land. But here the complexity of it would begin to bear in on her, for some of the people with a lot of money were common and ought to be below she and Claud and some of the people who had good blood had lost their money and had to rent and then there were colored people who owned their homes and land as well. There was a colored dentist in town who had two red Lincolns and a swimming pool and a farm with registered white-face cattle on it. Usually by the time she had fallen asleep all the classes of people were moiling and roiling around in her head, and she would dream they were all crammed in together in a box car, being ridden off to be put in a gas oven.[2]

Too much moiling and roiling brings on the Nazi mightmare.

Drawing upon her studies of nineteenth-century women's private writings, Nancy Cott describes the special class history of women that rests on industrialization and the subsequent removal of work from the home. As proliferating and male-organized institutions took over previously home-centered activities—religion, education, medicine, manufacture, entertainment—so the value given by both men and women to what women were left to do, declined.

Such deep social changes bore drastic results for women, relegating them to a "separate sphere,"

> not only because it was at home but also because it seemed to elude rationalization and the cash nexus, and to integrate labor with life. The home and occupations in it represented an alternative to the emerging pace and division of labor. Symbol and remnant of preindustrial work, perhaps the home commanded men's deepest loyalties, but these were loyalties that conflicted with "modern" forms of employment. To be

idealized, yet rejected by men—the object of yearning and yet of scorn—was the fate of the home-as-work-place. Women's work (indeed women's very character, viewed as essentially conditioned by the home) shared in the simultaneous glorification and devaluation.[3]

Historically and humanely, "work" more accurately than "blood" describes differences between social classes.

Using the word *class* in relation to work approaches the question from the subject's point of view, for women, and men as well, define themselves in relation to the work they do. Work colors their imaginings about themselves. Thus, for some women, work means what they do all day long, every day, whether they are paid or not; their lives depend upon it. For others work is elective, scarce, a form of petty administration of others' work, and not as crucial to prestige as their leisure. The terms "working class" and "white collar," imprecise enough descriptions of the male work force, need to be even more severely modified when speaking of women's work patterns. Most women whose work is paid, whether by hourly wage or salary, differ from their male colleagues in at least two respects: within the job they have less opportunity for advancement and mobility, and outside it they miss almost entirely the contrasts between work and leisure, because after work they must work some more, taking primary responsibility for housekeeping and child care (a state of affairs that also prevailed among families on the Overland Trail).

Those women who are not paid for what they do also present a different picture from unemployed men. Typically, men who do not work either are too rich or else too ill or derelict to do so. In the case of women, I would include nonemployed women in the "working" category if their entire day is taken up with cooking, cleaning, sewing, preserving, caring for chickens or other small livestock, and all the other miscellaneous tasks that indirectly supplement family income by drastically reducing expenditures. In the category of properly nonworking women I place women in either urban or rural settings whose families—husbands, fathers, brothers—count on their nonproductivity as a sign of their own prosperity.

Judging from textbooks alone, language instruction in the schools in the nineteenth century strongly advocated rising class expectations. In order to see how they envisioned their audiences, I have picked two of these books at random: *English Grammar* by Allen H. Weld (Boston, 1849) and *Rand McNally Primary Grammar and Composition* by William D. Hall (New York, 1897). Paying particular attention to the content of sentences used as examples, I have found, not surprisingly, that this language of composition differs markedly from the conversational talk encountered in the letters and diaries of working women. I infer that to improve writing one ought to eradicate oral mannerisms and mute the voice.

What do Weld's *English Grammar* and the Rand McNally say written English ought to be? Who do they think their students are, and what are they telling them they should become? Sample sentences in both books reflect social views that differ from those implied by flanged pulleys and tying comforters. These four come from Weld:

> He, the marquis of Cadiz, beheld from a distance, the peril of the king.
> To die in peace, is the privilege of the good.
> Evergreens only, among the trees, look verdant in the winter.
> Those who are obliging, may expect to be accommodated.

Only very nervous people talk in appositives and aphorisms or set their minds to such rigid categories: royalty and inferiors, good people and the no-good, evergreens and other trees, those who are obliging and nastier folk. Such stiffened arrangements of words are unlikely to occur either in literature or in life; they exist primarily in a grammar-book hothouse. For, in the jumbled comings and goings of letters and diaries, few categories emerge; though now and then someone sneers at "Norwegians" for encroaching in too great numbers, private writings are not in the habit of ranking people, or even of classifying plants and animals. They report individuals, not groups. Nor will you find in these letters the hortatory tone, the efforts to improve everyone's moral fiber, of Weld. Explaining the parts of speech, he uses uplifting examples: *good, great, wise, prudent* are his adjectives, *pleasingly, sweetly, cheerfully* his adverbs. Also, the bucolic scene so many of his sentences describe is foreign to the fields and barnyards of the letters, which speak of individual horses or grain harvests rather than of a wide-angle landscape. And Weld is more of a chauvinist: in a military conflict, American troops are sure to emerge victorious:

> The Americans conquered the Mexicans in the battle of Palo Alto.
> The army under General Scott captured the fine city of Vera Cruz.
> The robin sings sweetly in the Spring.
> The flowers bloom in the meadow.
> The lambs skip over the hills.
> Spring is the most delightful season of the year.

Whereas Weld systematically surveys every possible grammatical category, letters of working women avail themselves of far less variety, tending to avoid adjectives, adverbs, and subordinate clauses. In the main, the letters and diaries do not speak "about" subjects the way Weld's sentences do. Topics Weld beholds from a distance— war, nature, the Bible, proper behavior—these the letter writers miss because their focus is too close and particularized. The sample sentences imitate vocabulary and rhythms of the Bible and of inspirational speech making; they are strong on aphorisms and as distant as they can get from private, casual conversation.

> He had a poniard concealed under his coat.
> I saw him laboring in the field.
> Jesus, knowing their thoughts, rebuked them.
> To excel in knowledge is honorable, but to be ignorant is base.
> Not to use correct and elegant English is to plod.
> At Burlington I met an acquantance with many principal people of the province.
> Shall a barbarian have these cultivated fields?

As though by obligation, almost every sentence has at least one latinate word: *poniard, laboring, rebuked, excel.* Weld's sentences do not mention women and they consistently use masculine general pronouns. The grammar promises to rescue pupils from the perils of an inferior class, from the basely ignorant, the plodding users of incorrect English. Good writing is what sets the principal people apart from the barbarians, women included.

Published fifty years later than Weld's, the Rand McNally grammar also exhorts students to improve their social and economic opportunities by means of "correct and elegant English." If anything, Rand McNally insists even more confidently upon optimism and upward mobility.

> Short, pithy sentences are here used by preference; the works of acknowledged masters in English literature are preferable to colloquial examples, or to extracts from less eminent, contemporary writers. . . .
> Other things being equal, a noble sentiment or celebrated utterance shall be placed before the pupil rather than a negative or commonplace expression.

Virtually all the short, pithy sentences in Rand McNally subscribe to optimism and aspiring success, especially in commercial and military efforts, and they encourage writing a dialect as removed as possible from the presumably long, rambling, colloquial utterances of unknown people on negative and commonplace subjects.

> Rome is the most noted city in the world.
> A thing of beauty is a joy forever.
> Honor and shame from no condition rise.
> Education expands and elevates the mind.
> Let us have faith that right makes might.

Rand McNally bends sufficiently in the direction of colloquial minds, however, to include a brief section on letter writing, even though the advice for writers of personal letters would not seem to have been applicable to those we shall consider here.

> Letters of Friendship, which are familiar communications between friends. In character they should reflect the relations of the correspondents. They should be simple, natural, and individual. Being conversations on paper, they should treat subjects of mutual interest. The same care should be taken as in speech; the writer should not presume upon his correspondent by slovenliness, haste, or selfishness.

An exercise directs students to write a letter to a friend on each of the following subjects:

> Your trip to Niagara Falls.
> Your visit to the World's Fair.
> Planning a summer vacation with a friend.
> Asking for a book which you wish to borrow.
> Recounting the adventures of a week.

Letters of working class women that I shall describe are certainly conversational, and they recount episodes though not adventures, but few other interests coincide with those assumed here: there are no reports of excursions or vacations and no book borrowing. Rand McNally gives other advice that, for all I know, may be directed quite specifically against the letters working people write, for the "errors" chided here are legion. Students are told not to write in margins or to use figures and abbreviations; to "finish one subject before commencing another, and avoid, as far as possible, the use of a postscript." They should also "avoid all hackneyed phrases, especially such as 'I take my "pen in hand'" . . . . Some of these expressions are really impertinent; others are useless, or even worse, senseless"

(259). The book consistently bases its exhortations on the importance
of bettering oneself in class terms: "An illiterate business letter, in
which words are misspelled, grammar is violated, or other blunders
are made, often creates prejudice against the writer."

A local example of the optimistic, hortatory style is a book called
History of the Red River Valley Past and Present by Various Writers, which
tells of immigrant settlements in the counties joining the Red River
of the North in Minnesota and North Dakota.[4] From the adjectives
they used to describe the settlers it is easy to see what personal
characteristics were deemed important by authors who engaged in
such projects. They write of men who are "progressive and enterprising," "prominent and solid," "substantial," "busiest and most
genial"; of a "principal promoter," a "self-made man," a "famous
founder"; of citizens who are "enterprising and wideawake," "influ-
ential," "esteemed." Farmers are variously "prosperous" and "well to
do," "steady going and hard working," "thrifty, bright, intelligent."
Of one admired subject it is said that "his parents both died and he
was sent out into the world to hustle for himself." Most of these men
are married, and their wives and children named, but in only a
handful of instances are the wives described, and then very distantly.
One "cheerfully shared with her husband the trials"; another was
"active and efficient in church and missionary work"; there is "a
woman of fine attainments . . . an able and invaluable assistant to her
husband," "a true helper in her husband's work"; several women of
"refinement," and numerous "genial ladies." Here is one of the
longer descriptions: "Since the death of Mr. Evans and their son Ole,
Mrs. Evans has continued to reside in the beautiful family home,
surrounded by the refinements and comforts which years of work in
the pioneer days are the well earned reward." The men who purport
to have written a "history" of the valley have placed women in a
black hole of refined repose; they have not imagined them participating in whatever is meant by history. Louisa Wanner used not
one of these expressions about wideawake hustling citizens. It is as
though two populations, living in each other's company, shared no
common perceptions.

Fannie Dunn Quain, Doctor and Historian

I have been contrasting school grammar books of the nineteenth
century with writings of people who did not use them. What about

those who did? What difference did it make to those, especially women, who made an effort to conform to the optimistic, self-improving state of mind those books advocate along with their concern for correct sentences? Grammar books were, of course, only one source of many for people susceptible to rules of correct behavior; they reflected and furthered attitudes which also abounded in advertising, sermons, magazine fiction, etiquette manuals, and popular literature generally. All impinged more strongly on the lives of women of the middle classes than on most working class women, to judge from the way each group wrote. Fannie Dunn Quain illustrates the predicament of middle class women on the frontier. Many of her experiences were as crude as any endured by poorer rural women, and they are the experiences she writes most carefully about, yet her education, profession, income, and general status in the community endowed her with a language and strategies for describing herself that are different from theirs, and which produced their own ambiguities.

Fannie Quain was a doctor, the first woman in North Dakota to earn a medical degree. She also taught school, wrote newspaper articles on historical subjects, and administered various professional and civic organizations. Born in Bismarck, Dakota Territory, in 1874, she died there in 1950. Her father, John Piatt Dunn (1839–1917) had come to Bismarck in 1873 as a druggist, newly married to Christina Sykes, age 17, his second wife, and he prospered in real estate and politics, being elected mayor of Bismarck and county treasurer. Christina Dunn was one of the founding members of the state historical society and active in a variety of civic and charitable organizations. Such was the background of solid citizenry into which Fannie Dunn was born, the fourth settler child in Bismarck and the first in a frame house, though as she wrote about it, that was a dubious distinction, for her mother was obliged to worry that she would fall through the floorboards. The town burgeoned as Fannie grew through childhood, and she attended high school as well as elementary school there, unlike the sons and daughters of many prosperous settlers who were sent east to boarding schools. She certified for teaching at the normal school in St. Cloud, Minnesota, in 1892, and after some years of odd jobs including teaching, entered medical school at the University of Michigan at Ann Arbor, receiving her degree in 1898. She specialized in eye and ear, practiced in Bismarck, and became active in public health, especially in preventing tuberculosis. In 1903, she married Eric Quain, a surgeon specializing in abdominal conditions who founded the Quain and Ramstad Clinic in Bismarck. There were three children; the first died at birth. Their daughter, Marion Quain Kaiser, now lives in California; their son, Buell, born in 1912, died in 1939 in Brazil, where he had been studying native poetry and folk tales. Fannie and Eric Quain were divorced and he remarried in 1940, when he retired and moved to Oregon. He died in 1962. Fannie Quain had one sister, Elida, and a brother, John Piatt, who studied veterinary medicine and ranched near Bismarck.

Fannie Dunn Quain's writings include historical articles published in the Bismarck *Tribune* during the 1920s, short reminiscenses, and an autobiographical essay.[5] The collection contains no personal letters or diaries. Fannie Quain wrote in two styles: one reads matter-of-factly, like straightforward journalism, and the other decorates itself in purple passages. The plain writing manner enumerates factual detail—principal events for each year of the 1870s and 80s are summarized in the *Tribune* series—but it also omits, we later find, significant details which are unexpectedly supplied by the baroque pieces. In her plain style, Fannie Quain states almost no opinions. She notes the outward facts of suffering (a fire, cold weather, primitive housing) but she hardly particularizes them in the experiences of individual people. Her other, decorated manner, which now looks stilted and rather dated, full of circumlocutions and clichés of the period, she uses to say things that she apparently could or would not in the plain style. It turns out that she does after all have strong reservations about the pioneer heroism touted all about her, and uses the style made for euphemism angrily to say so. There are two subjects in particular which Fannie Quain writes about often and in both manners: her memories of her mother, Christina Dunn, and her own efforts to earn money for medical school. Though we may never understand what she truly thought on either subject we can see how vexed and complicated her feelings were.

Twice she briefly tells of her mother's arrival in Bismarck, giving the event short shrift in a typescript mainly about her father: "In 1873 Mr. Dunn married Christina Seeley Sykes (St. Johns, N.B. 1856–Bismarck 1940) and brought her to Crystal Springs on the Northern Pacific work train and from there overland to Bismarck, a bride." In one of her *Tribune* articles there is a somewhat longer digression on the same event, when telling of a fire in March 1877 that burned several downtown buildings:

The first restaurant run by John Yegan since '72 was in that block of burned buildings also. Next to my Father's loss, Mother felt worse about this restaurant because it was where she ate her first meal in Bismarck and where she was introduced to a cup of the "purest water in the world" (a glass of mud) out of the Missouri when she asked for her first drink on her arrival in her new home town. This drink brought her first tears after a wedding trip of 10 days by freight car and wagon with rest on a bed of sacks of flour and no opportunity to clean herself up or relieve the strain of travel.

Her effort is to be light and witty, but she succeeds in saying something truer to her mother's experience than she does in the tear-less version.

The story of her own birth as her mother's first child evidently appalled her, and Fannie Quain tells and retells its strange details. One version incorporates the event among "firsts" in Bismarck—train, post office, names of new settlers.

When Mother arrived in Bismarck there were 147 shelters of one sort or another in the town. Many of these were tent buildings boarded up about halfway. The lumber came from Mr. E. H. Blye's sawmill on the bank of the Missouri and was all cottonwood. Our house was made of those boards and was the first frame building in town. These cottonwood boards warped and shingles warped so during the winter of '73, I brought a great blizzard with me and they made a tent of blankets over the bed to keep the snow off Mother and me. I cannot see anything very extraordinary about the Eskimos baptizing their babies in the snow. Mother tells of such cracks in the floor that she made herself a rug to place her chair on when she sewed because if she forgot to sit on the rug and dropped anything, it went into the cellar. Mrs. Humbert of Camp Hancock loaned mother the only sewing maching in town to make my first clothes.

The sewing machine, the 147 shelters, the holes in the floor of the cottonwood house all appear again in a longer and more baroque essay, a one-sheet single-spaced typescript.

A North Dakota blizzard stalked across the prairie the thirteenth day of February in seventy four. A blizzard that blows snow as fine as cake flour through every crack, around every window and door; tiny fingers of feathery snow outline cracks you have never seen before, and after a time your shoulders are damp because of it. The wood fire roars in its fight against the cold. A woman labors in a bed in the corner and the snow is sifting in so fast that a tent of blankets must be made over the bed to keep the snow out and help to save the expected babe from the cold. The young mother is a bride of less than a year and yesterday she answered the call of a sick friend. This friend was an old lady who was the wife of one of the army officers. She had allowed the expectant mother the use of her sewing machine during the months of the summer and fall to prepare the baby clothes. The army officer was seldom sober but he was very kind to her and had taken a great fancy to the young bride. He drove one horse hitched to an improvised sled made from a packing box. The snow was very deep and drifted into billows by the ever howling wind. When he had come after Christine the day before and announced that his good wife was sick and would like her to visit her, Christine went. They bobbed along over the drifts and made the visit but had to cut the visit short because of a very great distress which had come over Christine. So, as she lay there in the corner on the bed, she blamed herself for taking the ride and wailed, "Oh, if I had not taken that ride with a drunken man, my baby would have been a Valentine." Into that snow blown tiny house, on that terrible night, a girl child was born.

Mother loves her so, and Father is so proud of her that they give little thought what the world has in store for the girl. Men can work hard with the fellows and go to war with the bands playing and the other fellows marching, but if this piece of humanity fulfills her mission in life she must go down into the shadow of death three or four times for the good of her country. Every one is an added tie to the life that is filled with joy, fear, or sorrow, as the case may be. She must hold up her head and smile when her boy walks off to foreign research or to war; and when her husband goes off with another woman who has not borne children and hence has more leisure to be beautiful and attractive. As Dr. Hertzler says, "I cannot understand why anybody would call woman the weaker sex."

The town of which this little cottonwood house was a part, had 145 buildings in it. Most of them board sides and tent roofs. Some few, made of cottonwood logs, these were fit for habitation. Water was hauled about town in a big tank with a hose at the back, and delivered into barrels that froze almost solid in these poorly constructed buildings even though they stood near the stove. The cottonwood would not keep a fire through the night. The streets were deep with dust in the summer and deep frozen ruts during the winter when they were not banked roof high with snow. The lights were kerosene lamps that flickered and smoked because of the drafty conditions in the homes. All women baked their own bread and did their washing by hand with a tub and a wash board that took the skin off their knuckles. Then they hung these clothes out on lines in the deep snow and they were frozen onto the line as soon as they touched it. Each home had a hole under the floor of one room to help cool things in the summer and help to keep them from freezing in the winter. When our baby had a bath, Christine dropped about half of the tools on the floor and they went straight through a big crack in the cellar, the crack was not quite large enough to let the baby through. There were no street lights, no telephones, no ice-boxes, no toasters. Irons were heated on top of the kitchen stove summer and winter, and mother ironed the stiff dress up shirts.

For all the genteel "tiny fingers of feathery snow," this is an angry piece: anger at the imposition placed on her mother for the mere borrowing of a sewing machine, at the drunken army officer taking "a great fancy to the young bride," at the appalling physical conditions that her mother was subjected to, and, in her own behalf, she was angry from the start at the very condition of being a woman, at what had happened both to her mother and to herself. Focusing on their shared childbirth, she implied crossgenerational guilts, for she, Fannie, was the child her mother bore at such pains and with such hope, and yet she blamed her mother for her own life having fallen short of those hopes. But motherhood and childbirth are sacred topics in American culture, not often exposed to close inspections, and so Fannie Quain kept these reservations bound within pious sentimentalities of genteel writing, even though clichés compounded the angers.

Yet even so, the story is not complete. What did her father have to do with the affair? Where was he when her very pregnant mother was taken off through a snowstorm in a horse-drawn packing-box? One wonders whether it was derring-do and pioneer spirit that brought people to such a frontier town, including young women inevitably pregnant, or men's sadistic folly. What she says of "going down into the shadow of death" in childbirth, of losing sons to war or to "research," and of husbands abandoning wives for younger and childless women—these allusions sound mysteriously histrionic, until one knows that Fannie Quain's own childbearing was difficult, that her third child did die in "foreign research," and that Eric Quain at retirement married a younger and childless woman.

The third-person narrative gives Fannie Quain's sentences the appearance of detachment; it is no more than an impersonal story, being retold yet another time, but this device calls attention to omissions, the words that were not directly spoken. A tent of blankets "must be made"—by whom? Who besides Christina Dunn, was in this clammy room, and, more to the point, how did Fannie learn the story? Her conventional expressions constitute what little is left, in Fannie Quain's telling, of the manner in which the story first came to her, and they betray severe editing. Her narrative so insistently refuses to admit a voice speaking directly that we are all but deafened by the indirect speaker who is nowhere and everywhere. In Fannie Quain's less detailed newspaper account, it is easier to hear her mother's voice: "Mother tells of such cracks in the floor that she made herself a rug to place her chair on when she sewed because if she forgot to sit on the rug and dropped anything, it went into the cellar. Mrs. Humbert of Camp Hancock loaned Mother the only sewing machine in town to make my first clothes." Names tame the account, and one can imagine that Mrs. Dunn herself saw some humor in her experiences. But in Fannie Quain's essay, there is no trace of humor or adventure or pioneering firsts (the "only" sewing machine).

Sometimes Fannie Quain's descriptions hover on the bizarre, evoking much but explaining little. A single carefully written paragraph titled "Custer's Dogs," for all its intimacy, again leaves out her mother's thoughts except for a parting witticism.

General Custer was a great lover of dogs and raised a number of fine purebreds. Doctors were forced to use all available relief for their patients at the time because they were without the supply depots for instruments and apparatus needed for special treatment. When I was looking for my first nourishment, Mother's breasts were in terrible condition. She had had more milk than it was possible for one small bundle to care for and there was not a breast pump this side of Minneapolis and nothing but the pony express to bring it through one of the worst blizzards the prairies have ever seen. The old army doctor had to use his head. This he did. General Custer had a new litter of pups and when he made his next visit he had his pockets filled with little round dogs so little that they did not have their eyes open. These he applied to the distended breasts. Their paws kneaded the glazed surfaces until the natural color was restored and their tiny mouths healed the nipples. One small dog after the other took his turn and ate until he fell exhausted and as Mother tells it, "You could crack a louse on his belly he was so full." Others may have the distinction of being the first baby born in Bismarck, the first to do this and that but I have the undivided distinction of have been raised with General Custer's pups.

Fannie Quain could no more have recorded this episode from observation than she could her mother's packing box trip, but her manner of writing about nursing puppies is less bitter and more direct. Tall tales on the frontier are the impetus for this story, not secret resentments.

Fannie Quain's opinions about her mother were ambivalent. She tells an unattractive anecdote about her in a description of celebrations in Bismarck of the passage of the Enabling Act in 1889; she viewed her mother both with empathy and hostility.

> The Methodist Ladies were feeding the celebrants that day at the old Athenaeum which stood on Main just east of the Lamborn Hospital, later St. Alexius. The Ladies fed 1500 people and among them were 40 Indians. Mother was a little girl in Minnesota during the uprising of the Indians there, and she did not like them very well. In the rush one freezer of icecream (in those days everything was home made) had gotten salt into it and they had regretfully set it aside. When Mother saw the Indians she said, "Give them the salty ice cream." Some of the ladies thought it was not just right, their Methodist conscience plagued them a little, but the Indians liked it. They took the ice cream and mixed it with baked beans they served for the lunch and ate it all with great relish.

For all the wealth of experience and information that Fannie Quain has at her disposal, we strain through her writing to puzzle what it means to her. Women's lives on the frontier were as ambiguous as they were physically precarious. Primitive and dangerous living conditions, not surprisingly, were paired sometimes with primitive moral values, yet Mrs. Dunn, who had given birth under a blanket tent to keep off the snow and had suckled puppies, fifteen years later was serving ice cream in a group of "Methodist ladies." It is of course an old observation that people try to preserve the social marks of their class regardless of other incongruities; Fannie Quain's writing also suggests how difficult it evidently was for individual persons (as here her mother and herself) to fit language, behavior, personal relationships, and physical conditions to a coherent pattern. There is so much she was unable to tell in more than disconnected scraps. A paragraph summarizing the society of middle class women in Bismarck leaves out much else one would like to know. The women's avowed mission was to make life minimally endurable while the husbands ran the town's business.

> All through these early years a crowd of women who came here in the first years of settlement, worked together. They had seen the suffering and endured the hardships of the frontier and there was a bond as close as sisterhood among them. They helped to build the first churches, entertained at the Lyceum Club, opened their homes on New Year's Day for the gentlemen of the town and Fort Lincoln to call, furnished society at the parties, nursed the sick, officiated at births, sat

by the dying and acted as undertaker for friend and stranger alike.
Nothing happened in the small town that these women did not help. A
woman who arrived later in the '80s, who admired the crowd very
much and liked to be counted in with their fun, jokingly dubbed them
"The Elephant Gang." They were all good sized women and the name
was immediately adopted. They were Mesdames Ward, Steyell, Dunn,
Suttle, Davis, Donnelly, Glass, Whalen, Wakeman, and Marsh. You will
find the names of their husbands in the list of the business men of early
Bismarck.

In Bismarck as in other communities, women established their separate "sphere" as much for their own survival as for the community's.
All these glimpses of her mother are like snapshots, rigid in time and
in Fanny Quain's memory without connections between apprecia-
tions and resentments of her mother.

Another puzzle in Fannie Quain's life is her parents' attitude to
her studying medicine and becoming a doctor. She begins her autobiographical essay of 1930 by referring to the several relatives in
her parents' generation who had studied medicine: her father, a
pharmacist; his brother, a doctor; her mother's sister and several
cousins, nurses and doctors. "This background," she writes, "may
have had its influence on my desire to study medicine." Yet it seems
to have had little influence in her parents' supporting her efforts,
for although she reports no overt attempts to discourage her, the
family apparently did nothing practical to help her.

Her medical career, then, was slow in starting, for she was obliged
to earn her own way. This she did in a variety of largely unsatisfactory jobs: typing for the surveyor general, teaching in rural schools,
and even running for county school superintendent. She lost her
first campaign because of ballot-box stuffing by her opponent, she
says, but the next time, after medical school and several years'
practice, she ran again and won, serving one term. But while she was
trying so hard to gather money to study medicine (at the University
of Michigan because, she had been told, it was a place "where
women medical students were well treated") no financial help seems
to have been forthcoming from her parents. In fact, on one occasion
when an offer of aid was made by another relative, her mother
would not let her accept it. She had applied for nurse's training at
Belleview Hospital and had been rejected for being too young.
"About this time my mother's sister who had studied medicine
wanted to take me to New York and let me go to school. My mother

knew that she lived in luxury, that I would be weaned away from home and family if I went, so decided against it." She nowhere comments on this lack of support, but in an essay entitled "The Pasque Flower and the Promised Land," the somewhat stilted and romantic writing reaches through to reservations she had not made in the more apparently straightforward pieces.

The essay is about the six months Fannie Quain taught in a country school, beginning in April of the year she was seventeen. The autumn before, there had been a very large prairie fire over the county to within twelve miles of Bismarck, "leaving a black desolation in its wake." Her father drove her with horse and buggy, and all the way from Bismarck to the school thirty miles away, she saw nothing but burned earth to the horizon.

> It was about two o'clock when we reached the top of a small elevation and looked down upon what was to be my home for the next six months. We were looking at the home of Ole Anderson, a cluster of sod buildings of all shapes and sizes grouped around a well. The well was conspicuous because it was the only thing in the collection that did not have a wall and roof of sod out of which were standing the dried heads of last year's sunflowers. This place was known to the neighbors as "Sod-Town." One could hardly distinguish the buildings from the surrounding gloom.

She went with her father to the top of the hill to say good-bye; it began to rain and did not stop for five weeks; the Andersons spoke only Swedish; the small part of the sod house curtained off for her bedroom had to be shared with two daughters; and most desolating of all, there was no word from her family until a "small note" came in the third week saying that they were quarantined for scarlet fever. Gloom permeates her description of the school room.

> My school house is another story. It was not a school house but a granary that the school board had partitioned so that the school room was about ten by sixteen feet with two windows. One on the east wall and one on the south and near enough together so an aisle arrangement could hold a black-board about a yard square between the two. A kitchen table and chair for the teacher stood near the black-board and the home-made desks were along the wall and back into the dark corner. These desks were made of two upright boards with a board slanted at the top for the desk and a shelf six inches below for books. There was a narrow shelf about sixteen inches from the floor to form a seat. This was attached to the front and served to seat the pupil who sat

at the desk ahead. There were about six of these desks and ten or
twelve pupils as weather permitted. This room leaked all around and
the floor had come to life. Every two boards made a tent clear across
the floor and the water stood between as we had to walk on the ridges
to keep our feet dry. It was cold and damp and the first few days we
had no stove where the children could be dried when they came to
school wet. This was improved when a stove was set up in the dark
corner.

Not surprisingly, she was homesick and unhappy. On the Monday
morning of the sixth week, she awakened to sunshine, and looked
out of her window to see the pasque flowers in bloom, which "com-
pletely hid the burned grass and had transformed the hills to a pale
blue." She speaks of this as a miracle—the sunlight and blue flowers
after all the rain and black—"framed by the casing of that deep
window of a little sod house on the prairies of North Dakota. I wrote
my mother, Mrs. John P. Dunn, that I had looked into 'the Promised
Land.'" But the visionary ending of the essay, however beautiful and
surprising the scene of blooming anemones must have been, does
not cancel out the details of her abandonment to pools of water in
sod-town. What had her father been thinking of to leave her there?

Johanna Kildahl: Self-Help toward Education

It might be supposed that nineteenth-century women of the professional class would be less inarticulate than their sisters, thanks to
their education and relative economic security, but such was not the
case. In fact, professional women were especially apt to take an
indirect approach to the truth. Finding acceptable language in which
to write about themselves was apparently difficult, and seldom attempted. For example, a major crisis in the lives of numerous
young men and women, then as now, was the struggle to earn
enough money for college. Yet whereas men were likely to make a
heroic story of their hardships, women feared they would be accused
of bragging, and wrote deprecatingly so as not to attract attention.
Thus, Fannie Quain turned the misery of sod-hut boarding into a
triumph of resurrected pasque flowers. When Johanna Kildahl told
a similar story, she hid her angry suffering behind joking satire, but,
as in Fannie Quain's accounts, factual details belie the hearty tone.
The year she graduated from the University of North Dakota, 1898,
Johanna Kildakh read in chapel an essay called "Self-help." It is as

close as she can come to telling what it has taken for her to get an education, yet it strains not to make a public disturbance.[6]

If college students took to heart the prolific literature on self-help, Johanna Kildahl says, they would achieve "independence, humility, charity, trueheartedness, decision, and . . . success in after life." She laments the loss suffered by those whose parents paid their way to college, thus depriving them of the benefit of overcoming enormous difficulties. Her own parents made it possible for her to put off college for six years while she nursed her ailing mother; only then was she free to begin teaching long enough to earn the money for university. She boarded in a sod house where she was given a very small room: "I welcomed every obstacle as so much towards the development of my character. The room contained one window of six small panes, two of which were broken." During several consecutive days of rain, she came home one evening to find half an inch of water on the floor. "My clothes, which I had hung up on the wall, were all wet and little rivulets were trickling down the walls, with a sweet musical sound, forming delightful little pools on the floor." She got into bed, the only dry place, and read her self-help manual, "having time for reflection." She had even more time the next day when she took her clothes into bed with her and covered the bed with oilcloth, the roof having begun to leak there as well. The next night she spent in the school house, sitting up. "My thoughts wandered and I grew homesick," and she decided to give up and go home. But then she was inspired with providential visions of self-help and resolved, underlining the sentence, *"As long as I could keep my head above water I must stay;* it would be cowardly to do otherwise. It continued to rain for three more days when the rain turned to snow." When school was finally over, she looked forward to her own schooling, only to learn that she was not to be paid until the following autumn, and that her clothes were ruined, "so I was compelled to remain at home, my coveted education still in the offing. I did not mind these little trials in the least for I knew what I was gaining in discipline." How she eventually did arrive at the university her essay does not say.

Almost thirty years later Johanna Kildahl wrote of an earlier attempt to earn money, when she was fifteen and hired to teach five pupils in a school six miles from home (in "My First School," 1922). In order to accept the position she needed a certificate, which involved a trip to Crookston, some forty miles by foot, wagon, and

train, to persuade the school superintendent to give it to her in spite
of her being under age. This she accomplished by refusing to leave
his office for several days, though once she began to teach, she was
able to remain only a few weeks before being called home to nurse
her mother for the six years prior to her next teaching effort. Again,
she concludes the account with mild irony: "As I have looked back
on that event, which at that time was all important to me, I could see
how an All-wise Providence intervened to protect my too kind-
hearted Mr. Brown from the retribution he had invited upon himself by violating the law, myself from the results of participating, in
deed at least, of being the co-partner and the mainspring in the
crime, and the children from innocently suffering therefrom; also
how vain it is to hope to profit from ill-gotten gains." Yet her
desperation comes through in spite of the mannered writing. When
she reappeared the second day in the superintendent's office for her
certificate, she told him, she says, "that I could not go home without
it; that the dream of my life was to get an education, that I had to
make my own money to pay for it, that I had a school engaged, etc."
On the afternoon of the third day, she realized that she was running
short of money: "I put in my time planning how to make it possible
for me to prolong my siege until victory was mine. I decided to find
a place to work for my room and board. The possibility of failure to
obtain the certificate never entered my mind. My only concern was
to be able to stay until Mr. Brown capitulated." When he finally did,
addressing her always "Now little girl," she walked the eighteen
miles from the train station in Grand Forks to her home, with ten
cents left to buy milk at a farm on the way. She got lost in the dark,
and fell into an excavation. She had her victory, but there is so much
Johanna Kildahl said nothing about. What of her family? She mentions in passing that a sister had taught in the school before her—
was there no one who might have helped (self-help notwithstand-
ing)? Was her family opposed to her ambitions, or did they not
notice? She is silent on all of that.

Lives like Johanna Kildahl's are half lost to us. In the file of her
typescripts at the State Historical Society in Bismarck, there is, besides the two autobiographical essays, one called "Reminiscences," as
well as six political essays on the subject of world peace, dated
between 1919 and 1924. "A Demand from Woman Voters: Recon-
struction of International Law" proposes that any peace conferences
"be composed of a Jury, comprising all truly neutral, civilized na-

tions, and barring all belligerents from participating in the framing of peace terms, thus discarding the unjust and barbaric custom of dictation of peace terms by the victors." There are clippings from Minneapolis newspapers reporting her activities in behalf of the League of Nations as well as her letters on world peace addressed to Presidents Woodrow Wilson (1–15–19) and Warren Harding (12–30–20).

Great seriousness and grueling determination must certainly have marked her character, as well as considerable intellectual achievement, yet over a span of forty years, her writings about her personal life succumb to the numbing optimism that she found ridiculous in the self-help books. Her "Reminiscences" of 1936 tell of moving from the farm near Grand Forks to one in the Mauvaise Coulee Valley in August 1883, and arriving at "a small frame house and a tent, after a week's riding in a prairie schooner behind a team of oxen." Devils Lake, the nearest town, was three days away by oxen, to which "the ladies," she says, "made one trip, in the fall." The family raised cows, chickens, a big garden, as well as wheat, and planted thirty acres of trees. Her father, who she says was "not able bodied," cared for two hundred chickens; there were an older sister and three brothers. Her mother was bedridden for five years, having arrived by train on a cot. She describes her mother as "a tower of strength in our family; her marvellous cheerfulness, amiability, undaunted faith and courage, which never recognized an obstacle, and her wise counsel never failed and was a constant encouragement and impetus to all of us to do our best, and carry on." Even so, this mother, by keeping Johanna home to take care of her, was the primary impediment to Johanna's own carrying on. So strenuous an adolescence followed by a professional career of such high social purpose (she received a Ph.D. in biology from the University of Chicago in 1904)—one wants to know how one led to the other, how the young girl who walked twelve miles after straying cattle, and made the trip to Crookston, became obsessed with the precarious fortunes of the League of Nations.

Grace DeCou and Adah Bickford, Relieved of Husbands

None of the rural and working women whose letters and diaries I have been reading is wealthy, although only a few are intermittently very poor. As one woman puts it, "I am not Aristocratic and am not wealthy neither one." Some earn a living: as hotel chambermaid, proprietor of a store, seamstress. Some depend on the earnings of husbands or fathers who chop wood, load cargo on produce boats, or perform unspecified odd jobs. Several share homesteading or farming with parents or husband. These writers have had enough schooling to write fairly standard English in a legible hand. They give virtually no information about culture, politics, or the arts, and they almost never express an opinion. They observe—minutely, repetitively, sometimes in flashes that show things not seen elsewhere. Such reading, admittedly, takes patience.

The distinctions I have been making among styles of writing have included gender differences between men and women, as well as distinctions of class among women. For, from the examples I have read of private writing, it has seemed to me that all men, regardless of class, write in a larger circumference than do women. It is easier for me, a stranger, to understand what men's letters and diaries are about than women's; it takes less time to realize where they are, what they do for a living, what are the relationships among people they mention. Those kinds of details are what people mean when they ask what something is "about." When they write privately, men appear to assume that writing is a form of public declaration, to be conveyed a considerable distance between themselves and their correspondent, regardless of who that person is. Their writing is not necessarily less intimate than women's, but it is, I think less elliptical, perhaps in part because, more surely than women, men are writing about themselves. Charles Forbes stood in the center of the wheatfield landscape he described to Beulah. When Hubbel Pierce, as we shall see, prepared his wife Viola for her trip from Michigan to Dakota, he too described himself at the center of the venture.

Thus it may be said that men write in order to make distinctions, to assert that some events are more important than others, and all of us are schooled to this view when we learn to write—drills in composing topic sentences, outlines, introductions and conclusions on demand. But working women entertain other, and nearly opposite, ambitions. They write in order to assert a pattern and to blur distinctions between recurring and unique events. In this view, keeping the pattern intact day after day is the mark of a well regulated and successful life. Their effort is not, I think, to belittle their own value; indeed, as we shall continue to see, working women typically write with considerable assurance and self-regard. Rather, their writing emphasizes patterns because patterns compose their days, and they do not see time as a succession of discrete or climactic events.

The writing of middle class women, those who have enjoyed education and some professional experience, uneasily approaches both modes without resolving the contradictions. Serious ambiguities in writings of women like Fannie Quain or Johanna Kildahl are at least partly attributable, I think, to their supposing that they ought to write (and also to think) in a hierarchy of events and ideas, as indeed they must if they intend to succeed in education and professions. But convictions waver; their hearts are not always in the effort, nor do circumstances in their lives always permit it. Fannie Quain was too aware of complicated textures of everyday living to condemn her family, the farmers she boarded with, or the weather for her miserable sod-house teaching venture. Johanna Kildahl also was too caught up in the daily complications of her mother's illness to be able to cut herself away, and as a result, both women appear now somewhat victimized by their circumstances. They knew too much, as it were, to make clean separations both in action and in syntax that a man would perform.

To illustrate the unemphatic, short-reined perspective of working women's writing: Grace DeCou made daily entries for over forty years. The one for December 18, 1893, is typical.

Tuesday. Snowed. We washed. Jasper brought wood. He was here for dinner. Mrs. Schoentzow called and payed me one $1.00 she owed me, I called at Mrs. Walkers and brought Mrs. Roys dress home to make, went down town, got crackers .07 cents, cheese .17 cents, foolscap paper .01 cents, a bottle of Chamberlains immediate relief .25 cents.[7]

What is important to Grace DeCou, what does she see of her life? The weather, the names of people she visited with, and money, earned and spent. I gather that she was unmarried and lived with her widowed mother but nowhere in the three years of this diary can I discover what were the arrangements concerning a farm for which she gave Jasper $20 to pay the tax, who Jasper was, or what he did aside from deliver wood. There is a pattern to virtually all her entries: first the weather, then business, sewing, and visits, then shopping. And should anything out of the ordinary occur, that event is fitted as closely as possible into the pattern:

July 11, 1894, Wednesday. Jasper came at 5 am to take Mother to Isaac. Their baby is very sick. Isaac came up about noon. The baby died before Mother got there. Isaac went to Sam's for dinner. He wanted me to go down town with him so I called at Sam's for him. Flossie Taylor came after some pieces of Bird and Belle's dresses. Belle and Bird came after their waist, paid me $3.25. I went down town this evening.

Thursday was warm and windy; she went to Isaac's and ate supper at Jasper's.

July 13, 1894, Friday. Allie Underwood and I sat up all night at Isaac's. I ate breakfast at Isaac's. The baby's funeral was at the house this forenoon. They buried her in the Alexander cemetery west of Perm. I stopped at Stellie Tompson in Perm for dinner. Came home on the train, cost 17 cents. Went down town this evening. Called to see Julia Weaver.
July 14, Saturday. I washed. Went down town this evening.

Forty years later Grace DeCou had moved from rural Michigan to a suburb of Los Angeles, yet her diary for 1934–36 is in the same style. Sentence parts are short with almost no connectives except *and*; she uses few modifiers, a high proportion of short concrete nouns and pronouns, and verbs of simple action. Nouns and verbs repeatedly refer to time, to weather, money, business, domestic activities. Should anything out of the ordinary occur, that event is fitted as closely as possible into the pattern. At the time she moved from Michigan to California, Grace DeCou had married one T. H. Zintgraff. I do not know what he did for a living, who he was, or his full name. She makes only passing references to him in her diary until mid-April of 1935 when he took ill, and the doctor had to be called to give him a hypodermic. Grace the same week also entertained her visiting sister, went to a community sing, and made various purchases. T. H. worsened; there were more hypodermics; he "seems to be crazy"; she says she can do nothing with him. Then on Sunday, May 2: "Quite nice. T. H. is no better, just as crazy as ever broke a window pane with rocking chair. Mrs. Fisher, Mrs. Alexander called, Miss Stanzel came to see my new stove. T. H. passed away this evening at 8 PM."

The funeral was on Tuesday ("was cremated, his wish") and on Friday she had Mr. Wats put new glass in the window ("cost 87 cents, putty and sale tax"). So much for T. H.

More ominously, a year later she was rummaging for paint:

> Looked the things T. H. had in some cigar boxes, found something like red liquor in a small round glass in a small paper box with some thing like sawdust to keep it from breaking or moving, do not know what it was but thought it might be something dangerous T. H. had to do some one or some thing damage, so buried in as deep a hole as I could dig between the walk of our house and the neighbors. Did not know what else to do with it to keep it from doing no one any harm. Hope I have got it where it will do no harm. Mrs. Fisher called. I went to the store got potatoes 15 cts corn meal 10 cts, . . .

and so on. Grace DeCou's life has been made of hard work, meticulous care over small sums of money, an intricate network of friends, acquaintants, customers, and relatives, and, in her forties, marriage to a disagreeable and violent man. But more telling than these "facts" of her life is her way of seeing them, so apparently without selection or perspective. No one event appears to color or displace another: prices, visits, trips to town—the pattern invariably reasserts itself.

There are no remarks in Grace DeCou's diaries to make one think that she was writing them for anyone to read. She does not even comment on the fact of her writing, although she never missed a day's entry in the three notebooks I have read. She never directly mentions what I learn only from relatives now living, that she was active in the Christian Science Church. Why then is she so reticent, even about T. H.'s outrages? These omissions are not that, I think, in her mind. Her habit is a very close focus. She does not generalize or abstract, and details are everything even though they reveal so little to an outsider. Their focus is too close.

The diary of Adah Bickford, of Kempton, North Dakota, for the year 1910 also illustrates the secrecy of women's writing. The success of a woman's life traditionally is judged by the skill with which she manages to keep undisturbed the smooth pattern of daily living. Any happening is a disturbance, unless it can be shown to fit into the pattern. Adah Bickford's diary hides the desertion of her husband in the interstices of the very patterned order of her day. She keeps her housekeeping intact and preserves self-respect by not attaching herself to events, certainly not in the way most men define their importance in what they do. To decipher her diary needs some sleuthing.

The Bickford family ran a combined store, pool hall, and livery service for which the son, Merle, drove a taxi. Earl Bickford, Adah's husband, worked also at a mill, but on March 3 left for Nevada, California, and later Bowbells, North Dakota. Adah records his movements in her laconic way:

> Elmer left this AM on the 10 o'clock train which was two hours late. Did not tell us where he was going, but said he would write. Had trunk checked to Larimore. I asked him to stay but did not say very much as we saw by letter he wrote to *woman* in Cal. that *he was* going back and he had told us he would not stay, also had packed his trunk several times to go. Said in letter to her that he came back to us only to get things in shape to make a home for him and her there, so we tho't best to let him go before he got money in any way. Better now than later.[8]

(How did *she* know what Elmer said in his letter to the California woman?) Adah corresponded with hotel keepers along Elmer's route, and subscribed to two Bowbells newspapers in order to read the accounts of his doings there in the society notes. And yet she never says in her diary that these all are tactics for keeping track of him; she hardly indicates that he had disturbed the pattern of her life, which, judging from the form as well as the content of her diary, was a strictly regulated one.

The entry for almost every day begins with a few lines about housework: "Made belt collar and finished my black silk waist. Also mended a little and did a few other odd jobs." Then she skips a line and reports other events: Merle's trips with the taxi, letters sent and received, Merle's going to dances, Halley's Comet, buying ice cream and tending the store. "Merle and I washed then after cleaning up I did most of my ironing while Merle fussed with the auto, he also got supper while I ironed." She kept a tight rein on Merle (who was thirty-two at the time) and she never let her husband far from her mind. On May 3, "Two months today since Elmer went away." The last line of every entry reports the weather ("Rather cool and windy but not a bad day"). Adah Bickford was a woman for whom respectability was important; she enjoyed riding in the new car Merle bought, she went by train to Larimore and Grand Forks for shopping, the dentist, and opera, and she worked very hard keeping the store and her house and garden in order. She answered letters promptly. Her diary reminds us how important social class is to the way people think of themselves.

Adah Bickford almost never comments upon events; the fact of her reporting something is as much as she reveals of feelings or opinions. Certainly Elmer's defection was a strain on her respectability to which she reacted with iron impassivity, but she was not fooled: "See by Bowbells paper rec'd tonight that E. A. Bickford returned from his western and California trip to that place last Wednesday" (4–2). She is tough, but her diary notes so many brief instances of other lives collapsing as to make her hold on her own seem the more precarious:

> Letter from Sister Alice telling of Sister Ella's sad condition rendering confinement necessary all through the deviltry of her husband. (8–11)
>
> Little Bessie Aldridge died this afternoon of Infantile Paralysis. Mrs. Fredingerh came for me and she, Mrs. Olson and I made a little dress, skirt, and panties for her to buried in. (8–16)
>
> Heard this evening that Mrs. Hobie took a dose of carbolic acid this afternoon about four o'clock from the effects of which she died about two hours later. She telephoned for Mrs. Halverson and took it while she was there. (11–28)

There but for the Grace of God goes Adah, is what these notes imply. Achievement, success, and always optimism, are so strongly the code by which Americans are expected to live that women, to whom the code least applies, appear in their writing loath to admit otherwise. That, I think, more than sexual prudery, is what makes their writing appear reticent, and sends them to concentrate so hard on keeping to the surface pattern of their days. But the counterpattern is there, if we learn to read it.

Mattie Lampman, Klondike Diarist

One is tempted to say that diaries like Adah Bickford's and Grace DeCou's fall into repetitive patterns for the obvious reason that their authors' days were repetitious. The women were not oblivious to progress, their writing merely reflected the fact of their static existence. They were neither going anywhere, nor changing, nor achieving anything in particular. Yet when outward circumstances would seem to insist upon discrete, one-of-a-kind events, adventure even, women who kept diaries persist in thinking primarily about what happened over and over. Patterns emerge regardless.

In 1898 Mattie Lampman *was* going somewhere, from her farmstead in Grinnell, North Dakota (now under the waters of Lake

Sakakawea formed by the Garison Dam), to the Klondike. The diary she kept for that year, a miniature three-by-four inches, details virtually every town, fort, river, lake, and portage along the water route between Edmonton, Alberta, and the place where her party spent the winter, Snyetown, on the Laird River in the Northwest Territories.[9] This journey ostensibly was undertaken for the purpose of finding gold, and toward a specific although unnamed destination. One expects a progressive attitude from travelers: getting oneself from here to there ought to be a future-minded activity. No matter how amazing or impeding the scenery along the way, one anticipates arrival and then the beginning of whatever business had been the purpose of the trip. A tourist can afford to luxuriate in the journeying itself, but not a goldseeker. Travel hardly suggests repetitiveness—you do not pass the same place twice, least of all on a river boat.

But Mattie Lampman did, or might as well have. Her summaries day by day of what certainly was an unpredictable and dangerous progress do not emphasize distance achieved or obstacles overcome. Rather, she makes us remember continuous states: tedium ("floated all day," "patched some, walked some"), loneliness, and "dull days." Although not complaining, she resisted change and movement, doing what she could (however incongruously) to impose stasis and permanence. She wrote that she fixed up the tent, cooked, and sewed even on a moving boat, visited with other travelers and local Indians, wrote and read. Much of what she wrote conforms to observations by Faragher and others who have read diaries of the Oregon Trail, that men made major decisions and that work was divided along traditional male/female lines. Mattie Lampman uses the word "men" to designate a group that did not include her: "Men rested, I baked," "Men at the Snigh are all living in houses and making toboggans," "Men talking of what way to go and when to go," "I have nine men to cook for." The men hunted and she cleaned up the tent. She also steered a boat, walked much of the way, and at the end of a day still had domestic work to do. But her separation from men was more profound than continuing old habits of the womanly role. Mary Lampman imagined differently the sequence of days. Her writing sounds accurate. She was meticulous about prices, mileage, place names, but she does not arrange this information in a manner that inspires confidence in the journey. Her writing lacks the conviction I would think necessary to successful golddigging.

Mattie Lampman's entries conspicuously leave out comprehensive explanations of what was happening, what the purpose of the expedition was, even whether gold mining was the Lampmans' intent. She does not say where they expected to go, or how long they planned to be there, or even who people were—Tom, Nate, Lou, Mack—sons perhaps or close relatives. No women's names appear. Linden I take to be her husband and Booker a young son. She said they had a sale and dance before leaving the farm, and someone named Murry moved into their house, and "Ole Thompson came down, took our organ to keep for us," presumably against their return, but she does not mention selling house or property, or rental arrangements. The party left Grinnell on March 20 by wagon to Portal on the North Dakota–Saskatchewan border, then rode on a train through Moose Jaw and Calgary, arriving in Edmonton on April 11 after delays along the way, left Edmonton by riverboat on the 19th, and established their last camp on September 6 near Snyetown, on a day when the boat sprang an irreparable leak. Yet Mattie Lampman's diary never explains how close this was to their intended destination, assuming they had one.

She had almost as little to say about landscape and was vague about place, observing from the train between Calgary and Edmonton, "nice country, all timber and pine." On April 21, a few days after leaving Edmonton: "Fine weather. Writing by the campfire. Passed several creeks and lakes, reports of a bear along the road. About 25 camped around us," and at Grand Rapids between May 11 and 13: "Lots of people here, rough old place . . . rocks, rocks . . . I washed and baked bread and pie." Once, in mid-July on a day when the boat was floating easily, she wrote, "lovely country." Two weeks earlier she had "seen roses in bloom," and on September 2: "Seen the grand northern lights this eve." Otherwise, for all her activity out of doors, she wrote about the place she was only in a functional manner, not descriptively. She named rapids, rivers, high banks, crossings, such activities as berry picking, fishing, hunting. Every day she commented on the weather ("fine," "rainy," "cloudy," "nice weather," "snowed," "rather cold," "68 below, cold.") Variations in the length of days amazed her enough to write them down exactly, and to account for a three-o'clock-in-the-morning bread baking:

May 28, sun goes down here at 9 o'clock. June 3rd not dark at 12 o'clock at night. June 10 sun goes down 10:30. Fort Smith, Fort Resolution does not get dark can read or write all night. June 30 at Simpson,

July 24 it commenced to get a little dark about 10 o'clock. **Fort Laird**
sun goes down about 7:00. August 31. Snigh town November 11 sun
rises 8:30 and sets at 4:00. December 21 sun rises 9 o'clock and sets
3:30.

But Nature as something external to be accommodated, fought,
appreciated, or responded to in the many complex formulations of
our literature and mythology—this was not in Mattie Lampman's
understanding: "Rained all day. Did nothing but cook. Men all
loafed around." Generally she was not stimulated by the out-of-
doors. At Fort Resolution she wrote, "Bad looking old lake. Several
men here starting back home discouraged" (6–30).

The word *gold* appears three times. On April 16 from her tent in
Edmonton she wrote: "I baked bread and cake. Linden was down to
river watching a man wash out gold." On July 31: "Men rested,
looked a little for gold. Found quite a few specks. Had raspberry
shortcake for dinner. I had to wash a little, took bath." On Sunday,
August 21: "We are resting. Linden, Nate and Mack gone hunting.
Reed brothers prospecting, found several colors, more than before.
One boat passed." The urgency and excitement that we connect with
the gold rush hardly intrude into these idle remarks.

If she did not place herself geographically or in relation to land
and landscape, or within a tactical plan of action, Mattie Lampman
did write of other quadrants that told her where she was. Days in
Grinnell went at a steady pace, a rhythm that she tried to reestablish
from then on. In Grinnell she "ironed and patched," "ironed
patched and knit," "patched and knit," "washed, patched and knit,"
"baked and knit," "baked and scrubbed." She made shirts for the
men, a nightdress and aprons for herself, wristlets and double mitts.
Linden shod horses, did chores, got hay and a load of wood, tanned
deer hides. They visited other families and entertained guests and
went to a wedding dance. Away from home, she continued to report
similar repetitive activities.

> Made cookies on boat (6–25). . . . I made pies, took a bath (7–13). . . . I
> baked bread until 3:30 o'clock at night (7–14). . . . I made a little jelly
> and baked bread (7–20). . . . Rainy, men loafed. I made pair moosehide
> pants for Tom (7–22). . . . Had raspberry shortcake for dinner (7–
> 31). . . . I made some pies and took a bath (8–7). . . . I made 3 pillow-
> cases and a cap for myself out of mooseskin (10–21). . . . Lots of Indians
> came, I got a beaver hide for a dress (10–21). . . . I covered a vest with
> part of an old overcoat (11–1).

Dwelling places were important to her; they located her in comfort and order, settled spots from whence she could extend help to others and gather her own forces. On September 19: "We put stove into the tent. I made it look as homelike as possible. Squaw making moccasins for us. Poor outfit crying with hunger. We fed them. Linden cut wood. I baked. The men went hunting"; on the 24th: "I did a big washing. Booker took the tent down, put 2 logs around under it and put it back, makes a nice room. We cleaned it all out and put in boughs." Between the 5th and 7th of November housekeeping improved considerably: "Indian wants us to move into his house. . . . Men are fixing up Indian house. . . . We moved into the Indian house. Quite warm nice fire place. I went in to see the Indians, they are real friendly." On December 5: "Booker mudded the house. I scrubbed and fixed up the house." She wrote about these shelters as though she were achieving something, dry floors and fireplaces more to the purpose than specks of gold.

Mattie Lampman also placed herself among people, whether she knew them or not. In Grinnell there were names of those she visited or bought and sold things to, and on the trip she continued citings of whom she was among. During a wait of several days in Calgary: "A lady and I took in the town. . . . Our trunk came today. I was out for a walk with a lady." While waiting in Edmonton: "Living in tent, lots of tents all around us." On the way to Athnabasca Landing: "About 25 camped around us," and at the Landing: "Lots of tents and boats here. . . . I counted 75 tents from back of our tent" (4–19 to 4–23). There was a good deal of visiting en route, she even speaks of paying calls.

> French man and wife stopped here few minutes (5–14). . . . Had some music on Graphophone (5–22). . . . Lady gave me milk (6–2). . . . Gave a stranger dinner (5–4). . . . The Detroit Lady and crew got in last night. She and husband came to see us, afternoon she came again, she and I went to see Mrs. Booth, then all come back here (6-9). I gave some cookies and biscuits to Mrs. Bell and Reed. They gave us fish (6–28). . . . I went to Nagle's store to see the fur. Grand (at Fort Resolution 7-2). . . . L and I went up to the mission. Stayed for tea. 5 white ladies there, nice place (7–11). . . . Rained all night nearly. I am completely done up with steering and walking. About 30 men in this little place tonight (8–3). . . . I gave an old squaw medicine for Grip (8–4). . . . 2 steamboats got here. Men all came to our camp fire with music, banjo and concertina, nice music, singing (9–8).

Increasingly her sociability included Indian women:

2 squaws here all day and 2 children both belong to same man. Klondikers in and out all day. Squaws offered me some of their dinner, dried meat and tallow (10–23). Squaws to see me. I cook all day. Mr. Keats over in the eve with the music. Played for Indians (11–9). I baked and patched, went over to see the Indians. They are making us a snowshoe and duffles (10–12). Men planing boards, men up from Snigh town, old squaw over to see me. I went over to the Indian graveyard. 4 graves (12–12) [she had observed Indian graves several times along the rivers]. An Indian and wife here to supper (10–14). Had some company. Indians brought us some moose meat and 4 pr moccasins. I am trying to learn their language (12–15). Squaws over to see me. I had to doctor 2 babies (12–18).

Her entries for the days at the Athnabasca Landing, waiting for Linden to return from selling the team in Edmonton and their boat to be made ready, reveal how she was more likely to write about people she noticed around her and about cooking or sewing than about more general plans for the trip. The period is for April 26 through May 4.

Tuesday. First mosquitoes. Weather nice. I suppose Linden is on his way to Edmonton. Quite lonesome. Tom brought me some reading. 2 women came in, made a mistake on the tent. One was halfbreed. Men working on our boat.

Wednesday. Rained a little, windy. Long days. Linden will get to town today. I read most of the time or write. Minister and daughter called on me PM in tent. Men working on boat.

Thursday. Windy. Several people pulling out. A man with a Graphophone playing and singing "Goodbye my honey, I'm gone." Lou making oars. I made bread, lots of hammering.

Friday. Nice weather. Some people coming and some going. An old man died here last night. Lou making oars. I read, wrote, and washed a dress. Men working on boat.

Saturday. Windy. Rained some and thundered. I washed some. A funeral here today, an old man, hunter, trapper.

Sunday. Nice weather. Tom had me make some lemon pies. Boats sailing up and down the river. Church today. Very quiet. Lots of teams coming in. Looking for Linden.

Monday. Fine weather. I baked bread and cookies, washed. Three ladies called on me, one was a Hudson Bay lady, the other hotel lady, brought me a novel. Our things came from Edmonton.

Tuesday. Nice weather. I sewed on a sail all day. Lots going on river. Looking for L. all day. 4 ladies called on me in eve.

Wednesday. Nice weather. I finished the sail. Another lady called today. Detroit lady going to Klondike. Linden got home with stage. Brought 6 letters. Took most of stuff down to boat.

She did note, but without elaboration, that a boat was under construction, her own sail-making the only detail. "Lots of going on river" appears rather an understatement.

When deprived of the company of Klondikers, steamboat passengers, and Indian women, Mattie Lampman found the days dull, and when Linden was away getting supplies or hunting, she wrote that she was especially lonely. During a particularly slow day on the river, when they were moving only a mile an hour and she nearly upset her boat, she wrote, "Was alone PM, rather hard for me." In late September Linden and the other men were away for several days hunting, leaving Mattie with only Booker for company: "Makes it lonesome for me, I baked and cleaned up tent. . . . Booker and I are alone, long lonesome day. . . . Awfully lonesome, no one home yet. . . . Long lonely day, snowed considerable, all are quiet, I am alone with the mice" (9–24 to 10–2). She mentions sending and receiving mail once or twice, and once not having any letters when mail was delivered. All holidays were improvised. On the Fourth of July: "Nothing extra for the 4th excepting apple dumplings." Thanksgiving was trying: "Very poor Thanksgiving dinner, if this is Thanksgiving, baked bread and pie." For Christmas she made considerable effort: "We had chocolate cake for Xmas eve. Very quiet. . . . Xmas very dull day. We had moose meat and dumplings. Evaporated potatoes and apple dumplings with sauce. Best we could do. All wondering what folks are doing at home." She made a note of Linden's birthday, but not her own. On the last day of the year (it had been 68 below zero the day before), in the last entry in her tiny book, she wrote, "Men cut wood. We hauled 4 loads with the dogs. I wonder where we will be next December 31. I hope it will be at home. Pretty lonesome and dull here."

Whatever "home" meant to her, it was not in the Klondike, and whatever her adventure signified, it did not match in value her longing for home, much as she tried to replicate with dumplings, a beaver dress, and doctoring babies—the best she could do, but clearly not the same. In the extra pages at the end of the diary, Mattie Lampman wrote slightly fuller accounts of principal events, those presumably breaking the monotony of "dull days." All were catastrophes.

> May 11. Passed a birch bark canoe, and 2 men that had scurvy, could not move their limbs and teeth falling out.
>
> August 4. We just heard that the boat with 2 women in was tipped over and all drowned in the Great Slave Lake. A man here was drowned about 2 weeks ago. Jumped into water with rubber boots on and could not get out, only about 30 ft. from shore. He did not come up. They found his body afterwards.
>
> August 19. We found a corpse lying right at the water's edge. The skull was perfect and the brains still in it. Had a buckskin coat on. The clothing was all rotted. White man's skull.
>
> September 18. Sunday. Found a Mr. Keats that had been lost for 11 days, had only 7 hardtack for the 11 days. He was very weak and almost dead when found. He seen Linden away from him and he hallowed like a crazy man at him for him not to leave him. Linden took him to camp and kept him here until they came in. He eats all the time, can not get enough. He would not have lived two days more.

Mattie Lampman's diary is not a call to the wild. Despite the bears and a dead man's skull she tried her best to make life ordinary, to keep herself and others clothed, fed, warm, and unhurt. She liked having a little music and something to read. But her diary does not stir up longings for adventure, challenge, contests against the elements. The most singular things about the trip may well be that she never missed a day of writing in her miniature book, and that it has been kept all this time.

Jane Freeland on the Erie Canal

I have been emphasizing how little effect school grammar books had upon women's writing, particularly on the letters and diaries of working women. The insistence in these books upon conformity in mechanical construction as well as in social ideas and attitudes appears to have passed them by. However, it would be a mistake to suppose that women therefore were oblivious to matters of style, to the rightness that transforms language to literary art, for it is clear that they lavished upon writing the same care for detail and pleasure in design we see and hear of in dressmaking, embroidery, quilting, darning and mending, baking, preserving, arranging houses, and gardening. All these primarily utilitarian chores women often transformed (and still do) beyond practical use into art, and they did the same with writing.

None of the working class writers I have been citing say anything of imaginative literature such as poetry or fiction, and few mention reading books, and yet many letters go far beyond the requirements of "news"; they show writers who are shaping material at least as much for the sake of the piece of writing as for satisfying the curiosity of their correspondent. The writing of such letters is a deliberate and cherished activity, not merely a duty or indulgence. Read, for instance, this letter dated July 8, 1884, from Ella Abbott in Colebrook, New Hampshire, to Allettie and her mother Eliza Keyes in Dazey, North Dakota. Ella begins and ends complaining of having to write in haste and asking her friends to "excuse the shape" her letter is in, and we see that it *is* the shape that she so enjoys forming—what might be a listing of dreary calamities she turns to an exuberant joke.

Dear Friends each and all,

I have not seen the time since we have been here when I have had as little time to write as I have now. The 4th was a very nice day here. I hope it was there and that you had a very nice celebration out there minus mosquitoes. The band marched through the streets followed by the fantastics. There was a horse [race] in the day time and a promenade concert in the evening.

Now you have read so far and you stop look at each other and say with a long breath, Well I am glad they are where they can take some comfort on such days and how I wish we were out of this terrible lonesome hole. But we did not have such a good time as you think we did. In the first place as grandpa and grandmarm are very cross and fussy, the hired man and woman were not contented and went away quite a while before the 4th so that Frank and I had all the work to do until more help could be found. Of course that made it quite hard. Also the evening of the 3rd as grandpa and one of the neighbors were walking on the street a heavy team ran over grandpa breaking both bones of his left arm cutting a bad gash on his hand and bruising his leg. It was a great wonder he was not killed. So you see we did not have much of a jolly time.

We expect a man and a girl tomorrow and we will be very glad if they only come as we need help very much. I never worked so hard in my life as I have the last week. Girls are very hard to find here that want to do house work.

Grandpa and grandmarm have failed very much and are two very fussy

old people now. You would hardly know us we have developed into two
such steady old seeming people. I hope we shall live long enough to see
you all again. Now I shall have to call this a letter and send it along. We
are very sorry you have had so much trouble and if wishing could make
it any better, I would wish very hard for you to write us lots of news.
We think of you all and of H. and V. very often. Write when you can. I
will do the same. I write this in a great hurry and you must excuse the
shape it is in.

Yours with sincere friendship from both of us.

Ella Abbott[10]

Ella Abbott is a witty writer and a tactful respondent to whatever
troubles she had been told of. Though tired and bored, with elderly
people on her hands, her spirits rise as she writes, and we feel her
poised between the "steady old seeming people" she forsees herself
and her husband becoming, and the much younger person she still
is, excited by a Fourth of July parade and an amusing way of
describing a situation which in such better moments she sees the
humor of.

For over forty years a correspondent of Eliza Keyes and Allettie
Battey Mosher was Jane Freeland, who lived with her husband on a
canal boat in New York state—"We are all well as usual and here in
Buffalo for the winter. We just got here and that was all, we lie
frozen in here with a load of coal on it, is more comfortable. I hope
it will stay on all winter. . . . The paper states there is over a thousand boats frozen in along the canal. There isn't more than two
dozen boats here" (13–13–71). Her life is very hard and, to judge by
her handwriting and syntax, she has had less education than her
sister or certainly her daughter Maria; Jane Freeland's punctuation
is scanty and always writes the pronoun I in lower case. But she
is a distinctive writer; she so relives the event in its telling that she
takes us into the scene as into a work of imaginative writing. Her
letters contain if anything even more deaths and illnesses than most,
yet she makes of each a set-piece. There are fourteen letters between
1861 and 1903, none less than 500 words. Her nieces, not surprisingly, found her in later years rather pathetic. In the summer of
1904, Allettie with her second husband Emmet Mosher traveled to
Michigan and New York visiting relatives, and Allettie's sister Viola
Pierce writes from North Dakota, "Poor old Aunt Jane so glad you
have seen her at last. Oh how happy that would of made Ma if she

could of known it so hard not to have a dollar of your own. I will write to her before long" (7–18–04). Yet when Jane Freeland writes, she shows little sign of self-pity.

The first letter from Jane Freeland in the Mosher collection tells of the death of a daughter, Lelah. It is not a hasty letter written in emergency, but a scene re-created a month later; writing it down gives her power of recovery, as does the thought of going to her daughter's children next month, and recalling their hymn singing. She shapes her writing carefully:

My Dear sister and family,

With a sad heart I write you a few lines asking why you have not answered last letter. My health is very good at present and hope you are all alive and well.

Well I must tell you I laid Lelah away to rest the 23 of last month the dear child is better off she has no more trouble. O she died so happy the last words she said was take me Jesus. She had the quick consumption. I was with her six weeks until she died. She left a husband and 3 little children. The oldest is 8 years old his mother has got them. Lelah's family has been living there for over a year in the country. It was hard for her to give up that she couldn't live but when she did give up all for Christ she died so happy. O she clung so tight to me she couldn't bear to have me out of her sight. She knew every thing till the last. She took cold last October and had caught one cold and another until there was no cure. I didn't know that she was so bad as she was until she sent for me. They didn't get a doctor until it was too late. The first time he came he told her she had the Consumption and then she wrote to me and I went out there as soon as I saw her I knew her time was short. It nearly unnerved me at first the change made me sick and had to come home for 10 days. I went to the doctor and got medicine and went back and staid until the last. Lelah's husbands people were very kind to her and done all they could.

I expect to go out there next month for a while and help the old lady with the children's clothes, they are lovely children. It done my heart and soul good to hear them children sing hymns they learned by hearing their mother sing from the oldest to the youngest is 3 years old it used to worry Lelah thinking they would be brought up in the Lutheran faith if they lived it seemed hard for her to give up her children but I am so glad God used me as an instrument in his hand of pointing her to Christ. Give my love to all the children and accept a large share yourself.

Good bye these fine scrawls from your far away lonely sister,

Jane Freeland

In this, as in nearly all her letters, Jane Freeland meditated upon her own behavior during, and recovery from, the death of someone she loved. She pictured herself a "sad and lonely heart," and "your far away lonely sister," the one who had nursed and buried a daughter and listened with pleasure to her daughter's children singing hymns in their mother's memory. Her few pious phrases—Lelah's "take me Jesus," her being "so glad God used me" in "pointing her to Christ"—are certainly not perfunctory, but neither do they obscure complicated and contradictory feelings. What is important to Jane is that she behaved well toward her daughter and Lelah toward her, and that Lelah acknowledged her mother's importance at her death, and therefore in her life. Jane's story appears to ramble, but is in fact organized in terms of her growing ability to cope with the crisis. By the time she wrote, she had had a month to reflect upon Lelah's death, and to realize that she need not look upon it as a sign of her own failure. Of course Jane Freeland intended that her sister, reading the letter, should hear her voice, but she must also have derived consolation, in her loneliness, from hearing it herself.

Jane Freeland had three children in addition to Lelah: Sarah, Maria, and Charley. Her husband had been in the Civil War, and evidently there were family tensions, especially concerning Charley. Maria, less emotional but as observant as her mother, wrote to Eliza Keyes of the next family death, four years later.

> I did not tell you that father had been here did I? ["New York" is her heading; she says her mother is on the boat in Buffalo.]. . . He felt very bad about Charley's death he said that he had got things just as he wanted and now his hopes was all crushed to the ground. I thought from the way he talked he intended to put Charley to school or trade but he has gone where he will never need school or any of the world's goods it was too late I told father so and told him he could not blame any one else but himself for the position that the whole family is in it made him feel very bad he cried like a child. He is very tender hearted. . . . Mother says Charley is buried in a lovely place now I wish I could see it but will perhaps sometime. . . . Mother and all of the folks was there and the bell tolled for a funeral that was entering the Cemetery and Mother said it sounded more like a voice from the grave than anything else she could compare it to. It is a large tower where the bell is and where they transact business. My heart aches writing about it. (8–5–65)

Maria sympathetically catches her mother's tone in writing about the funeral bell.

Jane Freeland writes of the next death—Maria's—this time only a week after the burial, and again re-creates the scene from her participation in it.

> She lost the use of one side of her two days before she died her tongue too and laid five days as stupid. She had commenced when I wrote you last she didn't have her right mind all the time after the fever set in she would say a few words rational. She did not speak a word for two days before she died we went for Sarah Trebby the day she died but when she come she did not know her. I don't think she knew anyone for over two days the last she said to me I asked her if she thought she was agoint to get well she said O yes but I don't think she realized what she said for she began to talk at random. When Harlon died she said she wished she could die I said to her I should think she would want to live for her baby she said there was enough to take good care of it she dident seem to have any anxiety to live after he died for her whole mind was on him. O I think what a consolation it would been to us if she could of had her right mind and could have talked to us as much as bid us good bye but that was not to be. And I had to bear it seemed as though it would break my heart to part with her although I cant wish her back again for I know she is better off and I don't think she ever would live herself again.

Jane actively grieves both at the time and in the telling, but again also demonstrates her considerable powers of recovery in the prospects of caring for Maria's infant daughter.

> I have got the baby and shall keep it and the little thing is dreadful good and grows like a little pig she has got dark blue eyes and just such a head of hair as Maria had when she was a baby with dark brown hair. We calculate to go ashore this summer if we can sell for I am afraid we can't raise the baby on the water we will have to get so many kinds of milk. O the little thing is such a comfort to me in my lonely hours I have been almost sick.

Had the child's father not neglected to pay his insurance premium before he died, his widow would have received two thousand dollars:

> He was of an easy disposition naturally that was the worst fault he had. O dear I can't hardly make it seem as though they are both gone forever but so it is. The longer she is dead the more I miss her for I can't look in no direction in the cabin but I see something she has done or something that belongs to her. It seems sometimes as though I should fly it seems as though I have shed tears enough to almost float this boat. I think sometimes as though I have more than I can bear but as the saying is the back is fitted for its burden.

The baby continues to be an intense part of Jane Freeland's emotional life, which takes in the pain of other people as well as her own, and makes very complex her feelings and judgments about any situation.

> If I make many blunders don't wonder for Lelah is playing and talking to her dolly she comes up to me every four minutes and wants to write too. O she is a little witch if there ever is one she learns very quick and has got good memory I left her to Aunt Tilda's this fall while we went up the lake she was there nearly a week. She didn't want to come back, she cried to go back. She thinks everything of Aunt Tilda as she calls her and always has ever since she was old enough to know who she was I guess I will let Tilda take her next summer if she wants her. After Tilda lost her baby she was so lonesome she asked me if I would give Lelah to her I told her that was a pretty hard question to answer but I would rather let her go than keep her on the canal I guess I haven't written to you since Tilda's baby died she died the last of July. O how the dear little thing suffered she never was a well child. She had the scroffula, consumption the Doctor said she was just seven months old the day she died I got greatly attached to the little body before we come away as I used to tend her a great deal. (13–13–71)

Yet it takes so little for Jane Freeland's spirits to rise almost gaily: "Well you see by the date of this I commenced two days ago but I will tell you yesterday I went avisiting to an acquaintance of ours and today she and I went up town and done a little trading. I got me a new bonnet the second winter hat I have had since we have been married. I don't think I have been very expensive do you. . . . Well I have just put my little pet to bed and she was so tired it makes her as tired as it does me to go away from home for it is so seldom we go," and she ends with Christmas greetings.

Twenty years later, a month after her husband's death, Jane Freeland wrote about that. She is recuperating more slowly this time, for she has lost not only her companion but her home. Nevertheless, with as much energy as moves out of the letter itself, she shows considerable reserves, at least in her imagination.

> My Dear Sister and Family,
>
> With a sad and lonely heart I sit down to pen you a few lines. I am well as can be expected under the circumstances. I supposed you received the paper with the death of my Dear husband. O I hardly know what to write first my Dear sister I can sympathize with you in the loss of your companion. It is 4 weeks ago last Monday since he passed away. I had been away from home to work. He didn't seem to be any worse than he had been. I bid him good bye as we always did when going

from each other. The day before he went out to his last prayer meeting he said as I was getting ready to go to work that morning was I going to Trudy's before I came home. I said I did not know he said why not go and see how they are.

Well I said if you say go I will I did go and when I got home at a quarter to 3 I found him sitting in his rocking chair as I thought at first look asleep. The color hadent all left his face he died with out a struggle he had done the hard chores and built a good fire for me for the last time. O what a shock it was to me I never shall get over. I haven't no one to work for now, but I am so thankful he passed away so peacefully he is out of his pain and suffering he used to say he was never free from pain but he bore it all so patiently never would murmur. His heart was affected I think that hastened his death. Blessed are they that die in the Lord. He made arrangements about 4 years ago for his burial and had his pallbearers picked out but 4 of them had gone to rest. He used to say he dident want any corrupt hands to handle his body and there wasent. He requested his body to be buried from a dear friend's house of ours and I should have a home with them as long as I lived as they are good Christian people.

O it was so hard for me to leave the home we had taken so much comfort in but I couldent live there alone so I thought best to sell it there is a good Christian family that bought it so I feel at home to go there sometimes and now my earthly house is at present at Brother Ayres house, 444 13 St. Everything nice and comfortable. Yesterday was Thanksgiving day but it was a gloomy day as they all are, our winter's butter came today from the country he gave 10 dollars to a friend of ours but he wasent here to taste of it.

Now Dear Sister let me hear from you soon give my love to all accept a large share yourself this from your lonely far away sister Jane Freeland. (11–27–91)

Her life at the Ayres' continues placidly; she writes the next year: "I think you and I are afflicted about the same. My back and limbs are very lame at times but my general health is very good. I think the good Lord is letting us both down gently to our graves" (5–27–92). Always, Jane Freeland's letters convey her strong sense of the presence of the sister to whom she is writing: "After a long anxious waiting and watching for a letter from you at last I received it yesterday morning and O how glad I was to hear that you was all alive and well as you are. I was alone in the house and of course I had a good long cry as I always do when I get a letter from you" (5–2–93). She closes with the same phrases over the years: "this from your far away lonely sister may God's blessings rest upon you all, good bye, Jane Freeland." And this time she adds, "O how I would like your picture." One difficulty of her boarding arrangement was lack of privacy, and she needs privacy to write. "I am not alone much but there is some one in every evening and I can't write when there is any confusion. My old head aint as strong as it used to be" (4–8–02). "I wrote a letter to Viola yesterday I was all alone yesterday in the house and it was raining so improved the chance of writing and it is the same now for a short time as Mrs A had gone out so I write in a hurry for I can't write when there is any confusion around" (10–2–03).

The letter of May 27, 1902, is one of the saddest because briefest letters, this time on receiving the news that her sister Eliza Keyes had died. It is to Allettie Mosher, Eliza's younger daughter:

My Dear Niece,

With a sad and heavy heart I will try and answer your letter that brought me such sad news of my Dear Sister and your Dear Mother's death. It nearly unnerved me for a time but I have got settled down so I will try and write a little. It was strongly impressed on my mind when I read her last letter perhaps it is her last to me. I was looking so long for a letter from her but it came at last but not from her. Mrs. Ayres opened the letter directed to her husband. She came in the kitchen where I was at work broke the news to me and O I can't express my feelings. But I am truly thankful that she died in the Lord and that my Saviour was her Saviour too, and O I know you all miss her greatly for she was a good mother. I am the only one left of our family. God only knows why I am left but I will wait patiently for my time. I think sometimes it won't be long before I shall be with your mother. O what a meeting that will be.

Always Jane Freeland engages herself in the experience of others, however far away; this time she restores herself as best she can by thinking directly about her niece: "You ... seem very near to me although I never expect to see any of you here on earth but I do expect to see you all by and by, but I am so glad I have your pictures all but Violy it is a great pleasure to look at." She did, of course, see Allettie the following year on the visit to which Viola referred.

A Literature of Omission

In some respects these diaries and letters of rural working women in the last hundred years constitute a literature of omission. From the selections I have been quoting, it would be difficult to garner much information about the economic or even the domestic details of canal-boat life, the dressmaking trade, or the progress of the auto industry, although all are mentioned often. Even less do we hear about national or local politics, and nothing at all of cultural or scientific events. But if we are calling this a literature of omission, we need to wonder why it is these writings, satisfying so few of the usual canons of literary composition, can affect us so.

They affect us partly, I think, by their inevitable self-assurance. It may of course be true that it took considerable determination to write at all, so that those who did not possess the trait are forever dumb; nevertheless the writers I have been reading appear solid in their own eyes. The details of their lives are hard, goodness knows, full of the concomitants of poverty: they moved often, lived in rented rooms, and were separated for long periods from their husbands. Illnesses and deaths are staple subjects. There are family quarrels, disappointing offspring, and fractious aging parents, or, for the aging, indifferent and interfering children. The weather can go from dreary to calamitous. Through it all women are not particularly cheerful, but neither are they helpless. What they are is sure of themselves. Yet neither do they think of themselves as singled out or special for what they are doing: the word *pioneer* does not intrude in the writing of rural working women as an expression of the uniqueness of settlement experience. These authors were less strangers to a new land than familiars to a condition of living. Mrs. S. C. Cole remarks on the beauty of the Cheyenne River Valley, but nearly everything else she has to report could happen anywhere: being cheated by the railway company or snubbed by town settlers; delighting in the chickens she has brought with her. Sharecropping potatoes and housekeeping in a cramped shack inconvenience her, but so does the poverty which she would have to put up with anywhere. She does not sound as though she felt particularly displaced, or in any doubt about her abilities.

We have *not* got acquainted with *too many* honest men since we have been out here. The most of them have been *too sharp* for us & consequently my good man has gone over in town today to saw wood for some of the quality folks who are too much qualitified to do it for themselves. . . . We all have shanties exactly alike. Terant's family & us on the east side of the river & True and daughter Adie Bell on the west side. They live over in the *town* and we live in the *suburbs* along side of

the RR where there is to be a big town when some boomers take it in
hand. Snobs & saloonists comprise the majority of Lisbon society although there are some most excellent people who deserve a better fate
than to live among *sich*. Two of the leading ladies in town paid us a call
yesterday, Mrs Weisner & Mrs Harcourt both very nice & friendly but I
could not help feeling ill at ease in our present circumstances as my
poor daughter in law Ida says, she is so "darned poor" she don't want
to see anybody that is anybody, but I go to church every Sunday when
it is not too bad & have made the acquaintance of some of the best folk
there is whether they are the biggest or not. . . . You folks had better
sell out up there & come down here it is the prettiest place I have seen
since I have been in the territory; my chickens are in good order
especially Peter.

Rose Schools, a daughter of Mrs. Cole's, was farming hear Hope,
Dakota Territory, in 1882, and she too took for granted where and
how she was living.

We get along fine. EH and I does most of the cooking. Lydia helps
considerable we have a gay time are looking for Ma, Mat and Sister
Add tonight. . . . I would like to see you all so well. Peter is mean as
ever, fights Millie, Bella, baby Jenny is all right and we get eggs to
use. . . . I commenced this Sat. but could not get time to finish so will
try and master it now, but I am not sure I'll succeed as yesterday and
today was my "sick days" but got along fine. . . . We were up to Hope
Sunday to sunday school. We are going to try to go every Sunday if
possible, it was real nice to go to Church once more, they have Preach-
ing every two weeks they have a very fine Hotel there. Ma is going up
to work as chamber maid.

How close to brutality women were obliged to live also groups
them by class. They describe fire, flood, and the extremes of elements as assaults, as well as the human sort, and connect a sense of
personal worth with the precise distance they are able to keep between themselves and such violence.

Poor Mollie Kenes, daughter to Mrs. Johnstone Hogan, who for six
years served my mother faithfully, a woman of refinement and sensitive
nature, married John Hogan, an honest hard working man who looked
upon her only as a slave and almost dumb brute, and treated Mollie
harshly, and of course she (Mollie) married a man who is not only a
brute, but ignorant and treacherous in business as well. So it is said,
poor girl. (Lulah Cavileer, 2–10–14)[11]

You wanted to know about Biglow's folks. He is a miserable drunken
brute. He abuses his family shamefully. He has threatened of killing

and she left and was gone two days, left all her children with him but she had to go back on the account of her baby for she has not weaned it yet. (Eliza Keyes to Viola Pierce, 2–1–69)[12]

Poor Mollie Kenes's mother had worked for Lulah's mother, and was therefore at several removes from Lulah. Lulah muddles the one long sentence (it was Mollie's mother, not Mollie, who married John Hogan, and it was John who abused Mollie, his daughter), but we feel her indignation at Mollie's plight in going from an abusive father to a husband who is just as bad. But Lulah Cavileer is confused in her loyalties. Not wanting to show disrespect for Mrs. Hogan, her mother's companion, she describes her husband as "an honest hard working man." Yet this same man treats his daughter "as a slave and almost dumb brute." She uses "brute" again, applying it both to Mollie's father and to her husband. This, like other highly charged passages, contains an introductory and closing frame: "Poor Mollie Kenes. . . . So it is said, poor girl." Lulah Cavileer keeps her distance from these private woes, and it is an emotional distance that matches her distance in class.

Eliza Keyes's writing is so caught up in her outrage "about Biglow's folks" that she, too, cannot be bothered to sort out he's and she's. "You wanted to know"—and she tells as though in revenge against the outrages she reports. The next three accusatory sentences begin *he*: two short and a long one, full of consonants—the m, the d, the b's—("miserable drunken brute. He abuses"). "He has threatened of killing" reflects the disorientation it describes, for Eliza Keyes as a writer seldom confused grammatical structures, although her punctuation is rather loose. What she does not say about "she," the trap the woman was in with a nursing infant (who was it saw to it that the baby was fed for the two days? how painful her breasts were when she returned)—these omitted details fit the despair of the downward turn of the last phrase, "for she has not weaned it yet." Eliza Keyes, unlike Lulah Cavileer, makes no effort to detach herself from the Biglow disgraces, indeed, she makes us feel the woman's plight directly. Yet both writers, without generalization or figurative language, have described intensely violent events.

In 1866 Maria Freeland in New York State wrote to her aunt Eliza Keyes about her rift with her sister Sarah:

She has not been to see me since I have been keeping house which is nearly 6 months. Mother was here last fall 4 weeks and Sarah never

came to see her all that time. Mother and I went to see her one evening
and she was coming up here to see Mother the same week but do you
believe it she never came. Do you think she has a heart if so what is it
made of? . . . I suppose you are surprised to think that two only sisters
should live in the way we are but God only knows I do not wish to live
so but what can I do I am not Aristocratic and am not wealthy neither
one and do not want to be if it will cause me to forget the parents that
gave me birth. May my heart cease to beat when I do.

Such letters display not only self-assurance, but also confidence in
the person being written to. Nor do these women write in euphe-
misms; whatever they tell, they tell all, so that one is left to suppose
that if there are unmentionable subjects, these are simply not mentioned. I have heard people remark that the detailed and frequent
descriptions of deaths and other horrors sound callous; I do not
think they are meant to be, and would suggest that when it is not
possible to mask the indignities of so much suffering, then the way
to salvage self-respect and sanity is to describe fully what is going on.
And having described, there is no more to say. There may be also
some comfort in writing it down; forming the event into sentences is
a way of gaining control, when events themselves have proven so
unruly.

Victoria & Elias were here today. They have charge of the woman's
things that shot her husband the 5 of March. There was the man &
woman, two children 4 & 9 years old & a hired man. They were in
some quarrel & she shot him Sunday night. He lived until Monday
night at 11 o'clock. Sumner staid with him and was alone with him
when he died. He was an awful mean drinking man & some folks think
he was crazy. She is a little black eyed woman about as big as your
thumb. Both her & the hired man are in jail & an old dutch woman has
the children. Kincaid's folks have charge of the house & other things.
She has the nicest kind of things in her house. They moved here from
Milwaukee last July. She says he was trying to kill her. I am going with
Victoria to pack up her things. (Addie Kincaid to Mamie Goodwater,
Palmyra, Wisconsin, 3–18–88)

Mr Annable is very sick. He will soon be in his grave the doctor does
not seem to know what is the trouble with him he keeps failing and
wasting away getting weaker and weaker every day so he can't last long.
Mrs A was all summer same as she has been so melancholy and down
hearted until about two months ago. Now she is right the other
way. She got her a new crape bonnet a new black dress and shoes to
wear to his funeral. She has had them more than a month. All the time
she talk about him & his going to die she says she can never come back

into that house again. Ma says it is heart rending to hear her talk sometimes. (Emma Watson to Allettie Mosher, 2–26–88)

Some years later the same Mrs. Annable is writing to Allettie Mosher about people in what she now considers an unmanageable state, making no mention of instabilities of her own:

Took care of Mrs Samuel Vanhouten nine weeks and now have been taking care of Mrs Bevier. Since the first of June her and Mrs Vanhouten are both pronounced incurable by our doctors here in the Rock. Mrs. Vanhouten had a cancerous tumor removed that weighed 14 pounds also one of her kidneys three years ago and she has been having hemorrhages of the bowels over a year and is not expected to live but a short time. (10–6–95)

"You wanted to know how Matie was," an aunt in Flat Rock wrote to Allettie, and proceeded to tell her, perhaps more than we might now care to know:

She has went through everything but death since you was here last September she had peritonitis and when that was at its height Lee sent to Detroit for a doctor and he said if she lived she would have to have an operation and just one week Dr Parker & Dr Hyman came and put her under the influence chloroform her womb was turned upside down and grown fast and a growth that had to be taken away it was not cancer but would have been in time then when they got through with that they had to open her and take the ovaries they was one hour and a quarter doing the whole then the third day they thought blood poison would set in they had had to take the stitches out so they could treat the incision she had a nurse from the city for four weeks she charged $15 a week then they got a cheaper one she staid till about the middle of January then she had the gripp that used her up worse than the other she sits up in bed quite a good deal now and has walked a few steps and I guess in time it will come out all right but it is going to take a long time. (E. Harryman, 4–8–94)

She is forthright, neither embarrassed nor sensational, making plain facts the more harrowing for their plainness. Her writing is also acutely aural, addressed to the ear, not the eye alone, and shaped by performance time, not calendar time. "She has gone through everything but death." This is a "progress," a medieval harrowing by stages: peritonitis, chloroform, a womb upside down, a possibly cancerous growth, excised ovaries, blood poisoning, stitches removed, and an expensive nurse, each equally just short of death.

The words *and, then,* and *they* speed the voice on without subordinating pauses. Only the ending slows down the voice, when present time, "now," deliberates Matie's recovery, "in time" and "a long time" projecting healing into a slower future. There are seven months between September and April, and four from September to January, but Mrs. Harryman did not say whether she considered these periods long or short in regard to "time." She did not even say when, after September, Matie's troubles began.

There are other gaps in her recital, but one needs to stop listening to notice them. What became of peritonitis? Were there two separate operations for womb and ovaries, and what has the employment of nurses to do with surgical procedures? Questions like these intrude of course on Mrs. Harryman's recitation which gets it all over with as fast as possible, for how else to endure so much agony?

What is the source of such language, and what sources does it ignore? For it is so unlike any public writing of the period one can think of. The language of newspapers and other popular informative writing, as typified by the *History of the Red River Valley* is generalized, ornate, hortatory, and the letters and diaries are not that. They do not even give advice or urge industry upon their correspondents (though letters between men often do so). On deaths there are occasional scriptural cadences, but devotional literature is seldom quoted. Nor is the behavior of characters in sentimental novels reflected in even the most scandalous goings-on: no fainting fits, though people are reported very ill in disgusting and painful ways, they go mad, and they die on every hand.

Do we conclude, I wonder, that for practical purposes the newspapers, devotional literature, and sentimental fiction hardly touched working people? Were the popularity of elocution and rhetoric attempts to improve by artificiality the working person's plain speech? "The rain in Spain falls mainly on the plain." Shaw, Ionesco, the Czech playwright Václav Havel are among writers who have mockingly constructed versions of unspeakable speech. Havel's "The Memorandum" is about a new language, Ptydepe, invented entirely for bureaucratic use: the play begins, "Ra ko hutu d dekotu. . . ." Composers of school writing manuals wrote for other writers of public literature. Women in their letters and diaries wrote as if public literature did not exist, or, if education and social aspiration drew this public style to their attention, their attempts at imitating it were erratic.

The mode that I think does characterize the spare, plain style is conversation. This was to Mamie Goodwater from Gwendoline Kinkaid (6–29–98), whose talking voice awaited a listener: "It is a very pretty evening out, for folks that can go and enjoy themselves, but that's not me or you. I must close for this time. Now write soon, we can do that if nothing else. Good night and cheer up, from your friend Gwendoline" (9–11–99). A reading voice is able to supply transitions that appear less evident to a silent eye. Though there is frequent evidence that individual writers were conscious of shaping what they wrote, few worried about the letter form as such. They apologized for haste and poor penmanship, for using pencil or blueing instead of ink, for not having enough paper. But grammar, spelling, vocabulary, sentence structure, standards of epistolary style, they did not mention. While the grammar books urged virtually a separate language, away from speech, for what was to be committed to paper, women wrote in order to create substitutes for their own voices.

IV

"Don't Read Aloud": Class and Sexuality, Disease, and Death in Women's Writings

Public Health in the Nineteenth-Century Midwest

If women made a habit of dwelling upon that in their lives which was material and concrete, then it is not surprising that they wrote so much about sexuality, illness, and death, for what is more material than one's own body? Moreover, they blended the three. In our time, and even in the late nineteenth century, popular literature, especially romantic fiction, and advertising have treated sexuality, disease, and death as though they were separate and unrelated. Love is shown as the apogee of health, bound to transpose all, through sexuality, to heart-studded immortality. The diseased body challenges scientific heroics or ingenious and quick remedies for minor irritations. And death, when not responsive to euphemism, promises a glorious resurrection. Sexuality, and sometimes love, becomes in this view a problem in management, disease a problem for technology, and death a problem for the imagination. Much of the commercial success of popular arts including advertising depends upon our being distracted from seeing connections among sex, disease, and death.

It has taken psychology in the twentieth century, of course, to assert the opposite and to call attention to connections that have been made by art and literature since the time of the Greek tragedians, emphasizing that women themselves, because of their very sexuality, are primary sources of death and disease, as well as life and health. Woman is foul because she *is* the body, or holy because she is the source of other's lives—in any event magical, mysterious, fearful to men, who are their lovers, artists, and psychoanalysts.

Writings of women themselves that I have been reading speak differently than either popular or high art and psychology. While women's letters and diaries confirm connections Freud had made among sexuality, disease, and death, women do not often write, as far as I can see, as though they held themselves at fault for mortality. In their own eyes, they are neither Eves nor Virgin Marys. As with other matters, women flatten out what they see and make it ordinary, for sex, disease, and death occur daily and are hardly to be distinguished from each other. Emma Ladbury, who lived in Gallatin, North Dakota, and wrote to Allettie Mosher in Dazey between 1899 and 1908, responded strongly to the physical debilities of her mother and father and of other people she knew, but was not one to generalize from what she had seen and heard. Causes and effects were too mixed to separate.

> Geo. Saunders living across the river from us are having a hard time. I think poor Mrs. Saunders is having more than her share of trouble now, first Jim shot himself last harvest then Maggie was married in the fall, she was only married a short time when she was taken with convulsions, it took four men to hold her. Her mother had to be with her as soon as she got better the next girl younger was taken with fits it took two men to hold her and then they had the measles, just as the girls were getting better Will came home from the woods (last Sunday) sick with the measles. They were obliged to have the doctor Mrs. Saunders had all of them to take care of and now she is down herself just worn out. They were obliged to get Dr. Phillips yesterday for her, and just when the girls at home had the measles Maggie had the measles and pneumonia they thought she was dying several times and her mother had to go there. Isn't that trouble enough for one poor woman at once? (4–21–01)

"They thought she was dying several times": grammar and syntax, like Mrs. Saunders, break down from sheer exhaustion, suicide and marriage equally taking their victims in Jim and Maggie. No mention of George Saunders, except that his name identifies the family. It is Mrs. Saunders upon whom all the ills have been visited, measles undistinguishable from madness. The family fortunes hardly improved, for two years later Emma Ladbury wrote:

> There is lots of sickness in this neighborhood [a phrase she used more than once], it is mostly the mumps but some are very sick with them.

Will Saunders has been lying in Hope for six weeks with blood poison. I
suppose he suffered almost everything with it. The doctor says he won't
be able to leave there before June. I feel sorry for Mrs. Saunders if he
had died it would have been almost too much for her after losing Jim
the way they did. (2–27–03)

Physical details are all Emma Ladbury's writing stops for. She
concentrates on suffering, a word she used often.

I should have come down with Willie [a distance of about 35 miles] if it
had not been for so much sickness. . . . I am sorry to hear about Laura
Pierce it is so hard for a young girl like that. I think they seldom get
over them. Elsie Saunders never got over having fits her folks say she
don't have fits now but she does. She is liable to go into a fit any time
(3–1–03). . . . Poor Mrs. Monson is out of her mind. It seems to bad.
Ellen looks so care worn. She does not look at all as she used to
(3–8–03). . . . Poor Mrs. Monson had lost her mind entirely. She does
not know her own children. Fred said he would give all they have got if
she was only all right again. Hattie has a nice home it seems too bad
that she does not have anything to do with her folks you know how
much Fred used to think of her when we lived here now they never
speak. They say she said she never wanted to see her father again if he
was dead it seems to me that is a dreadful thing to say. (4–1–03)

The sufferings of the Monson family of Dutton, Michigan, where
Emma used to live, are no less complex than those of the Saunderses
in Gallatin. Emma's visit to her old home town in March 1903 is itself
threatened by disease: "Where they had the small pox in Dutton the
Dr disinfected the house on Sunday and the disinfectant he used
spoiled everything in the house even killed the house plants. I did
not know that they had to use anything so strong" (4–1–03). Returned to North Dakota, Emma found her father in a high fever that
was only slightly relieved by baths in warm salt water.

I wanted to come to see you so much but could not. Mother was very
sick for a week, for a while I thought she would not get better. She
looked so bad the last few days, the pain in her head and neck has been
so bad that I scarcely knew what to do for it. Yesterday I got a porous
plaster for her and today it seems some better. Father is about the
same, some days in bed nearly all day. His head is getting so bad he
can't bear very much noise, he keeps up as much as possible but I can
see he is a great deal worse than he was at this time last year. (11–15–
08)

Her relentless grip on details keeps the writing away from generalization or metaphorical comparison, or self-pity, for that matter. Sometimes sympathetic suffering becomes so acute as to cause mortal sickness itself.

> Mr. Axdahl that used to be in the drug store in Hope is dead, he was sick only 24 hours. Old Mr Dodd near Mr. Northrup's was found dead in his bed they think it was heart failure.
>
> I don't suppose anyone will ever know if there was any change in C. Palfrey before he died I think he was delirious the most of the time. They say he wasn't feeling well when his house burned and he slept in the barn and took cold he did not live but a short time after that. Mrs. Palfrey takes it dreadfully hard. I heard a person say it was the saddest funeral she was ever at. We did not go for we had the threshers ours was nearly the last job they had and the men were so anxious to get through so we had to thresh.
>
> Mrs. Neil Stewart is very sick with inflammation of the lungs. Mrs. Stewart is down taking care of her. . . .
>
> Did you know Mrs. Wilson that used to live near Hope? They were Scotch people. They went to Manitoba a little more than a year ago. Word came a few days ago that she was insane she was at home alone she took the axe and chopped one of her knees through and cut the other limb badly when they came home they found her lying on the ground she had fainted from loss of blood. She is now in the insane asylum at Brandon, Man. Some say it was religion that drove her insane but I don't think it was. (1–22–99)

Even religion, which might well be thought a plausible explanation for many ills, Emma Ladbury did not allow to be a generalized explanation for Mrs. Wilson's hideous madness.

> There is lots of sickness near here of typhoid fever and Lagrippi. . . . Will is not well has had a very bad cold most of the winter and is troubled with catarrh I am afraid he will get it the doctors in Detroit say it never was so bad and fatal as it is now in New York. They are dying off like every thing. (Helen Anable in Flat Rock, Michigan, to Allettie Mosher in Dazey, N.D. 1–11–01)
>
> There is much sickness around us and many deaths among the older people. R. Haynes was buried today, Mr. Anble Isaac, Mr. D. Cole, Mrs. Compow, and several very sick. Mr. Hiram Haynes is very bad with cancer, one eye is entirely gone. . . . Dr. Fox is still alive but pretty feeble and poor Willis is in the asylum. What was the cause no one can tell. He has two sons that cares for his wife. Seems so queer but I am so sorry for them all. Don't it seem such a sad thing, two husbands in the same asylum. (Achsah Mosher in Dutton, ND, to Allettie Mosher in Dazey, N.D. 2–22–07)[1]

General health in rural America a hundred or so years ago was poor. Patent medicines flourished because people were so chronically ill and because they were apparently receiving little help from doctors—explanations also for the flourishing of alternative medical institutions, such as Christian Science and homeopathy, both of which attracted and accepted women practitioners. "Heroic" medicine was the fashion—bleedings, purges, and major surgery—compared to which nostrums may well have seemed more soothing, depending upon the proportions of opium and alcohol.[2]

It is difficult, however, to piece together an accurate social history of mental and physical health, because historical emphasis has not taken that direction. Free land propelled people west to visions of prosperity and independence, yet from their own accounts many hoped even more fervently for improved health, some only to be disappointed by new diseases they had not yet encountered. After the Civil War more people in the United States than ever before knew how to fire a gun, and most veterans on both sides kept theirs, paving the way for legends of the wild and woolly west and for frontier violence. Many individual experiences after the war were intensely asocial, people living very separated and isolated lives on farms and ranches, lonely miners of gold, cowboys and sheep-herders, gatherers of buffalo bones trying to earn money while holding down a claim and waiting for the first crop. And the women who accompanied these men, most of them reluctantly, wrote to the friends and relatives they had left, longing to walk into their kitchens for a chat, their letters now their only sociability. Health—physical, mental, emotional—concerned everyone, a fact that partly may account for its not being given much prominence in accounts of railway expansion, Indian fighting, the homestead act, the discovery of gold, and the other more glamorous events of which standard history textbooks are made.

Malaria was so severe in the heavily forested Midwest that the eventual successful settlement of that region has been attributed to the persistence of continuous migration. Although settlers correctly associated malaria with stagnant water, they attributed the illness to "miasma" or "putrid exhalations" from the swamps, and not to a mosquito. Housing was crowded and inadequate, sanitation virtually nonexistent even in towns, water muddy and worse, and the diet chiefly meat and bread. People dipped their drinking water out of the same rivers and streams that had received carcasses and general sewage; pigs ran loose to scavenge. European travelers like Mrs. Trollope commented on these conditions, as well as on the personal uncleanliness and uncouth habits of people they encountered.

As malaria was the most prevalent disease in the Midwest in the early nineteenth century, so typhoid was in the latter part, though the two sometimes were mistaken for each other. Unlike malaria, typhoid did not cure itself with economic progress; it took strict sanitary measures to bring a decline in typhoid cases. Dysentery epidemics killed many settlers, as did erysipelas, especially dangerous to pregnant women. Smallpox continued into the twentieth century in spite of the availability of vaccine, and milk sickness flourished through ignorance of the poisonous effect of white snakeroot on cattle. Around 1900 there began large-scale efforts against tuberculosis in response to its high death rate. Goiter was prominent in the northern tier of states. However, typhus, yellow fever, and leprosy—diseases which immigrants had brought with them—did not take hold.

> It will never be possible to assess numerically the full extent of morbidity or mortality in the Midwest in the nineteenth century, but beyond any doubt they were gigantic, especially when compared to other western countries during the same period. The proportions are on the other hand understandable when we realize that we deal with a sort of invading army, one with a development so rapid that sanitation simply could not keep pace with accelerated growth. Only around 1890 did the Midwest experience the highly significant statistical shift from a summer to a winter peak of mortality which had been noticed in France by Vilerme in 1833.[3]

People's letters express their fear of living under such conditions.

> I was vaccinated over four weeks ago and have had a very sore arm and it discharges yet. I think I was as sick with it as most of them have been with the Small Pox. There has been a terrible scare here in town and the surrounding country ever so many families have had it here and they did say they would quarantine the town but they only quarantined the houses that were infected. There are lots coming down with it yet. Mr. Shoves family have all had it and their little babe only 5 weeks old has had it so bad that the Dr. has had to lance it in different places several times he don't think it will live. No one has died with it yet it has been in very mild form here and all over this year a few have died with it in Detroit it has been within a block of us the churches and schools was closed for a while there is one new case here in town this morning. . . . Cad Whipple has had Pneumonia on both lungs and her

mother and father Mr. and Mrs. Gifford has been staying with her and
taking care of her. Her sister Gertie died last fall of cancer and her
husband died only 5 months before her and left 4 or 5 children. I wish
you was well as I be I am very well excepting my arm and that is better
than it was with lots of love to all of you I close from Mrs. Anable.
(Helen Anable in Flat Rock, Michigan, to Allettie Mosher in Dazey,
N.D., 2–15–03)

Poor health caused acute anxiety not only to the patients but to
close associates as well. Women, being the primary nurses and wor-
riers, were especially prone to organic or psychological illnesses—la
grippe and fits—and these were inevitably exacerbated by the anxieties of marriage and childbearing. Women wrote about sexuality,
disease, and death as though they expected to slide by degrees from
one to the other, no condition, in their minds, segregated from the
others.

Birth Control

Women's letters to each other took for granted that the many
facets of their lives connected simultaneously. The tone of writing,
typically, was easy, and women told each other what was going on,
what they had done and heard of others' doings, all because they
were interested in this very connectedness. Work and health and
relationships to other people overlapped. Nor do writings sound
disapproving. They did not pass judgment but confirmed what
everybody knows, that life is complicated and difficult, funny and
sad at the same time. Ceal Coss in Wasioja, Minnesota, wrote often to
her cousin Mamie Goodwater in Grand Forks.

> Iva is married and has gone to keeping house in that log house as you
> go to the Center. People say it was a wood chuck case with her about
> getting married. (10–17–89)
>
> Oh! yes tell Henry Anna Cheney had a juvenile. Ed. Messenger was the
> father (you remember him). Cheney made him marry her the next day
> after it was born. (2–15–91)

Ceal's own behavior equally bemused her.

> Oh! Mamie I mustn't forget I have got a new beau, he is a dandy (I
> mean his team), *he* is a regular farmer. I had three beaus last Sunday,
> all with carriages, and then didn't have a good ride. Georgie Black

came over and staid with me, we had a nice time. . . . Well I must stop and eat dinner, and go to the field. I am a regular farmer. (10–17–89).[4]

The report by Viola Foote in Grand Rapids, Michigan, to her cousin Viola Pierce on the death of a woman named Ellen tangles personal feelings, family relationships, social observation, and illness. Viola was thinking primarily about Ellen's whole life, how awful that she died just when she was "getting able to enjoy living," and just when her death apparently implied the ascendency of someone Viola thought was evil.

> I suppose you have heard all about Ellen's death by this time. Maria was here some time ago and said she had written you about it. It was a terrible blow to us all. She had been so much better for the last few years did not have the head ache much and seemed so well. She was up to Emmas Wednesday afternoon and said she intended to come on up here, but E told her to come up Friday as she and Allie were coming so she said she would bake Thursday so that she could have the children's meals ready and would come and stay all day. The girls say she seemed unusually well that day. When Maude came home at night she brought some fish that Mr. Wallen had given her. Ellen did not know how to clean them so she ran over to Mr. Haddan's and asked him, then she asked Mrs. H to come home with her, as they were going to hear some music they went over together. Mrs. H went into the sitting room and E went to the wood shed to clean the fish. She came in when she had cleaned the fish as she entered the door she put her hand to her head and said O how my head hurts in a breath she said I will lay down a minute and see if that will help me. Maude and Mrs. H followed her to the bed and rubbed her with camphor May ran for Dr. Mcpherson just two doors away and when they got back she was gone poor Ellen. Why should she be taken from her children when they needed her and she was just getting able to enjoy living and that old *she devil* left to be a curse to everyone who comes in contact with her. She is the meanest human being I ever knew. (5–27–84)

Even in less dramatic moments women wrote as though few details, even about their own mundane physical state, were unworthy of report. Thus Addie Kinkaid, another cousin of Mamie Goodwater, wrote from Palmyra, Wisconsin:

> I have had the tooth ache ever since Christmas. I tried to have it pulled but the dentist broke it off and it swelled my face up so that I couldn't shut my mouth for two weeks. Did you ever have the tooth ache much? I thought I should fly I couldn't sleep or anything else but it is better

now and I am in hopes to not have it any more. The rest of my teeth
are all right. (2–13–88)

Writing of this nature presupposes, I think, an ideal correspondent, virtually a second self who can be depended upon for her
interest, her empathy, her acceptance and lack of reserve. Such
writing does not explain or argue, but takes for granted an entirely
like-minded reader, who, for most women, is another woman. These
unreserved correspondences contain almost nothing constrained or
covert, no visible distance between what the writer does say and what
she might say. It is not out of character, then, for correspondences
such as these to light now and then over the years upon topics of
central and urgent importance to these women's lives. Here for
instance, is Rose Williams to Allettie Mosher on September 27, 1885.

> Well now I should say & did say "who would have thought it." You
> better bet I was surprised when I read your letter, you never let a
> fellow know you even had a fellow. . . . You never sent a piece of your
> dress as you said you would. You want to know of a sure prevenative.
> Well plague take it. The best way is for you to sleep in one bed and
> your Man in another & bet you will laugh and say "You goose you think
> I am going to do that" no and I bet you would for I don't see any one
> that does. Well now the thing we [use] (when I say *we* I mean us girls) is
> a thing: but it hasn't always been *sure* as you know but that was our own
> carelessness for it is we have been sure. I do not know whether you can
> get them out there. They are called Pessairre or female prevenative if
> you don't want to ask for a "pisser" just ask for a female prevenative.
> They cost one dollar when Sis got hers it was before any of us went to
> Dak. She paid five dollars for it. The Directions are with it. . . . Reece
> just told me to tell you to wear a long night dress with a draw string at
> the bottom and a lock and key for if you was in separate beds you
> would crawl over together . . . & would not like to have someone else to
> get this. It would spook them sick I wouldent wonder . . . let me know if
> it does.

Between 1895 and 1904 Gwendoline Kinkaid (whom Mamie
Goodwater visited in Wisconsin) wrote a great many letters, and long
ones, to Mamie in Grand Forks. Gwendoline displayed her confidence in Mamie by discussing birth control, that enterprise made
commercially illegal by the Comstock Act in 1873.[5] Gwendoline
wrote as though she and her acquaintances fairly consistently had
pregnancy on their minds, and while she lovingly describes the antics
of small children, she almost always dreaded the prospect of another
confinement. The women kept each other up to date. Thus Gwen-

doline wrote to Mamie on March 17, 1895: "That is too bad about the woman being in the soup. Thank the Lord I am not—I went over time that was all. Came around the 10th. Don't let anyone see this letter." And three months later:

> No you will not have to come to a bee to my place I want to know what you are going to fix me with. Sure that is the receipt I am using. You know we don't sleep together. Don't read aloud. I say that is a good reason you are using it because Ben is not to home. Oh say I have got another now. I bet you will laugh. Tell how much faith you have in it. *Just blow on your wrist.*

Over the next six years Mamie had a second child and Gwendoline three, and Gwendoline wrote to Mamie for more drastic measures than blowing on her wrist. "Are you all right yet. I am yet but one can never tell how long that will last" (1–10–01). Being "all right," or being "sick" (menstruating) or "going to be sick" (due to deliver) are recurring phrases over the years, and reflect, we may now suppose, societal attitudes about women which they could not help sharing, though skeptically. One wonders, for instance, whether much of the secrecy associated with menstruation might be a denial of illness. Women who did not consider themselves truly sick had no way of proving that they were not except by not disclosing at all the fact they were menstruating.

On March 5, 1901, Gwendoline wrote to Mamie:

> I wish I could see you and find out your remedy. I think you might write it to me on an extra sheet and I will promise you I will not tell, for it isn't likely we will ever see each other again. I am so anxious to learn everything I can to prevent for I don't want to have any more . . . Well good night and write soon, and don't forget to tell *me all you know,* and how did you find out so much out of a book.

On May 5 she had some news for Mamie:

> What Isabelle sells is in a liquid tablet. Mamie I am going to send you an ad I answered. The lady has sent me several times her circulars, and I will send you one. I think the pills would be fine, for just what they say in case any one should get caught; if they could have them they would be all right, but they are awful dear. I haven't sent for any yet. I don't suppose I ever can.

Yet she must have been managing somehow, for she wrote on August 13 of the next year, 1902: "Yes Mamie I am all right I guess for I am sick today. Two women in our neighborhood will be confined this winter, Mrs. F. Dongdon in November, her baby will be a year old this month the 26 I think. Mrs. Rosa Baldine in January. I am thankful I am not in it any more."

Someone less all right was Gwendoline's cousin Mary Kincaid. On February 28, 1896, Mary wrote:

> Mamie, I got two hard months before me yet that if I count right, I just dread the time coming. I aint any bigger than Gwendoline was when she come home, but I am different shape that she was. I stick out in the back as much as I do in front, so you might know what kind of a looking thing I am. O Mamie I wish there was no such a thing as having babies. I wish I took George Willard's receipt and left the nasty thing alone. I will next time you bet I not have any more if I live through this time what I hope I will. Well Mamie it is there and it has to come out where it went in. Well might as well laugh as cry it be just the same.

Her count was correct, for she reported at the end of June that her baby boy was two months old and weighed 16 pounds: "I tell you Mamie I don't want no more babies. We all think lots of the baby and the neighbors all was so kind to me. They brought all kinds of fruit and everything I wanted to eat and they are all good to me. Yes I am glad to have good neighbors, I don't know what I would do."

That December Mary did not know whether she was pregnant or not, she had not "come around" for three months, but her husband's mother thought she might be "having a turn of life, but time will tell." And she went on: "I don't care, I just as soon have one more as not. All I hate is to have it, if I could go to sleep and wake up and be all over with I like it." In mid-December, Gwendoline wrote: "Yes Mamie there is something the matter with Mary all right. She is quite big. I never see anyone grow so fast. I think she will be pretty sick, so many years apart and she is quite old. I hope she won't be, as it is bad enough if it is as easy as can be. I am glad I am through with it." (12–11–96)

Mary's pregnancy in December of 1896 may have been a false alarm, for in March Gwendoline writes that "they are weaning David from the night," when he would have been just under two years old. But by then Mary was desperately ill and died on May 11. "The doctor said it was her heart." Gwendoline sent "particulars," and like so many writers of the period, she is very good on deaths.

Mary was buried up to Ottawa in the Catholic Church yard beside her brother and everything was done Catholic, her wish. The last thing she done was to kiss the cross. After she died she wanted the center table to stand by her and the candle burning and the cross and bottle of holy water to stand on it. And it was. The priest came three times to see her. Her mother sent him down the first. I was there when he came. After he went she told me she was reconciled now. It is too bad she couldn't live. But everything was done and she had everything she called for. That is what we all have got to do some time, and she is through with it and I hope she is in a better place. She looked very nice such a quiet and peaceful expression. She was laid out in her black dress. (6–29–98)

Mamie Goodwater had access to information in a book, she claimed, and so did many women, for although increasingly professionalized, wealthy, and powerful male doctors engaged in the lucrative effort of professionalizing the invalidism of upper middle class women, as recent scholarship has shown, women also had access in their own right to medical information by and for women. These and other studies show the reluctance of the medical profession to accept the idea that one might be both healthy and female, for it was assumed that debility was proof of femininity and that, like Tantalus or Sisyphus, women always reached for but never achieved curing. For women, nearly all ailments that did not clearly manifest themselves as contagious diseases or broken bones centered, according to popular professional views, in the womb.

But judging from their own writings, women worried about a far broader variety of ailments, including the health of their children, husbands, family, and acquaintances, the physical accidents and contagious diseases of sometimes epidemic proportions that all were threatened with. When women concentrated on their own female complaints, what they most wanted to know, apparently, was what doctors least wanted to tell them: how their reproductive organs worked and how they might prevent conception, and sometimes even how safely to induce abortion. For information of this kind the many home medical books must have been invaluable, as they were virtually the only source of information other than advice from other women. These books were cautious; their tone highly moral, advocating always the instinctual joys of motherhood, but many were thoughtful and compassionate as well, recognizing the often insupportable burden of continued pregnancies. Their thorough manner of classifying herbs and compounds for every imaginable ailment leads one to assume that at least some of them were indirectly aimed at women who were seeking remedies for an unwanted pregnancy.

Tokology, A Book for Every Woman, by Alice B. Stockham, M.D., takes its title from the Greek word for motherhood, and it speaks strongly for social reform in the interest of better maternal health.[6] The dedication sets the tone:

> TOKOLOGY IS DEDICATED First: To my Daughter, whose faith in the physical redemption of woman by correct living has been a constant inspiration in the production; Second: To all Women who following the lessons herein taught will be saved the sufferings peculiar to their sex.

Alice Stockham was moved to write the book by the very catch-22 situations that current writers have been describing:

> We find in women of superior education and marked intelligence an exaggerated development of the emotional nature, and a correspond-ing deterioration of physical powers. Weakness, debility, and suffering is the common lot of most of them. Not one in a hundred has health and strength to pursue any chosen study, or to follow any lucrative occupation, and what is vastly worse, most are unfitted for the duties and perils of maternity. (19)

She was a strong advocate of planned parenthood, explaining that "Fewer and better children are desired by right-minded parents." Nevertheless, some of her instructions for limiting births could not have been very helpful, for she instructed, like most physicians of her time, that ovulation takes place during menstruation, and that to avoid pregnancy, one should postpone intercourse until two weeks after menses, a version of the "rhythm" method that would have resulted in maximum fertility. Her awareness of ovulation, however, led her to discredit the theory that conception "is under the control of the woman's will; that by avoiding the least thrill of passion herself, during coition, she can prevent the ovules being displaced to meet the male germs." Dr. Stockham gives directions also for "sedu-lar absorption": "In this, intercourse is had without culmination. No discharge is allowed. People practicing this method claim the highest possible enjoyment, no loss of vitality, and perfect control of the fecundating power" (326). But she thought withdrawal was "incom-plete and unnatural" and equally "disastrous" as masturbation: "In the male it may result in impotence, in the female in sterility. In both sexes many nervous symptoms are produced, such as headache, defective vision, dyspepsia, insomnia, loss of memory, etc. Very many cases of uterine diseases can be attributed solely to this practice" (325). The emphasis of the book is on pregnancy, birthing, and infant care, with short shrift to sexuality: "Coition, the one important act of all the others carrying with it the most vital results, is usually committed for selfish gratification," such as drunkenness, licentiousness, or "parents producing offspring while laboring under great mental strain or bodily fatigue" (323). Women's maternal instincts would more than prove their success in bearing children, Alice Stockham reassured readers, and the best prevention for too many children, she advocated, was the "law of continence."

On the subject of induced abortion she was adamantly unambiguous: "The woman who produces abortion, or allows it to be produced, risks her own health and life in the act, and commits the highest crime in the calendar, for she takes the life of her own child. She degrades the child of the right to its existence" (246). In the event of early signs of miscarriage, she recommended doses of either aconite or cimicifuga, which, were one wanting to encourage the event, presumably one might omit. A woman wanting to abort might also try some of the practices Dr. Stockham warns against: "lifting, straining, a fall, a jar, a blow, a violent cold, or an acute attack of disease, sudden mental emotions, etc," although she cautioned also that the system might develop a habit of aborting. Other hints are there in her advice for curing amenorrhea, the absence or suppression of menses, which generally is best treated, she says, "with plenty of out-door exercise, congenial employment and freedom from care. . . . At all events, in treating suppression avoid using strong remedies, such as old fashioned tansy tea, steel filings, and ergot. These produce congestion, and may be the source of serious chronic ailments." Social and moral reform, in Alice Stockham's view, were the only permissible ways to avoid unwanted pregnancy.

> Women must learn the laws of life so as to protect themselves, and not be the means of bringing sin-cursed, diseased children into the world. . . . As long as men feel that they have a right to indulgence of the passions under the law, no matter what the circumstances, what the condition of the wife, or the probabilities of maternity, so long will the spirit of rebellion of women and the temptation enter their souls to relieve themselves of this unsought burden. May the day soon arrive when men will learn that even passion should serve reason, and that gratification at least should not be sought at the expense of conjugal happiness and *unwelcome children*. (251)

Compassionate instruction in health and morality were Alice Stockham's aims.

Reading a book like *Tokology* "in reverse," so to speak, presumably provided some women with information that had been denied them by the passage of the Comstock Act in 1873, which in many states prohibited the sale of contraceptive devices as well as the publication of contraceptive information. One learns to read other medical guides, herbals, and home remedy publications for the germs of similar forbidden information. There is, for instance, *The People's Home Medical Book.*[7] Here is *People's* treatment for amenorrhea: "Improve the general condition by giving a preparation composed of arsenic iron and nux vomica. Take four tablets a day. You can buy the tablets in any drug store" (364–65). *Nux vomica* is made from the poisonous seed of an Asian tree called *Strychnos nux-vomica,* which is also the source of strychnine.

According to *People's,* the tansy tea Dr. Stockham had warned against "is excellent for its tonic action on the stomach. Good for menstrual troubles and hysteria. Aids in bringing on the menses. A tea made of the leaves and seeds is good for worms in children." Even more hopefully suggestive is the description of Swamp Snake Root: "Good for coughs and consumptive habit. Good also for female debility due to irregular monthlies and has been called 'the female regulator.'"

The People's Home Medical Book takes an even dimmer view of sexuality in marriage for any other purpose than bearing children:

> Never have anything to do with a young man who is 'sowing his wild oats,' or who has sown them. This may mean more than you think. Ask your mother and she can, if necessary, find out from the family physician what it means to the young man and what it would very likely mean to you if you married such a man. Never marry a man to reform him. Leave those who need reforming severely alone. . . . Marriage is a lottery. You may draw a prize, or your life may be made miserable. It is so much better to remain single than to make an unfortunate marriage.

(Statements like these may be helping to foster the idea in our time that "companionate" marriages in former days were rare.)

> Not all women should marry because all women ought not to be mothers. A woman with poor physical or mental health should not marry, for such a woman as a rule will not bear healthy children. . . . Women who intend never to bear and rear children have no right to

marry for this means the taking of measures to prevent conception or the getting rid of the product of conception and the latter is, in plain English, abortion.

There is a great deal of abortion being produced in all classes of society. Abortion is not only dangerous to the woman's life (and of course it destroys the life of the child) but it injures the generative organs. . . . Abortion is frequently caused by women themselves either by the aid of medicines or mechanical means and, to the shame of my profession, it must be said that there are medical men who do it for the sake of financial gain. Whenever abortion is performed, not only the health but the life of the woman is at stake.

As to the prevention of conception, most of the means used are very injurious and especially so to the woman. During my thirty years of the practice of medicine I have seen a great deal of trouble and sorrow caused by the production of abortion and by many of the means used for the prevention of conception, (389)

Men

For day-to-day emotional sustenance as well as remedies for aches and pains, women turned to other women, companionable mothers, aunts, sisters, cousins, friends—allies of a lifetime. However, it was inevitably men who, when it came down to it, made most of the critical decisions in their lives. Traditional relationships between women and men have been described in terms of women's dependence on fathers, brothers, husbands, sons, and employers for economic sustenance and social usefulness, even for their very name. In the age of professional specialization that the nineteenth century increasingly became, women grew more and more dependent upon clergymen, doctors, and commercial entrepreneurs to tell them how to think, how to feel, and how to buy. Women's history, in this traditional and admittedly oversimplified view, is a history of following directions from men.

If men were so important, why was it that women wrote so little about them, paying nowhere near the attention to men that one might expect given women's alleged social and economic dependence upon them? Often men appear as immovable objects to be sidled around. Men emerge, in women's writing, chiefly in three conditions: those held in high regard by women; those present but not well noticed; and those who are essentially enemies. Some of women's most explicit descriptions of men have come at times of great happiness. Two women connected with Allettie Mosher expressed joy in their husbands. Maria Freeland, a cousin, wrote from New York State to Allettie's mother, Eliza Keyes, when the Keyeses were still living in Michigan.

> O Aunt I wish you might be here today it is so pleasant we have been cleaning and I look around and am not ashamed to have any one look in my cabin for it is clean and neat if I do say it myself. Harlow said I should tell you that the next time I write you should have our picture. We will have them taken in Buffalo when we get back there. O Aunt I wish you knew him he is one of the best men he is not pretty at all but homely people are always the best you know I did not know as there was so much goodness in him (or in a man) until after I had married him. (6–6–64)

Rose Williams wrote to Allettie in Wilma nearly twenty years later.

> Well here I am gabbing away and never told you the news. Reece and I will be married a week tomorrow. We came from Lisbon week yester-day got out about two miles from here Sunday and they thought they would stay there awhile as we could not get to work and Monday morning Reece and I got in the gib wagon and went back to Lisbon got there about twelve. Was married between one and two o'clock got our dinner and started home about four, got in five or six miles of camp by dark, and raining like everything so we stopped right on the prairie and stayed there till morning. Got home in time for breakfast. We had a covered wagon but got rather damp. Now was not that a grand affair. I think I have got the *best husband* in the world. (7–2–82)

Maria was the daughter of Jane Freeland, and her life was often made difficult by poverty and family disruptions. Nevertheless, she was able to savor happiness when it reached her (although not for long, as she and Harlow died five years later, within six weeks of each other). Rose Williams's happiness with her husband also came in the midst of difficulties. In 1882 she visited her mother in Lisbon, Dakota Territory, and then returned to Ohio when Reece worked on produce boats in Florida and Rose and her children moved in and out of boarding houses or houses shared with other relatives. Never-theless, in spite of poverty and frequent separations, Rose Williams wrote intimately and affectionately about Reece, as in her earlier letter to Allettie advising "female prevenatives" when she quoted Reece's drawstring remark.

Emma Seaton and Allettie Battey were friends in Michigan. Emma's letters to Allettie between January 1876 and September 1880 (when Allettie moved with her mother and brother to Dakota Territory) speak mainly to three themes: Emma's affectionate delight in her husband, a strong regard for Allettie, and a watchful eye on the affairs of everyone she knew. Husband and friend were not rivals for her affections. Although Will Seaton determined Emma's daily circumstances, Allettie remained a constant reference. Emma's first letter commemorated, in literary diction, the first year of her marriage, as though she knew of no other words to express her truly happy feelings for Willie. But, with a single exception, a later death, she did not again diverge from concrete and material language.

> Yes Lettie there has been many changes since we stood over in that room one year ago. That evening which was the happiest I ever knew, the evening in which I made a vow to leave home and obey my husband. That vow has been faithfully kept for I do love I do honor and it is easy to obey for he does not command me to do anything but that which is reasonable and right. And how happy I was on the first anniversary of our wedding eve. I thought and wondered if you thought of that evening and here you must have been writing at that very time. Willie and I sat up very late that evening reading and talking of one year ago, and I told him how much more I loved him on this Newyear Eve that I did on the one a year ago. I loved him then but I had not learned to love him with that reposing trust and confidence that I now do. But you will think that this is a love letter; I must stop this and go on. But I was so taken up recalling the past that I forgot myself. Excuse me this time I will not do so again. (1–5–76)

Emma gave her attention to Will Seaton easily and without anxiety.

> Did you get April fooled? I did not but Will tried to fool me. I fooled Will twice. The first time though he was not fooled very bad. I blew the egg out of its shell and had boiled eggs for breakfast and I took out the one that I had fixed and asked him to see if it was done, but he found out that it was for a trap before he broke it. But for dinner I sat an empty dish on the table right before his plate and had it covered up with a plate and a spoon on the top of it that fooled him, he expected to find a nice dish of something. . . . I hear Eillie whistling so he can't be far off, so good night from your friend and sister. (4–5–76)

The Seatons were not wealthy enough to afford a house of their own: "We have moved up to Will's folks, but we are keeping house by ourselves. We have the front room and the front room up stairs" (12–3–76). Emma Seaton's regard for Will did not lessen during the five-year correspondence, but neither did it displace her love for Allettie, "Dear friend and sister" as she repeatedly addressed her. Writing to Allettie she had in mind the expected crises in women's lives, marriage and childbirth. On April 24, 1876: "What did you mean I should understand by your finery. Shall I suppose that you and that Sidney Pierce are going to strike up a match or simply you are getting your summer goods early. You must tell me in your next letter which it is." It was neither. Sidney Pierce was a brother to Hubbel Pierce, married to Allettie's sister Viola, but Allettie did not marry Sidney. Her husband later in the year was Tom Battey, a Civil War veteran and frequent caller for many years, according to other letters of Allettie's mother. Emma Seaton next referred to Allettie's marriage on October 21, 1877 (there may well be letters missing in the series): "By the way Lettie it is creeping along toward the last of October and if anything should happen to you before you answer this tell your Ma to pen me a few lines as soon as she possibly can to let me know all about you for I shall be awful anxious about you now remember." Five months later: "(In Confidence) Let if nothing happens to me I expect sometime between the fore part and middle of next month to get a boy to marry your girl. There I suppose you are suprised. Well next time I write perhaps I can tell more about it but not at present" (3–5–78). Discretion, tact, and warm concern mix in her words.

But before Emma could write to congratulate Allettie on the birth of her daughter Inez, she heard that Tom Battey had died. Her letter, for all its literary diction, takes for granted that Allettie was bound to be very sad at his dying, but it does not assume that the event meant a termination also of Allettie's existence. Her friend was alive in Emma's imagination independent of any husband's death, or of marriage or childbirth for that matter, crucial as those events were bound to be.

I heard Sunday that your dear husband was dead. O Lettie I cannot express my sorrow for you. At first I could not believe it. It was but a few days before that I received your letter telling me of your dear little baby and then to hear so soon that it was fatherless made me feel so sorry for you but Lettie your baby will be such a comfort to you in his absence. What was it that caused poor Tom's death. Some say that he fell from a building and some that he had the cholera of course they have so many stories about it that we will not know what is true till we hear from you. Well Lettie you must try to bear it with the patience that every poor afflicted mourner is bound to bear trials, it seems harder though for you have only been married such a short time, but we ought not to complain at the will of God for he doth all things well though it is hard to see clearly why it is done. I do wish that you could come out here and make a good long visit it would help to divert your mind. You would get over your sadness sooner. Why don't you do it. I wish you would. I do want to see your baby so bad while it wears long dresses. (11–23–77)

A letter written the following summer graphs the manner in which Emma's affections easily glide from husband to friend and include both. She was speaking of dances and of an "excursion" she had been on.

Will could not go but insisted on my going with George and Bessie. They went together while they were down from Detroit. They were pretty loving, I don't know if it will amount to anything or not. I am alone through the week now for Will has gone threshing again this summer. I do not have so much to do now for whoever works here now boards himself but I am so lonely when Will is away he was away all last week and is going again tomorrow. How I do wish you were here to stay with me. I have a young lady friend that stays with me nights but I wish it was you instead. (7–28–78)

Emma had seen another couple, unmarried, being "pretty loving" to each other; although her husband was present as she wrote, she dreaded his inevitably leaving again for his days of farm work. This emotional trail of associations brings her to long the more for Allettie, not as a substitute for Will (which she had in the woman who was staying with her) but for her own sake, his absence in fact making easier the prospect of Allettie's company. Emma's last letter in the group anticipated another sorrow, Allettie's leaving Michigan for Dakota Territory, a deprivation that threatened to displace a center to Emma's life.

I received your letter a few days ago containing the mitten string and was glad to hear from you again while you were in Michigan. When I think of your going away it makes me feel so sad. To be sure we shall always write to one another, but O Let I am afraid that we shall never see each other again in this world but let me believe that there is a better world in store so let us try to live so that we may meet where parting is never known. . . . Well Let I guess I shall have to close as I am near the end of the sheet. If you can just drop me a line the last chance you get before you start and send me the Dakota address and I will send a letter to you so that you will get it soon after you get there if it is just a post card it will do. I received your card the same day that I

sent the other letter well Lettie good by for the last time in Michigan
but not for ever for if you went to the end of the world I should write
as long as I knew where you are. (9–5–80)

The bulk of Emma Seaton's writing could be called news or gossip,
depending upon one's point of view. She had a watchful reportorial
eye, taking for granted that all events in the lives of others are
potentially valuable to one's own. She wrote energetically, with good
humor, only disapproving of meanness.

> My brother Will was married 4 weeks ago tomorrow to Miss Libbie
> Burgess that Libbie of whom you must often have heard me speak. She
> lived near Trenton. They had a very nice wedding, but I did not think
> when I read your letter in which you said you supposed the next one
> you heard of would be Will. I thought I guess not for all I knew he was
> going with Libbie and thought perhaps they would sometime marry but
> I did not think it would happen this winter, but it is so. . . . I expect that
> the reason of Will's getting married this winter was to keep in the
> fashion. Everybody that can find anybody that will have them is getting
> married this winter. Since I wrote you before Ches Hitchcock and Cad
> Thorn (she is Gardiners daughter) have been married also Eva Baker. I
> can't think of her man's name. And Eddie Romine married some
> preacher's daughter, and Clint Chamberlin and Stell Lawrence, and
> Lumis Chamberlin and that Mate Chapin, and Willie Wagar and a girl
> by the name of Libbie Butler, she lived down near where Will's girl did,
> have all hitched traces to trot in double harness for life I suppose.
> (3–5–78)

> You also asked of Aunt Julia and Ann Webb. Aunt Julia lives with Ann.
> I saw her last Friday. She is real smart yet she has not changed much
> but they all say that she is as ugly as ever. Ann has that Abe Bush living
> with her. He is her cousin they say that he and her will soon be married
> but I do not know it seems that he wanted her before she ever married
> Arthur and just as soon as Arthur had been dead a little while he
> parted from his wife (for he was married) and brought his furniture
> and traps down to Ann's and has been living with her ever since. People
> talks a great deal about them for living so but if they marry as some
> think they will I suppose they think it is all right. He is nothing
> handsome. (9–5–80)

This correspondence probes subtle connections between two
women's feelings for each other and for the men important to them.
While Emma's writing amply demonstrated that she placed Will
Seaton firmly in her consciousness as well as in her affections, it
nowhere indicates that she felt dominated by him. Nor did Emma
write as though she expected Allettie to be permanently devasted by

Tom Battey's death, sad as it was. Her chatty view of things does not miss the inexorable interweavings of sexuality, disease, and death that occur in most lives, including her close friend's. And she succeeds in revealing more detailed information about her husband than one usually learns about men from women's writings, chiefly, I think, because she so enjoyed his company.

Mamie and Ben Goodwater wrote to each other as though their intimacies also meant a good deal to both. Ben's letters to Mamie while she was with relatives in Wisconsin during the winter of 1895 express both affection and sexual pleasure: "About coming home I don't think you had better come till the last of the month. It will be warmer by that time and it will give me more time to get the money in. I wish you were here now but seeing you ant why. Stay and have as good a time as you can and we will try and make up for lost time next summer." (2–4–95) Ben's letters sustain an erotic tone by reporting sexual scandals because he thinks they are funny.

> You know you said your father wanted to know what Charly was doing. He is working at his old trade holding down the bed, he is afraid the bed bugs will carry it off so he stays right by it to watch it. I don't think they can beat him he is too heavy. Oly Johnson stays there too. She has Ben eating dried apples and drinking hot water, I should say by the looks of things. I heard Nancy was coming home this week. Tom Hill's pocket is getting low I guess so they say. (1–15–95)

> Does your father ever say anything about coming. I don't want to hurry you any, I want you to have a good visit and a good time. Tell your father I asked old Maggie if she wanted him to come home and she only twittered and laughed. But Charly said they wanted some money that was all they wanted. Nancy stays to home again. The whole mob is there now. Tom Hill comes sometimes but don't stay long. Nancy goes off with him she doesn't stay up there with him. Mrs. Hill was after her with a gun so they say and the police are watching them now trying to catch them together. (1–27–95)

> You wanted to know about Oly Johnson. She don't stay with Maggie now she stays to home. Nancy run her away wouldn't have her stay with Ma Ma any longer so she said if anything should happen they will blame Ma Ma so she said she stays with Tom Hill again she says Oly is taking stuff the kill the little devil. I don't know suppose she is though Charly says it belongs to Perzett him that is in the candy store with McHeall. They used to be in the Oprie Block you know. (2–4–95)

> By the looks of things Oly Johnson's fellow skipped the town to parts unknown. She feels pretty blue so they say. They thought he was going to marry her he told her he would so to get time to fly the town she might have knew he would not if she had been half witted. (2–17–95)

Five years later, when Ben was working on the streetcar line in Minneapolis, their letters show that he might tease Mamie, but she was able to return in kind:

I found a card on the street the other day. It said it was the

Ages of Love
17 to 20 Night till Morn
20 to 30 Night and Morn
30 to 40 Night or Morn
40 to 50 Now and then
50 to 60 Billy knows when
60 to 70 Amen.
(from Ben, 4–12–04)

According to the age of love your age is pretty slow, ten years more it will be Amen. I must send that to Nell tell her you sent it to her. I haven't been to any dances since I came home but could of went to two but when I do go I dance more than three times. Couldent you find any one to dance with, you done better than that up here. O yes Nell and I had a few pictures taken. She wanted me to send Henry one so I will send it to you so you can see it and then give it to Henry. I thought there was no use of send one to you to carry around. Tell me what you think of it,' tell Henry to write. (from Mamie, 4–14–04)

Well Mamie I think that is a nice picture of you and Nellie. I thought it was mine till I read the letter. I will send it to Henry today so he will get it all right. (from Ben, n.d.)

In regards to the picture I did not send one to you as you would only have to carry it around, but if you want one of course I will send one. (from Mamie, 4–21–04)

More often, as I have said, women's descriptions of men are apt to be blurred, just out of focus or to one side. I had to read a long time in Grace DeCou's journal before I realized that T.H. was the man she was married to, and I have not been able to piece together what it was the Kinkaid men did, for all Gwendoline's long and frequent letters. These men were not central to their perceptions, although they may have been a considerable worry and annoyance. Goodwater men were particularly trying, according to Mary Kinkaid: "Sumner don't do nothing but horse trading. I tell you that don't get anybody a living makes me almost wild. I worry so much, that's what keeps me down so poor" (6–38–96). Twenty years earlier, Mary Ann Coss, Mamie Goodwater's adoptive mother, wrote to her mother from Grand Forks to tell her "that we are yet alive and well and doing well pretty well, but I have to do it all alone." She was keeping boarders.

> The steamboats comes in every day right close to the door so we can get a lot of passengers if Warren would take hold as he ought to, but he don't care as long as he has bread and tea he thinks that is enough but I have all to see to. . . . Mother I wish that you could see Warren, he is so fat you would not know him hardly, and as lazy as can be. So is Charley, they don't intend to do any more than they can help. Indians plenty here. (8–4–77).

Gwendoline Kinkaid was bemused and somewhat annoyed by her husband's labor pains, and she expected more real sympathy from Mamie Goodwater to whom she was writing than from the man who ostensibly was suffering with (or for) her.

> Brink has been sick so we had to have the doctor. He was took sick the night I was. I must tell how queer it was. The minute I called him and woke up he was sick. He went down stairs and vomited. He said he never felt so queer before, but he kept up that night and the next day he had to go to bed. He was sick for three or four days in bed, so you see it made it quite hard for his mother, three sick ones to wait on, besides the work. U[ncle] Warren said what ailed Brink, he felt my sickness. I have heard of that before, did you ever. (12–21–96)

Some private writing can only be called adversarial, treating women and men as enemies, the greater casualties falling among women for whom sexual relationships can become fraught with fear and danger. Thus William Coss's announcement to his sister and brother, Helen and Warren Coss, of his intentions to marry. William Coss was an uncle of Ben and (by adoption) Mamie Goodwater, whose own attitudes toward each other were markedly less adversarial.

> Now Helen a word to you. You want to know whether I was a going to be married or not. The truth is I expect I shall be in the course of about 3 months if nothing happens do not talk it all over the country. There is no use of saying that because that will do no good because it is impossible for a woman cannot keep anything 24 hours it nearly kill a person to do it. A fretful scolding woman is worse than the devil all to pieces. She is good looking pleasant and knows good manners and that is a fortune in itself. Her name I will inform you at some further period.

Instances abound of reported violence between men and women. Of the same generation as William Coss, Henry Fellon wrote to Eliza Keyes, to whom he was related by marriage. Whatever the facts of the court case, Henry Fellon was not strongly imagining wrongs done to the dead wife.

> We are having quite exciting times in our court about these days from the trial of Robinson on a charge of trying to poison his wife. You will see it in the papers I have sent you. They are in the defense now. He's believed by the respectable part of the community that it is an infamous conspiracy to ruin a very worthy and respectable man. Except for this story [illegible] by burglary, he stands as fair as any man in Rochester. The trial will last several days yet. When finished and decided I will send you the result if I can get a paper. (1–18–58)

Such instances have little bearing, of course, on statistical rates of adult abuse, but their being written about at all, and so vividly, speaks to people's awareness. John Engstad, who began practicing medicine in Grand Forks in 1885, described in a journal he kept of his patients the dangers that marriage held for some women. Living in rural poverty made survival precarious enough, what with inadequate nutrition, tuberculosis, and continuous pregnancies. Violent husbands, in John Engstad's mind, were insupportable.

> September 4, 1890. Mrs. Martin le Aanes, McKenna. Age 29. Had four children, one dead, oldest eight, youngest five years. Seven years ago after the third confinement she was taken with cramps, constipation, and a general weakness. Had to wash her children on the second day. Up the second or third day. Had to work in the fields and in the house over her strength. Had to carry water up a steep hill rain or shine. No closet in farm. The husband a devil. Will not allow her to do any fancy work or anything that would be a pleasure to her. Cries a great deal and depressed. Very neat and attractive in her dress and appearance. Erysipelis lasted fourteen days. Vomits every morning. Belladonna and alum pills and solal for the pain.

Not all husbands were devils, but few contributed as much to women's well-being as to their pregnancies. Engstad again:

> July 7, 1886. Mrs. Peter Wjoberg. Acton, Minnesota. Age 35. Has had seven children, two living and five dead. Last spring lost one child after a lung sickness and after that time she has lost considerable weight but her mind has suffered most from melancholia and it is so marked now that she has a staring look, talks to herself. "I do not sleep," and sit all

day shaking her head. Imagines that her feet will dry up as she asserts there is no more circulation in them. Refuses to get well. All organs OK. No pain in back. Tendon reflex almost lost. Very forgetful, forgets to dress or do anything only to sit and meditate.[8]

Death

Conventional wisdom in our age has it that the time of the late Victorians was chiefly marked by materialism and sentimentality, that people were so driven by progress and respectability that sexuality seldom entered their thoughts. The large families of our grandparents and great-grandparents came because children were needed to work on farms and to inherit businesses. They filled those huge mansarded, porticoed, and turreted houses; and everyone in those days liked children better than they do now. Prostitution flourished to be sure, the myth continues, as part of the urban blight that can be expected to accompany prosperity, for something must be provided for men's insatiable animal nature. Talk was of "limbs," doctors' discretion prevented their examining undressed women, or looking at private parts, and a "womanly woman" was all things but sexual. Strong bodies, pure thoughts, fresh air and cold hip baths for men, and a predisposition to consumption for women ensured virgin brides, motherhood, and a solid bearded citizenry who left their mark in commerce, on the land, and in the features of as many descendents as they and succeeding wives could manage. Ann Douglas's study of Victorian mass culture in America[9] connects proverbial reticence about sexuality in the nineteenth century to people's very vocal expressions about death—speaking of death took the place of speaking about sex:

> I have already said that women and ministers, in an effort to rationalize and glamorize their position, were engaged in subordinating historical progress to biological process. Barred by external taboos and internal anxieties from elaboration on the overtly sexual acts of impregnation and childbirth, they concentrated on illness and death: they were more interested in the moments at which crude energy failed than in those at which it accelerated. (242)

Douglas also shows that biographies by and about women tended to focus on the subject's "being" rather than doing, and often dwelt at length on her lingering and early death, since they were obliged to invent patterns that contradicted conventional male histories emphasizing accomplishment by action. Certainly Ann Douglas's points are well taken: death as a preoccupation for popular culture in the late nineteenth century does appear to have had the prominence that sexuality commands in our day, and may well have been for many people a substitute expression.

Nevertheless, evidence from women's writings invites additional observations. For one thing, women have written intensely and consistently about sexuality, working women with considerable frankness. In addition, many more people two and three generations ago experienced death at close hand than do now. Deaths of infants and small children were so frequent that women wrote as though they hardly took the fact of their living children seriously. Rose Williams promised to send a picture of her infant daughter Mattie "if she lives till I get short dresses on her" (to Allettie Battey 12–4–83). Rose and other young mothers virtually collected infant deaths:

> A new little girl baby at Frank's about noon that day. Babies seems to be plentiful there as well as back here. One of our young married girls had twins last week, girl and a boy. The girl died soon after it was born and the little boy died day before yesterday. She had been married little over nine months they were only seven month children and they were the littlest things I ever saw did not think both together would weigh more than four pounds. She felt so bad because she lost both. (8–24–84)

And Gwendoline Kinkaid to Mamie Goodwater:

> Charley said Mrs. Miller's baby died when it was two or three days old. What was the matter did you see it. Oh Hallie Arris baby is very sick, I guess this one will die. You know we went to her baby's funeral the last Sunday you was here.

Gwendoline did not even think about living very long herself: "Cora goes to Sunday School every Sunday now. Next spring I shall send her to school if I am alive" (6–29–98), and "Wednesday I will be twenty-four years old. I am getting old I think" (9–11–99).

Nearly always, someone they knew was dying, and because women were the ones who nursed the sick, and also the ones to write letters, it is not surprising that they gave the best of their literary skill to composing death scenes. Thus Rose Williams, then in Ohio, to Allettie Battey in Dazey, Dakota Territory, on the demise of one of her family in Lisbon, Dakota:

I thought I had told you what was the matter with Wit. She had the Meningitis of the brain took sick on Monday and a week from that day was buried she never was conscious just suffered everything would talk and yell they had to hold her in bed in her deliriums. Said she wanted to go home they told her to quiet her they was taking her home and she shook hands with Sis and Mantie and said she was glad to see them and asked them what they called their children and she thought they were Ett and I for she said she wanted to go and see us. But she died very quiet went off as if she was going to sleep poor girl. It is just impossible to believe she is dead she was to commence at the Lisbon school the day she was buried had it engaged for a year at $40 a month. (12–14–83)

Gwendoline Kinkaid lavished details on the death of her grandfather:

Well Mamie Grandpa Kinkaid died Thursday five minutes past twelve October 4, 1900. Oh he was such a terrible sufferer, you never see any one suffer so. He was three days a dying. He never told anything to us what he wanted done. He realized to the last but he couldn't talk nor swallow a thing for three days before he died. You know the doctor said he had consumption and heart disease. They had a post-mortem examination after he died and there didn't a thing ail him that the doctor doctored him for. I will tell you what the doctor told us. One of his kidneys was enlarged and as rotten as could be. The liver was enlarged and hung right over this kidney and had gall stones an inch square. His left lung was entirely gone and full of cancers. He had a large cancer in the stomach and all down his left side and his throat was cancers. The right lung was so filled with fluid that it pressed on the heart, and that was what made the doctors think it was heart disease, but his heart was all right only from the pressure of that lung. Wasn't it awful, we never thought of such a thing as cancers. Just think the awful condition he was in. The doctor said I didn't see how he ever kept about so long and lived. The doctor said if they had known there had been no help for him, it would of been better for him not to of taken any medicine. He was ailing for three years, and the last year he was very bad off. He was in bed almost seven weeks I think. Grandma took care of him night and day up till the last week. His funeral was held Sunday afternoon two o'clock to the house, October 7, 1900. Funeral was conducted by the G.A.R. Post, his request. He told Mr. Porter, one of the soldiers, he wanted to be buried by the Lodge. . . . The singers sang three songs. They were Rock of Ages, Down in the Valley and Rest Soldier Rest. They sang very nice and the pieces were very pretty. Grandpa's text was taken from the 90 psalm and tenth verse, the last part of the verse, He Flyeth Away. (10–16–00)

Virtually no other event stirred such passionate writing.

Aurie Carreau, Her Euphemisms

Women's writings on the subject of death sometimes call attention to the quality of their class aspirations. Working class women like Jane Freeland, Gwendoline Kinkaid, and Rose Williams used crude and graphic language to write about sexuality and death. But for women of upper middle class aspirations, words could impede thoughts and feelings. These women's words on death were as fraught with euphemism as they were haunted by sensuality. A correspondent whose writing illustrates these complexities, changing her style as she changed her social aspirations, was Aurie Carreau, of Grand Rapids and Detroit, Michigan, who wrote to Allettie Mosher in Dazey, North Dakota, between 1918 and 1933. In particular, her manner of writing about family deaths grew vaguer and increasingly euphemistic.

The first letter in the series is for October 7, 1918, and it begins with a death.

> Well poor old Uncle was laid at rest on Friday 4th of Oct he was glad to go he suffered terrible but Nora was so good to him I thought of it so much how glad I was he had some good wife to care for him in his last days. And he was too for no one can care for the other like husband or wife. We went out to see him twice while he was so bad it seemed to bring our dear Mother's death all back to us and I thought of how badly she would feel were she living he longed to see you all so much in his last hours and complained because we none of us come more often but my health has been so poorly up until we moved here the Dr told me to get where it was high and dry so we are at the highest point in city 3 blocks west of Division on Gardner 1934 off of Burton St and I am so much better which I am very thankful for. We got our car and that too I think has had a tendency to help me.

The state of her own health somehow takes precedence over the death of poor old uncle; it is even prepared for by his demise. In spite of her sentimental description of his dying, Aurie Carreau does tell of seeing him, of his wife's nursing, and of his feeling neglected. But typical of her writing is its gravitation toward her own affairs. She justifies not seeing the man more often by praising his wife and then reporting her own sickness; her attention moves next to a new house and car, subjects that recur often in her correspondence, measuring prosperity, social status, and better health. A year later the car, real estate, and economic well-being are even more strongly on her mind:

> I never enjoyed anything as we have our car. We are still living in the same place and we have bought us a lovely lot and will build next spring at the corner of Wever St and Union Ave. It's a short street running east from Madison all improvements and ½ block north of Burton. Carrie and Henry bought a lot next to us more for speculation I think. Ward has an elegant position and they gave him a $50 raise the first of July and we are getting along so nicely seems too good to be true. . . . Well Lettie its eleven years today since dear old Mother passed away and I miss her more every day. I often wish she could see how nicely we are getting along now for so often she used to say don't get discouraged children it can't rain always and a poor beginning makes a good ending. (10–31–19)

In August of 1926 she plans a trip by car to California with a stopover in North Dakota, and remarks about the traffic in Detroit:

> Its true one never feels safe on the roads now days so many Autos and presume round these parts are much worse on account of the big cities. I never saw anything like it we was in our front window on Sun nite and counted 118 autos in 1½ minutes so you know the traffic that goes past here and now they are packed with luggage going both ways from every state in the Union.

She is an onlooker to a more and more mobile, and dangerous, world.

Aurie Carreau's responses to family deaths, one is bound to observe, grow increasingly sentimental and remote from her willing conscious experience. On February 12, 1919, she responds to the news of the death of Viola Pierce, the sister of Alettie Mosher whom she had been including in the salutation of her letters: "We are so very sorry poor Auntie had to leave us and well know how lonely it is for you but the dear old soul in her last letter to Carrie she said she didn't see why she was left alone and why couldent she have gone instead of Uncle Henry. So we have the consolation of knowing she wanted to go." Viola had died of influenza.

Eight years later Aurie Carreau wrote another letter of condolence, this time for the death of Allettie's daughter Inez, and her formulas sound even more distant.

> It is with regret I must write this letter to tell you how very sorry I am

to hear of poor Inez death it is indeed sad to think one must be snatched from this earth at such an early age [she was 50] but God knows best and she has only gone to prepare the way for those left to mourn her loss and its only a few short years when we must all go on the same road. . . . I am kept so busy I neglect my correspondence and I am always sorry afterwards but never the less my heart is always with you all. You see Leona went back to school last fall and she has made high school in 3 years carrying 7 solid subjects two side subjects night school twice a week and in a night school play with a leading part.

The bragging about Leona may not seem the height of tact when she is writing to another woman on the death of her daughter. Though Aurie Carreau's ambitions for Leona were much more immediate to her than her sorrow at the loss of Inez, she sounds nervous, as though it were necessary for her to list things in order to make them real: "And I must iron do some pressing and scrub besides cleaning up the house. I worked so hard yesterday did not sleep much last night so I must bring my letter to a close and get to work." Precise as her style is in speaking of her own affairs, the mention of Allettie's affairs provokes her to flat abstraction, not imagination or under-standing. Her letter closes: "Now once again I want to tell you you have our sympathy and I trust God will bless and protect you all that are left behind and some day you will all be happy together again, and dear Gladys [Inez's oldest daughter] our hearts ache for you as well as brothers but all be good so some day you can join dear mother in heaven." (Gladys in 1927 had a child of her own.) For Aurie Carreau, language is a mask of feeling, not an expression of it, and gives her little power.

    I have said, in describing such writers as Grace DeCou, Ada Bickford, and Gwendoline Kinkaid, that they seldom make abstract or general statements, that they write in a literal way about what is immediately to hand. Their acceptance of social status likewise does not appear to vary; they show no signs, in our jargon, of being upwardly mobile. But Aurie Carreau makes a habit of gen-eralizations, many as uncertain as her abstractions on death, and she is self-conscious about self-improvement. In regard to her daughter Leona, for instance, she expresses contradictory attitudes in succeed-ing letters. Just a year before the account of Leona's academic triumphs, she wrote that Leona had been ill and stopped going to school, as a result of losing 90 pounds in six months "on a diet for her flesh . . . Dr. said she could not go back until next September and she says she won't go back then, she is so much comfort to us and trust God will spare her for us a good many years, she has never caused us a heart ache yet and will be 19 years old the 19th of April. Has never had a real beau goes out with a nice boy now and then but don't give a hang for them" (3–1–26). Yet five months later: "I am glad you have grand children to enjoy by the looks I will never be Grandma for my girl never sees anyone she cares a hang for so I am out of luck I guess being a grandma but wish I might for Ward and I both love children. Leona will be 20 years old next April and not even a beau she says I love my mother and Dad too much to be bothered with men" (8–9–26). In January of 1928 she writes that Leona had started college that fall but had had to stop in spite of high grades on examinations, for "she simply can not stand such hard work," and planned to go to work as an interior decorator in Detroit with family friends. "And we will probably go back to Detroit if she goes for she is all we have to live for and want to be with her while we can. . . . She may not be able to even stand that but will try it out if she isn't we will take her and go to California." Aurie Carreau writes as though she wanted Leona simultaneously to be sickly and dependent upon her, and a school "achiever"; she both praises Leona's aloofness from males, and regrets her childlessness at age twenty. At times her optimism has a sting: "I feel the best I have in years its been nearly six years since my goiter operation and the Dr said it would be about that long before I felt good and it was so we always have something to be thankful for don't we? I know you must be lonely for Inez poor girl, but she probably is far happier than you are for she was a good girl" (1–30–28). Leona lost her job as a decorator in 1933, and Ward Carreau also found himself out of work, and Aurie writes angrily about the "rotten disposition" of Nell, the relation for whom Leona had been working:

I get on with her but she quarrels with her neighbors and every one I really feel ashamed of her for its so humiliating for me as I usually get on with every one. And have an abundance of friends. They never go anyplace, never have company and sore if company comes and holds up their work in their yard. . . . Well I like my friends and its as Dad says amusing when I go into our auxiliary of 400 women first one grabs me than another and a hand goes up way at one end of the room then at other and its a wonderful feeling to say and see friends every where I love them all I love life I love God and what a consolation. I am glad I can see the good in the world and yet I am poor. Money isn't all happiness not a jug full. (4–7–33)

Also unlike correspondents I have been citing, Aurie Carreau sometimes comments on the political and social scene. In 1918 she is vehemently anti-German, and writes that "Dr Barth is in awfully bad, he they say was injecting and spreading the Spanish influenza in the local camps here and his uniform was taken from him he had no authority to have a uniform they say at all, he is a German Jew . . . . I say if its true Barth has spread this he should be strung up" (10–7–18). "Dr Barth is free as usual . . . such scandals its terrible and so much graft" is her disgruntled report of February 12, 1919, when she also says "I registered and will vote and I think every woman should," but two years later, when some steel plants had closed, she disapproved of women working: "but the factory that do work employs so many women Yet I think it a crime when so many men have families starving" (6–16–21). In the same letter she disapproves both of socialists and people with too much money:

> We hear Nell is building another house she will soon be so rich won't know what to do with her money but what is money without a peaceful and unselfishness in life. I don't want it if I have to be a traitor to everyone to accomplish it, do you? The socialists have been working hard here but with little results several have been deported and they should be if not true americans.

In 1933 she strongly objects to communists she has heard about. Michigan had repealed the 18th Amendment and there was drug trafficking in the schools, she says, and the mayor, it was discovered when some "sorrowful mothers" requested an investigation, was "right in with them," all this after "we had a recall of Mayors and took from office a KKK leader to put this fellow in, and our city is the melting pot of the Communists they have their head quarters here and have 27 posts here and are even instilling it in our schools in grades as young as 8 yrs and sending our money to Russia. I really do not see what its all coming to" (4–7–33). However, she favored pensions for veterans of the Spanish War:

> and at their ages it would have been a terrible thing especially after such a crisis as the country has gone thru the past three years, so we got together and injected a clause in the bill and we will receive them until the 1st of July and perhaps longer. We have our 28 wonderful attorneys still fighting for us at Washington. We had some mighty good Senators and Rep from Detroit that fought for us as well as one of your North Dakota Senators. (4–7–33)

Expressions like "instilling in our schools," "crisis the country has gone through," "wonderful attorneys" are nearer the clichés of public writing than the direct intimacies of conversation.

Aurie Carreau, it seems to me, is far less secure, less in control of all aspects of her life than are other correspondents I have been citing. The calamities which they report are disturbing enough, but they are pretty much to be expected and only mysterious as is the eye of God. And, for the most part, these writers possess a satisfactory language to describe, if not always to explain, each episode as it comes along. But the words at Aurie Carreau's disposal are insufficient to meld into the pattern of her day such disruptions as German Jews, factory closing, competitive schools, women in the labor force, migrating populations in heavy traffic past her door, to say nothing of socialists and communists. It is all too much, especially as the economic circumstances of her own life are not changing perceptibly (they certainly were not keeping up with the successes asserted all around her).

Private writings by women in the late nineteenth century repeat common topics: friendships with others, far away; relationships with men, housekeeping, worry about illness and death, the care of children. Women's outlook was primarily material; they wrote about things, people, happenings, and always money, some women virtually measuring days in coins. I see greater variation in the ways most women thought about their lives than actual differences in their circumstances. Working women like Eliza Keyes or Mamie Goodwater generalized so little about what happened to them as sometimes to be nearly unintelligible to an outsider, so near was their focus. But women of upper middle class aspirations, like Aurie Carreau, used language in order to stretch distances between themselves and everyday events. They tried to write, I think, as though such elements as sexuality, disease, and death were separable after all, but at the same time reported behavior that showed they acquiesced to the same *in*separables as everyone else.

Thus Aurie Carreau suspected conspiracies at the bottom of her troubles at the same time as she held death at arm's length, writing of Inez Mosher's death as if she had been a stranger and not someone she knew well. She sentimentalized her daughter Leona's sexuality as Eliza Keyes did not that of her two daughters. More so than her Dakota correspondents, Aurie Carreau wished she might live by the precepts laid down in grammar books, in newspapers and

magazines, in popular novels, her aspirations quickened by urban
living. Women who were more settled than Aurie Carreau in the
upper middle class felt severely inhibited when they looked for
words to say anything directly about sexuality, disease, and death.
Elsie Hadley White—married to a state governor and elected to
major office of the National Federation of Women's Clubs—wrote
fluently, sometimes scathingly about her husband's election results,
but remained mutely inarticulate about her personal life.

Elsie Hadley White, Political Wife

Elsie Hadley was born in 1864 in Indianapolis, of Quaker parents
descended from Cotton Mather, and died in 1925. Her father, an
inventor of machinery, was so ambitious for her education that he
enrolled her in a pre-college program at Earlham College when she
was thirteen. She graduated in 1882, taught in several high schools
in order to go to graduate school in mathematics at Michigan State
University (although her father wished she would let him pay her
way), completed in 1892 the first Master's Degree at Michigan State
to be earned by a woman, traveled for a year, then taught mathematics at Valley City College in North Dakota. A year later, in 1895, she
married Frank White, a Valley City farmer and engineering graduate of the University of Illinois, and a man with political ambitions.
These he realized after a year in the Philippines during the
Spanish-American War, when he returned to be elected for two
terms as North Dakota governor on the Republican ticket. He served
in France during the First World War, and as U.S. Treasurer from
1921–1928.

Elsie Hadley's ambitions were every bit as energetic as Frank
White's, and she fulfilled them in ways that were at the time, and for
women, just as highly approved of as his were for a man. She was
thirty years old by the time she had her Master's Degree and faculty
post, and had gone about as far as a woman was likely to—that is,
academic prospects at Valley City were not bright. Once married,
she channeled her considerable energies to caring for her husband
and son, Edwin. When Frank sailed for the Philippines, she went to
California to see him off and was on a boat to meet his ship when it
came in. She did not accompany him to the Philippines only because
a doctor forbade her to bring the rather frail three-year-old Edwin.
During World War I, when Frank White was appointed colonel of

the Second North Dakota regiment at Camp Green and Camp Miles at Newport, New Jersey, Elsie White lived in a tent across the road from his headquarters and mothered the soldiers before they were shipped to France. Again, only strict army regulations prevented her from accompanying her husband when he went to France. During the war she was given charge of the Registration Women's Committee of the Council of National Defense, North Dakota Division. She wrote a poem, "The Soldier's Mother," which was widely printed and distributed by the YWCA. She learned quickly about politics and herself moved into administration, becoming state president of the Federated Women's Clubs and the national chairman of the membership committee. By all accounts—and her scrapbooks preserve many newspaper clippings—she was a successful woman and much admired.

In matters of politics, of social obligations, even of family distress, Elsie White's writing was straightforward, practical, in the plain style of her Quaker heritage. In a journal she kept from August 1, 1899 to the end of February 1902 (intended for her son Edwin), she wrote, shortly after moving into the governor's mansion in Bismarck:

> On the evening of the 5th Alice McDonald came from Valley City to spend a few weeks with us and be a friend in need to me. She has taken the responsibility of the culinary department off my hands. In view of the fact that we have company all the time I value such loyalty more than I can express to her. . . . Our dinners have been simple but well cooked and nicely served. Only one girl to do all kitchen work and a man who helped in every way he can makes work for all. I am well satisfied with results so far. The Ball came Friday night when over 100 couples were on the floor. The chairs were taken from the House chamber and a canvass spread. Frank and I did justice to the occasion and had a fine time. . . . We both wore the same suits that we were married in and attended a like function six years ago. My white satin was made over in the late style and was indeed a beautiful gown, thanks to my dear Mother. (1–13–01)[10]

Two years later on a visit home at the time Frank was running for reelection and her mother was very ill, she wrote to Frank:

> Saw Dr. Wehoman today. He says a trip to Dakota would do Mamma good so I think we will go in two weeks or so if she improves. He says her trouble is all due to poor blood. It does her good to have me here. (10–30–02)

> Mamma is poorly today. She does not eat enough to keep a chicken alive. Everything she takes in hurts her and tonight she looks so pale and thin. (11–5–02)

> It was a great shock to see Mamma so thin. This last week she has been able to eat again but her liver seems almost inactive at times. Her face is so wrinkled she looks seventy years old. (11–13–02)

When she can look at matters with a managerial eye, Elsie White writes in a straightforward manner. But anything of a more personal nature she responded to with embarrassing sentimentality. Her letters to Frank alternately gush and nag. He sent her a careful counting of votes by counties, to which she replied: "I am indeed very glad that all is so well. I believe if thee had worked hard in Grand Forks and Cass as thee did in Barnes County it might have been still better" (11–7–02). Frank never wrote enough to suit her: "Well my precious, I must turn in now and I hope thee will not fail to answer this as soon as thee gets it so I can hear oftener than once a week. . . . Be sure and write Edwin, some day thee may want him to write to thee" (nd 02). Her first letter during a visit to Indianapolis to visit her sick mother, written on the day she arrived, begins:

> My Dearest, This is the evening thee became "my dearest" at this very house nine years ago and tonight I am here without thee and I do not know whether thee is at the farm or at Bismarck. I only hope thee has said some of the nice things on paper that thee did so long ago.

She returns to the theme at the close:

> My dear I must say good night—it is ten and no bath yet. . . . All these nine years have been so varied and yet how much better we understand each other than we did for the first few years. I know that I have grown more jealous of thy love all the time and only hope that the next nine years may find me as bound up in thee as I am now. Help keep the love warm and thee can have one woman who would sell her very soul for thee, my darling. With a goodnight kiss from Thy affectionate Wife. (9–19–02)

Seventeen years later, when she was expecting Frank home after the year in France, her protestations sound equally insecure.

> It rather seems to me that April 12 [the day she was writing] was the day we used to remember in our early married life as the day in the little old room over Anderson's store when thee first told me thee was

serious. Am I right? Is it not the day? Those were wonderful days. For me it seemed so strange for a man who had known so many women to be seriously interested in me. . . . I told thee then that my whole being would be thine with a devotion unswerving. It has been true and with our small ups and downs we have grown more dependent upon each other all the time. No other man has ever had a thought from me nor has it ever occurred to me that I could ever think of another in this world even if I were left to "carry on" alone in later years. Two of thy pictures are looking at me from the top of this little desk, two more are on the dresser so thee sees I can not get out of thy sight here. I carry one in my bag and show it and Edwin's a dozen times a day. Papers look as if treaty was near completion. God speed the day and send my own back to me "heart whole and fancy free" to me alone. Thy own devoted Elsie. Easter will find me not with thee in body but in spirit.

This shy insecurity pervades her letters to her husband even before they were married. She visited his relatives in Chicago during the summer of 1894, and wrote back to him: "Thy sister thinks thee should be married soon as thee can and I guess we are of the same opinion. . . . Dear boy, the time will go by soon and none too soon for me. I am anxious to know that nothing can come between us as I feel there can not" (6–16–94). (He was also her "dear farmer boy" and, when at war, "dear soldier boy.") By August of 1894 she was with her family in Indiana making wedding preparations, and the prodding began: "I found yesterday that cards such as we want will cost $6.50 for the first hundred and $3.00 for each additional hundred. Is that more than thee can stand? They will be folded and everything ready for addresses. We can do that the day or so before the wedding while thee is here" (8–3–94). The letter ends: "O my love, thee has entered into my life, and loving thee seems the most pleasant duty before me."

Two days later she spent a night with her friend Dr. Reba Rogers: "She told me some things I ought to know too before I go to make my home with thee. My dearest, I do feel a great deal of responsibility when I look forward to the years to come. We will be of one mind on most matters I think. I do love thee, I feel, enough to be all a true wife ought." On the 9th she visited Dr. Wehoman: "(nothing serious, only having the wart taken off my nose) . . . I told him I expected to live in Valley City and he gave me a great talking to about a wife's duties. He says she can make a man if she has the good sense to do so. I agreed with him in most all he said. He is a true German, but a good smart man. I *believe* he is true to his wife." On the next day:

"My loving boy, it is not hard for me to feel that thee will ever be constant and faithful to me. Thee is so honest and that has been half the battle."

What battle? What did she expect? What was she afraid of? It is impossible to imagine the Whites joking together about a drawstring on the bottom of a night shirt. There seems to be almost nothing that Elsie did not feel had to be said, and yet she could not come directly to any point that mattered to her. She could be matter of fact about the wart on her nose, but her husband's affections, the likelihood of his chastity, and all the prospects of sexuality tortured her and her language. One can only wish that, like Rose Williams she could have had a rainy wedding night in a covered wagon somewhere five miles from Lisbon.

Fannie Tenney, Civil War Widow

In these writings, descriptions of deaths are longer, their details probed more obsessively, than any other topic. A strong eroticism often marks these watchful deaths. Death is written about less as a substitute for sexuality, I think, than as a means to erotic experience in itself. If women typically regarded courtship as a joke or an embarrassment, death scenes gave them permission to luxuriate in erotic suggestion, as with this letter in the Mosher Family Papers:

> We are all well now Albert died the sixth of Nov. He was a great sufferer all summer but the last two months worse his disease dropsy of the heart his body and legs were swelled as full as the skin would hold on the 3rd the Doctor taped his legs from the knees down the 5th he strapped him up to the thighs the water ran out all the time until he died he was conscious until Tuesday noon he fell into a sleep from which we could not wake him he died about 9 o'clock in the evening he was the most patient person I ever saw sick and live so long he could not lie down for over two weeks before he died he sat straight up in the chair when I would think he was in great distress I would ask him what is the matter his answer was nothing a few days before he died I asked him if he had any doubts if he was ready if he should be called away he said it made no difference he was waiting his master's bidding. Tuesday morning Mrs. Jane Thorn had been here all night. I was going to lie down a while he had been very restless all night he says Mother kiss me I done so he kissed me he says now lets pray the last of that prayer I shall never forget if it be thy will that I suffer thy will O Lord be done it is very consoling to know that when our friends leave this world that we may know they have gone where pain sickness and sorrow is not known. (11–25–88)

Although women often wrote about the work, travel, health, some-times the opinions of their husbands, they had much less to say about the amount and kind of attention they received from them, and almost never bothered to mention kissing or extended conver-sations the way Jane Freeland did, repeating the last words she and her husband exchanged. Some of the eroticism in passages about dead husbands, then, is attributable to the concentrated attention these dying men lavish on their wives. One senses that it comes not from power over the beloved, the usual source in erotic writings by men, but from attention. These women enjoy being noticed. Deaths of husbands may also make women feel safe. Sandra Gilbert and Susan Gubar in *The Madwoman in the Attic*[11] have said that much of Rochester's attraction for Jane Eyre, at least his acceptability as a marriage partner, is due to his being blind and therefore harmless, deprived of threatening male violence. It seems to me also that passages about husbands' deaths sometimes express erotic feeling because for once women focus in unusual detail upon themselves, elaborating upon how well and thoroughly they have cared for their mates. These writers are excited, I think, to notice themselves, to have been noticed, and to be free from any coercion, regardless of how genuinely fond they may well have been of their husbands. The writing of these death scenes is as complex as it invariably is intense. Fannie Tenney, as an example, found a way of breaking through to write about her marriage although only when it was over, at her husband's death.

Sometime after 1916, when she was in her mid-seventies, Fannie Tenney saw to the selecting and copying of her husband's letters, which were bound into a volume of 150 single-spaced typed pages. Other than a few notes to bridge gaps, during periods when the Tenneys were together and therefore not writing letters, there are no indications of omissions and no other editorial information. The letter-book begins with eight pages from Luman Tenney's diary of 1865–66 upon his return to Oberlin, Ohio, after serving in the Civil War; the rest of the war diary was published in 1914.[12]

Luman Tenney was born October 1, 1841, in Amherst, Ohio. His father was a doctor. Luman enlisted as a private soldier in the Second Ohio Cavalry, rose to major, and took part in several major battles, including Lee's surrender at Appomattox. He had been especially fond of a younger brother, Theodore, who was with him in the war, and saw that brother die at the battle of Five Forks, April 1, 1865. His subsequent public record reads well. An entry about

him in the *History of Clay and Norman Counties, Minnesota* emphasizes
Luman Tenney's importance to the community of Glyndon, twelve
miles east of Moorehead.[13] In 1869 he had moved from Sandusky,
Ohio, to Duluth, Minnesota, selling real estate and insurance, and
from there to Glyndon in 1872, as agent for a Philadelphia land
company. He promoted what was known as the Elgin agricultural
colony which settled in Glyndon, and he started a general store and
the North Pacific elevator there, as well as taking a soldier's homestead. He organized the Congregational Church in Glyndon and
served as superintendent of schools for Clay County.

But Luman Tenney was never able to achieve real financial security, and he died young, age thirty nine, a typical casualty, I would
suggest, of the Civil War. The generation who experienced the Civil
War in their late teens and twenties, raised families in the 1870s, and
were in middle and old age at the turn of the century, in effect
experienced the war for their entire lives, for they give evidence that
that event may well have affected the health of the population as
drastically as it did economics and race relations. Of the correspondents whom I have been reading who were directly engaged in the
war, virtually none subsequently ever reports himself altogether in
good health; these men also wrote of themselves as particularly
unsettled, and their wives appeared even more "nervous" than other
women. Many Civil War veterans survived primarily as casualties,
and Luman Tenney, I think, was such a man.

What became of the veterans of the Civil War was a question that,
at the time, virtually no one cared to ask. Another was how their
wives, parents, and children fared. The war had of course been a
damaging experience, economically, physically, and psychologically,
and the country probably simply wished to forget. Casualty rates
during the war had been high, with twice as many deaths from
disease as from battle wounds. New recruits quickly contracted
childhood diseases, if they had not already had them—measles,
mumps, whooping cough. Entire regiments were sometimes put out
of action by epidemics of diarrhea and dysentery, malaria, or typhoid
fever. Nutrition was poor. In hospitals, the wounded were further
endangered by unsanitary conditions and poor medical care.[14]

Bad as all this was, it was feared by the few who did care enough
to notice that the long-term damage done by the war was just as
great. One man who cared, an Ohio physician named William
Caldwell, noted in 1888 that, according to figures furnished by the

pension office, the average death age of veterans was only fifty-six years, (and of their wives, only sixty-one years), and offered some sorrowful conclusions to his tentative investigations of the remaining survivors:

> What we do find, even after this interval of time, is some form of continued irritation, a susceptibility to unfavorable impressions, or a liability to exhibit perverted physical conditions, with an intolerance of pain, an inability to withstand the extremes of heat and cold, or the ordinary vicissitudes of life, the prostration of any special part or function of the system, sleeplessness, irresolution involving a spirit of unrest, with a loss of power to concentrate the thoughts or energies, and often there are unexplainable, constantly recurring symptoms.[15]

In relation to Luman Tenney and to other men who had experienced the Civil War in their teens (Hubbel Pierce especially, among persons considered in this study), Dr. Caldwell's observations are important: long-lasting effects of the war were severe enough to shorten men's lives noticeably, although little public attention was paid to their plight. Even the much celebrated Grand Army of the Republic, ostensibly organized to promote veterans' benefits and pensions, in fact did little after successfully mobilizing veterans to vote Grant into office as President.[16]

Fannie Andrews and Luman Tenney were married on April 16, 1867. They lived in Duluth, Glyndon, and Minneapolis, and had four children. Luman Tenney's profession was "business," mainly selling grain, real estate, and office safes. He traveled often to Philadelphia, New York, Chicago, Minneapolis, and intervening towns, and once, in 1871, to Salt Lake City where he rode horseback through the mountains looking at mining prospects. Fannie and the babies lived either with her parents and brothers in Oberlin for very long visits, in boarding houses, or in cramped sections of houses that the Tenneys owned but rented the larger portions of to others. Luman Tenney's career appears typical of that of numerous Civil War veterans: first in his never settling into the prosperity that so many other men achieved in the late nineteenth century, and second in his ill health. He died February 10, 1880, age 39.

Fannie Tenney intended that the volume of her husband's letters be a tribute to him and to their marriage. She quotes a letter to her from the man who had bought their house in Glyndon, written April 10, 1916: "This community is everlastingly under obligations to the late Mr. Tenney for a number of good things, not among the least of these is the great benefit he bestowed on the succeeding generations of this place by his tree planting. They constitute the finest kind of a monument to his memory." (149) Luman and Fannie Tenney were both active in the Sunday School movement. Luman wrote of teaching, going to regional meetings, and attending both church services and Sunday School in several churches on a single Sunday when on his travels. The chief topics of Luman's letters are travels, business arrangements, house hunting and managing, and his health. He worried about Fannie's health and her recurring "delicate condition" between the birth of their first child in 1868 and their fourth in 1877. He resolved frequently to become a better Christian, and even more often declared his affection for Fannie. He writes as a conscience-driven man. The last letter of his to Fannie to be included in the typescript is typical of his messages to her. He was in the Merchants' Hotel in St. Paul on his way home to Glyndon, and Fannie and the children were visiting her parents in Oberlin.

> I arrived safely at 10 o'clock this morning. When nearing the city I couldn't help wishing that I might meet my beloved here. I dwelt upon it until I became nearly foolish for tears began to come to my eyes. Do you say "Strange that Luman should be so tenderhearted and loving when we are separated. I wish he would be less forgetful when he has me with him"? Well, it is a hard world, but trust me for it, I am going to be just the best old husband any woman has. You shall be at the top of the heap yet. You have waited patiently and shall have your reward. Have faith. . . . It seems as if we had been separated a long time.

He had walked up a hill to look at lots he owned: "I am not sure that they are worth more than the mortgage on them, but it is pleasant out there and they may have value after a time as St. Paul seems to be improving nicely," showing a lack of business sense that may explain his always insecure financial status, for he goes on to give Fannie detailed instructions about return travel arrangements from Ohio: "If I return home soon enough I shall try to send you enough more money to give you a chance to pay your debts and get home. If I should fail you will not suffer for you have got your hand in at borrowing" (7–16–79).

It is hard to know how he seemed to her, or how to judge his extravagant expressions of affection. He often calls her "dear child" though she was only a few years younger than he. He was away a great deal and wrote longing for her company, yet repeatedly he prolonged journeys, and when she was in Oberlin said he yearned for her return at the same time as he told her to stay away as long as she wanted to: "The yearning of my heart is for my Fannie" (3–23–73). But there also is a lack of intimacy in his writing to her. Their third child had been born on August 27, 1872, while Luman was away, and five months later her parents had not decided what to name her.

> Last, but not least! I put you off for the leisure moments and they generally come after bed time or near bed time. Your letters of Jan 2 and 6 I found here. Thanks for the many little details, which are very interesting to me. I like to know how everything you do, each hour, each minute. I am sorry you have so much care in the baby, Mary Louise. The name pleases me; I always liked Mary, particularly as I associate it with sister Mary. So we are finally settled, I guess. (1–10–73)

But not quite, for Fannie's answer reads: "Oh she is such a darling. I just wish you could take her into your arms. She has been remarkably good for a week past. Our dear little Mary! I love the name Mary; but instead of Mary Louise, suppose we call her Mary Emeline? Now, if you say so, we will call it *settled*." (1–16–75) Luman's profuse and emotional expressions of affection sound befuddled:

> It takes patience to get thru the world; but I enjoy this life very much, and shall be very happy when we can *live together,* will it not be glorious? Five weeks tomorrow since we separated. (1–19–73)

> To tell the truth, I really feel homesick tonight, and if I were merely a boy away at school I think I would try a regular boohooing. I want to get home; I want to see you; I want to live with my family. I am heartily disgusted with the terrible demoralization by strong drink of beings supposed to have been created in the image of God. . . . Your two letters . . . did me a world of good. What could I do without my sweet precious wife? I feel that you are in many respects my guardian. The idea of calling the baby Emeline pleases me very much, if you like it too. . . . It is settled, Mary Emeline, you know well that I love her too. May she be spared to us many years, and grow to be a good and useful woman. (1–23–73)

Travels, business, longings to be home were the staples of Luman's letters; Fannie's consisted of children, church, and Sunday School affairs, inquiries after Luman's health and activities. He praised her and made resolutions to improve himself; she never complained. Yet for all its volubility, the correspondence reveals little. How necessary and productive was all that traveling, or was Luman a very restless man? Did Fannie have anyone to talk to aside from her small children when he was away? When she wrote "Baby has been a good baby all day, so that I have sewed considerably" (1–16–73), did she mean that she was nearly distracted by the children most of the time? Each seemed to be writing in order to stave off the other's anxieties. They strain to keep cheerful. Both were very serious and earnest persons, not given to jokes or irony, and no letter shows them angry or excited.

The last letter in the volume is Fannie's to her parents, written three days after Luman's death. It comes as a surprise, for it is less guarded and far more explicitly detailed than all the rest. It opens in a stilted fashion: "Yesterday at this hour, between eleven and twelve, we were on our way to the cemetery with precious Luman's body, where we laid him to rest. . . . The hack stopped at the open grave, close by the trees that line the river, where we could see the coffin, with a beautiful cross upon it, lowered." Then the letter details the end of his illness which had prevented a trip Fannie and he were to take to Florida, and enumerates horrifying scenes whose meaning we can only guess at. "Monday morning I told him I thought he would not live a great while" Fannie explained to her parents: "He required almost constant changing of pillows the last two or three days." His partner, a Mr. Barnes, intimately participated in the scene, taking turns holding Luman and helping to change the pillows. "He wanted me to keep the children out of doors a good deal. He was afraid that Bernard [their oldest child] might be troubled as he had been." (The symptoms she describes suggest tuberculosis, though no one clearly explained what ailed him. Luman had, some years earlier, refused to see a doctor, though he had complained of ill health ever since returning from the war.) The narrative continues: "While Mr. Barnes was sitting by the bedside Monday afternoon, with Luman's head in his lap and I, close by, fanning him, Luman talked by littles a good deal about the business," including schemes for improving churches, adding a reading room to the town hall, furthering temperance in Glydon. Mr. Barnes, Luman told them, was

one of God's noblemen, but that God had a little against him, as he had told him when he was well, that he wanted him to take more of a stand and do more for him. Mr. Barnes' tears rolled down his face and he said that he would try and thanked him. . . . He told Mr. Barnes that he thought that on account of my nervous state it would be better for me to have all business closed out at such a time as it could be done without loss.

That night Luman felt enough better to want to sit up. "So, as he had done before, Mr. Barnes got upon the bed, leaning upon the headboard and with pillows between his legs supported Luman." The doctor applied another blister to his chest, and later Fannie and Barnes and her brother Charles got Luman ready for the night, and the ensuing events were macabre: "Luman then seemed to settle down, wanted me to hurry and get ready for bed, to come and lie with him, and as I kissed him and put my head down upon the pillow he said 'Goodnight.'" She sang hymns to him ("Hush my dear, lie still and slumber"). But it was a restless night, and next morning Fannie called the men from their breakfast. The writing at the end of her letter is less controlled than at its beginning:

> They tried to change pillows a little to ease him, but he soon put out his arm, putting it around my neck and said he must say "Goodbye," but drawing me so close to him that I rested my head on his neck, clinging his arm still closer if I tried to move so as to look at his face.
>
> Oh I cannot tell you the agony of those moments, as the breathing grew harder and the film came over his eyes, the blood filling his mouth, he taking his arm from my neck to try to wipe it away, then the clinging of my hand and the last breath.
>
> I could not look away from earth to heaven as I wanted to. It all seemed so terrible to me. I do say "God's will be done" but I cannot look up as I want to. There is no other for me to go to but to God. If I did not know that there is help in him I should despair. I am physically nervous, more so than it seems to me I ought to be. I do not get the comfort I feel God has for me, but I will leave myself in His arms and trust. Yours in deepest love, Fannie.

Nothing in the rest of the correspondence resembles the strong emotions and raw anguish of this letter. Her report of family losses in the Chicago fire, for instance, was sympathetic but not emotional: "Theodore and Junius Cobb's houses are not burned, but of course their store is, and Uncle Lucius' library and home are burned. The fire came within two blocks of Theodore's and was only saved by blowing up the building before it. They had $60,000 insurance on them, but probably will not get any" (10–11–71). On very rare occasions she permitted her husband a glimpse of what she called her "nervous state" when she admitted to being harried by the children: " I must confess that I am a little down-hearted tonight. I long so for a home of my own, with my own dear husband and children with me" (she was on a year-long visit to her parents in Oberlin during Luman's trip to Utah mines). "The children are both well and I have very much to be thankful for, but Bernard is so fretful, and so impatient." Bernard tormented the younger child, and stammered. "I feel so sorry for him; but I didn't intend to write all these unpleasant things when I commenced" (7–31–71). Unpleasant things were so seldom written by either of them that the undeniable unpleasantness of her husband's dying released from Fannie expressions she had not used before.

Two factors permitted her to be so frank: the shock of his dying, and the fact that it was socially acceptable to write in intimate detail about a death. As Ann Douglas has shown, one was permitted, even encouraged, to do so, at length and at a high emotional level, a freedom permitted to no other subject. Even so, this letter to her parents raises more questions than it answers. What was Mr. Barnes's position in the household, and how strong an emotional bond did his business and religious interests make between himself and Luman? What did Fannie mean by saying she was "physically nervous, more so than it seems to me I ought to be"? Her brother Charles and his wife shared the house with her. She was thirty-six years old in 1880, with four children aged three to twelve. Though she seldom mentioned friends, she was active in church and civic affairs in Glyndon and was on good terms with both her own and her husband's families. And, with Luman away so frequently, she had had long practice at being on her own. Before her marriage Fannie had studied and taught music. She wrote of practicing six to seven hours a day and of teaching five pupils, and of attending a conservatory run by George Steele. In only thirteen years of unsettled housekeeping, children, and intense absorption in her husband, her psychological state seems to have deteriorated considerably, and yet she lived on to collect Luman's letters thirty-six years after his death.

These letters between herself and her husband which Fannie Tenney had typed and bound in his memory describe a career and marriage of utmost respectability and confused distress. The two hardly saw each other, it seems, let alone "kept house" very long in what might be called a home of their own. His letters are replete with promises, hers with forbearance, but why this was necessary is never clear. What is clear is his restlessness—the many rushed train trips, strange towns and hotels, and her anxiety—where to live, how to borrow money to live on and from whom, how to endure small children and control her "nerves." The letters take refuge in vagueness as to specific physical details (health, finances, daily living). Only Fannie's last letter, written in shock after Luman's death, confronts physical details, and then in so raw a manner that one can only guess at plausible interpretations.

"Nervous Impulses"

In the twelve letters she wrote to Allettie Mosher between January 1899 and November 1909, Emma Ladbury mentioned by name six persons dead, twenty-three ill, and seven mad ("insane," "fits"), in addition to more general reports that "there is a lot of sickness here, the La grippe I mean," and the hundred cases of smallpox she heard about during her visit to Michigan. As actuarial statistics over a period of ten years, her figures are no more impressive than they are reliable, but their prominence within the context of her letters tends to give the impression of a high percentage of ill health and an equally high mortality rate. The earliest letter, for instance, named four dead, five sick, one mad, and only seven others engaged in ordinary activities (a total of seventeen people accounted for, her idea of "news" being the doings of people she and Allettie knew). One needs to remember, of course, that in her day and location few sick persons were removed to hospitals, asylums, nursing homes, or otherwise taken away from full view of kith and kin. Still, it is interesting that her preoccupation is with death, madness, and disease. This was a time when daily life was made more precarious by petty crimes, brawls, occasional murders, and—in rural areas—accidents caused by farm machinery, animals, and firearms. Yet Emma Ladbury hardly ever mentions such an incident. She does make one confusing reference to being in court for litigation over a land dispute, but in general her letters and those of other women say little about such more public disturbances. If they did, I think the writing would convey a world no less dangerous, but one more controlled by chance and human action. The suffering from disease that women have concentrated upon is brought on by things in the air, miasmas and epidemics, pregnancy being yet another condition that overcomes one. Women have not written as though they thought that one might be separated from bodily events. C. Palfrey's dying "delirious most of the time" after catching cold from sleeping in the barn Emma Ladbury attributed to his "not feeling well when his house burned." In her view he was the victim of his unhappiness, not of infection or foolishness. Of course, she may well have been correct.

But the accuracy of these diagnoses is less the point here than their effects on the women themselves. Women recorded what they observed around them in patterned interconnectedness. Virtually no detail was irrelevant, none discretely separated from another. Such writing sometimes was highly insightful, and sometimes reflected behavior rendered nearly paralytic. Fannie Tenney articulated only with great difficulty what she wanted to say about sexuality, disease, and dying, partly because she could not really differentiate among them, even though sometimes in her confusion she arrived at startling truths. To her parents she unburdened herself of a dozen years of marriage during which she had been virtually a bystander, if also the principal prop that made Luman's way of living possible. It took his death for her to speak plainly about him, and it took the writing itself to expose her own erotic feelings.

Recent books like *The Physician and Sexuality in Victorian America,* or *For Her Own Good, 150 Years of the Experts' Advice to Women,*[17] have explained how in the late nineteenth century increasingly professionalized male medical practitioners located a vast array of events in women's wombs. All activity related to women's reproduction was then scrutinized for potential illness, and virtually all illnesses were blamed on the womb. The growing professional, economic, and political prominence of doctors in the nineteenth century depended largely, these books claim, upon doctoring women, and can be compared, I think, to the similarly professionalized alliance between women and clergy that Ann Douglas has commented upon, in that both alliances enjoyed women's cooperation. Private writings that we have been looking at suggest how it was that women were so vulnerable to this influence. Although some doctors clearly damaged women in their zeal, women were prepared to cooperate. Their assuming such close and inevitable connections among sexuality, disease, and death—an understanding with considerable validity to the human condition—as well as their relative lack of attention to discrete acts of violence, mistakes, or accidents, this attitude of mind can only have eased the way for the idea that women are sick because they are female. (The prevalence of the attitude does not appear to depend on the presence of doctors. The writing of women who used home remedies was similar to that of those who called in doctors.)

An example can illustrate how the female condition was judged differently than the male on the basis of sexuality alone. Men were endangered by potential professional medical abuse when it became fashionable to decry masturbation, described as "self-abuse," "the sin of Onan," the wasteful "spending" of "seed" in a sexual economy of scarcity. Steven Marcus has written of the English urologist William Acton who based a successful career on scarifying prognostications of what would befall the man or boy who masturbated.[18] John Engstad worried about such cases in Grand Forks in the 1880s.

> May 11, 1886. Age 22. Strong but not well nourished. Lost in weight last year. Rather pale and very nervous. Family history very good. Appetite fair, but digestion not very good. Bowels regular. Lungs strong and well developed. Heart apex in line of nipple and two inches below considerably enlarged. Can not work for any length of time. Lack of strength. General neurasthenia and suspect masturbator but of course denied. Tonic and advice.
>
> November 23, 1880. Age 17. "Onanist." Had convulsions last July after a warm day. Appears in morning when just awakening, last ten to fifteen minutes. Face turns blue and whole body stiff. Looks consumptive and pale. Oil and mercury with ether when in the spells.[19]

However misguided such diagnoses, however bizarre the devices that went with them to prevent males from masturbating or experiencing inadvertent erections, the idea that the desire to masturbate came from a diseased imagination was a relatively short-lived fad, and men were not declared basically ill because they were men.

But in the case of women, medicine, psychiatry, religion, personal relationships, family finances, and social reputation all converged upon the womb in a crazed but ordered pattern all its own, as the following example illustrates. Two letters by a woman who complained of fatigue, weight loss, and insomnia tell a story of medical fashion at its worst.

After a courtship of six years, much of it by correspondence, Ora and Morley Edmunds settled in Grand Forks, North Dakota, where Morley was employed by the Union National Bank, eventually becoming cashier. He had grown up in Drayton, a few miles north of Grand Forks, Ora in Wisconsin, and they had met as students at

Hiram College in Minnesota. Morley completed his studies there, and Ora returned home to teach in a number of schools for short terms, interspersed by long convalescences from undetermined illnesses. For six years, Ora wrote to Morley nearly every week, sometimes every day or twice a day and he evidently replied, although not quite as often (most of her letters, though only a few of his, survive). A recurrent motif in her letters is indecision. She said often that she did not know whether or not she would apply for teaching, or if she did, whether she would accept a job, sometimes hinting that she expected Morley to preempt her moves by marriage. Once teaching, she complained of dull and recalcitrant students, of unsatisfactory landladies and boarding arrangements, and uncongenial women among teachers and other roomers. Yet after any occasions when Ora and Morley did meet such as for holidays, relations seemed to cool for a time and letters decreased in frequency and in enthusiasm. Eventually they married, and the correspondence stopped.

Between September and December of 1911, Ora Edmunds visited her parents in Oshkosh, Wisconsin, taking with her her daughter Leal, then five years old. Most of the letters in this sequence describe family outings and Leal's antics, how much she ate or how well she slept. Then in mid-November, Ora sought medical treatment for chronic exhaustion, underweight, and sleeplessness, or, as she put it, for "mental work." One doctor spoke to her about "getting the channels inhibited and new gates opened and fixed," an effort in hydraulics designed to cure her "nervous impulses." Her explicit letters to Morley on the subject need to be read in full to catch the tone of all her worries. Complicating matters is the fact that she had felt better and slept well since being in Wisconsin. She liked being pampered by her parents, and also knew she would be obliged eventually to "enter the harness again" in Grand Forks. The Edmundses had no other children than Leal, and it is not explained whether "pessiary" early in the first letter refers to a contraceptive device and only that, or whether it and the "support" she refers to in the second letter were intended to prop a tipped or collapsed uterus. For all their astonishing confusions and strange episodes, these letters lead us among the patterns of Ora's thoughts, patterns that repeat themselves in three generations of women. She herself, her mother, and her daughter were all nervous, all light sleepers and eaters, and all apparently assumed that every difficulty was of a piece with every other part of their lives, responding to nothing less heroic than surgery or mesmerism.

November 7, 1911

Dearest,

Leal is helping Mama clean up for a girl from Ripon who is coming to dinner tomorrow, so I will try to write an account of my visit to the Dr. yesterday. The first time I went I did not talk to him at all and he saw what shape my general health was in and as he expressed it "the complexity of the pessiary" and that the only thing was an operation. Yesterday he found everything in good shape and said he could not see why there was "any trouble there to warrant reflex actions to result in such fatigue, loss of flesh, insomnia etc as I had." He said I had had quite serious derangements there, but they were on the road to recovery and rather than have an operation to wear that intermittently when I had to for years if necessary.

I then told him all about myself from a child and also something which I did not know myself until this fall. Aunt Maggie told me under promise of secrecy. I knew there was something mysterious about Mama's long sickness from 14 to 18 but did not know what and once when I asked her if she used to be able to read with eyes bandaged she flew very angry and laid it to Gertie's telling me (which was true), and told me never to mention such a thing again. So I didn't. But Aunt Maggie told me thinking it might enlighten the Dr. and told me not to tell her I knew.

For 4 years Mama was sick abed, and had what is called a double personality. The other one was like one of Miss Meuchamps, a dreadful profane one. They took her to Chicago when she was 18 and had mesmeric treatments which were a crude form of the present day hypnotic treatment. They did not know that the Dr. was a spiritualist until after he began to help her and then they let him alone at it. He said Mama was material for one of the best possible mediums. She could read with eyes blindfolded, tell who came from trains downtown, tell events transpiring in other places and all the other stunts. The treatments cured her largely but she ran away and got married at 19 and I was born at 20, just two years after, so it is no wonder I yelled incessantly nights till I was 3.

I told Mama the Dr. said it was hebelrirea, a case of inherited neurosis, and he could do nothing. I mentioned in a casual way that he said it was inherited nervousness and she said it could be nothing of the kind. That [with] all her sickness she had never been nervous. I said, "Why I always thought that long sickness you had of 9 months (I was purposely inaccurate for fear she'd suspect Aunt Maggie) was some kind of nervous breakdown and she said there was none at all, that she had spinal meningitis. So I rather felt that she would not serve very well as a source of authoritative information and did not push the matter. I'd be inclined to give her the benefit of the doubt and say she did not remember it, if she weren't so touchy about it all. So I easily said when I saw how she felt that I probably inherited it from papa's insane half brothers.

To return to the Dr. He said he believed the rest and quiet I got here would help me if I staid longer but did not believe the effects would be lasting without some special nerve treatments. He asked if I had ever had any suggestive work brought to my attention. I said I had been reading it ever since I came. He was rather horrified and said I ought not to read any more. I told him he should not worry I was not looking upon myself as a bundle of obsessions, phobias, fixed ideas, hysterics, etc. In fact I concluded after reading what the real cases had I was creating a good deal of disturbance over nothing. He said most women would have the whole category after reading a book that described them. He said I could not do much for myself and he thought the only thing for me to do would be to get rid of some of the nervous impulses and ideas by getting the channels inhibited and new gates opened and fixed. He said he did not know of any one but doubtless there was someone in Mpls and of course in Milwaukee or Chicago. He said I ought to go to some very reliable general doctor or specialist and ask to be directed to such a one in his city and get myself built up at once.

Now I do not know what such a course of behaviour would cost. If I should go to Mpls Mama would bring Leal up when I got through—it usually doesn't take long in a disease like mine—or I could go to Chicago and get Leal here on my way home. Mama said that Dr. Sheldon of Madison wanted her to take Leal to Fallows in Chicago. He does not charge anything and Dr. Sheldon would not be apt to direct her there if he were not all right. He himself prepares his patients for an operation by using suggestions given by a Dr. Scientist living in Madison but of course he tells the healer what suggestions to make, so no harm could be done by wrong suggestions. Moreover I am not sure there is a neurologist in Mpls, but could have Roy ask Dr. Cobb before I went. At St Paul I could stay at Gerties but could not keep Leal there on account of the cold. So Mama would have to bring her up when I got ready for her (I suppose you know Bishop Fallows is a bishop of the Episcopal church and does his work in connection with his church just as Dr. Worcester and Dr. McComb do in connection with the Congregational church). Munsterberg does not approve the church healers in general. He does not mention Fallows but does exonerate Dr. Worcester. He says the "originators of the Emmanuel movement are above reproach and capable psychologists, but their followers who try to do the same work are not.

Could you see whether your chances of a raise are at all favorable or is it too early to mention. Also let me know what you advise and if it could be managed financially. The regular neurologists fee and fare to St

Paul for Mama to bring Leal would equal my fare to Chicago and board while there I presume. If you want to talk with anyone I'd rather not have you, I think. We owe Dr. Woutat a good deal and I'd rather he did not know anything about it till it is done. It is cheaper and more pleasant by far than an operation. Mama just said she would let me take the money but I can see she rather hates to. It is all they have only the notes I guess. She says there is a clinic of Doctors etc just like the one in Boston and they won't treat without a written Doctor's diagnosis and seeing the patient. I told Mama we could pay back $10 to $15 a month by letting our other bills run and I thought she seemed a little relieved. I suppose she thinks it would be paid about as rapidly as the cloak money. She says she does not believe I'd have to stay more than a week. I do not know the fare to Chicago and it is pouring so I can't ask Mrs. Plakka. She goes home every summer. Let me know what you think. I'd not mind your talking to Charley if he is really interested in the subject excepting that I don't want him to know how I am and I think for mental work the fewer people there are interested the better the effects. That's one reason I don't want Dr. Woutat told. He has seen so much of us I think his knowing might have some distracting effects on me. Not that I believe he could present any medical influence on me except for a notion of my own that I don't want him to know until I am well.

I will write for some of Bishop F's literature and requirements today and ask him if he would take me. I feel as if I could only get a start in the right direction I could get well. I'd have Dr. Combs write my letter about myself for me.

I must close. It's taken an awful time to write this. Baby and I send our dear love and Kisses. Ora.

Same to same, November 14, 1911.   Tuesday.

Dearest,

Perhaps you may take the hint for paper. It is still cold and baby is still coughing. I have a lot of those tablets Dr. W. sent us in St Paul. I guess her nervous naughty spells are over for a time. She has been lovely and sleeping perfectly for four nights now. I notice that those spells are always much worse when she isn't sleeping quietly at night.

I thought I told you what Dr. Combs said. He thought the support a very trying one to wear and said he should not like to let me go without seeing me again to see what may have taken place after removing that. I do not know of course whether it was simply to work in another call or not. He said he did not think I could ever be well until I had the operation, and that it ought not to be delayed till too near the period that isn't very far off now. Of course we know that from Mrs. Perrott's mishap. He intimated the possibility of a more trying nervous break down if this trouble was in hand while I was having the *change*. If I go to him again I'll tell him all the trials to have the baby and get her started together with the extra sicknesses of entirely foreign matter I have had and see if he does not think my lack of flesh and general condition may not be partly due to that as well as to the displacement. I'd feel different about going to Dr. Cobb or to a nerve specialist or whatever I ought to see if I had any idea of what a consultation would cost.

I am much better now but do not know how much is due to a life of absolute idleness and irresponsibility or how much is real improvement. It will show that when I get back to Grand Forks and enter the harness again. I think if I don't get too tired out again I can sleep. I seem to have learned to put myself to sleep at last and I'll get to bed as early as I can and try to have the nights as nearly like these as I can. If I go to Dr. Combs again I'll write just what he says. I'd awfully well like to see a straight nerve doctor but they cost so much and I might strike one no good that probably Dr. Combs or Dr. Cobb would be as good. I must close and let Mama take this. You need not be worried about either Leal or me. We are both far better than you've ever seen us the last five years.

We sent our dear love. I thought to send baby pictures but I get home in 2 or 3 weeks guess I'll wait.

Ora[20]

They're awfully sweet.

V

Viola Pierce, 1845-1919

Viola among the Keyeses, 1862–1875

My discussion so far has arranged private writings in topical order, selecting examples that support my contentions, for instance, that theories of literary criticism about regionalism are not pertinent to women's writing, that working women, like Grace DeCou and Adah Bickford, especially favor repetition, and that women have had much to say about sexuality, disease, and dying. I now want to shift the emphasis to provide a closer look at a few individuals. The subject of this chapter, Viola Pierce, had connections primarily with rural working farm people. Two women described in the following chapter, Julia Carpenter and Emma Mott, lived and worked primarily in rural towns but also experienced both city and farm living, and they practiced professions. Selections from the private writings of, to, and about these women will illustrate, I hope, how complexly the various topics are interwoven.

Viola Pierce came to Dakota Territory from Michigan in 1879, a few months after her husband, Hubbel Pierce, began settling a homestead near Valley City. Her widowed mother, Eliza Keyes, subsequently made the move also, bringing with her a second daughter, Allettie Battey, also widowed, Allettie's three-year-old daughter, Inez, and Eliza's youngest son, Edward. The Keyeses homesteaded north of Valley City, near Dazey.[1]

Eliza's was a large and scattered family. She was born Eliza Bristol, in upstate New York, in 1824, one of three sisters and two brothers. The brothers became merchants and farmers; her sister Kate mar-

151

ried a farmer, Matt Harmon, and lived for a time near the Keyeses in Michigan; her sister Jane remained in the vicinity of Buffalo and married Tom Freeland, a canal boat pilot. Eliza herself married a farmer named Stephen Keyes, moving with him to several farms in Michigan. They have five children: the two oldest, Henry and Stephen, remained in Michigan when the three youngest, and their mother, moved to North Dakota a few years after·the death of their father in 1875.

Keyes and Bristol women tended to be long-lived: Eliza lived to be seventy-eight; Jane was still alive in 1903; and Kate Harmon wrote letters from California at age eighty-five. Allettie lived to be ninety-seven, and Viola and Hubbel were in their early seventies when they died in the 1918–19 flu epidemic. Inez, Eliza's granddaughter, rather an exception, died in 1927 at the age of fifty of heart disease complicated by kidney trouble and overweight. More usually it was the men they married who died young, as Tom Battey, Allettie's husband did, before the couple had been married a year. Jane Freeland's husband died in 1891, and she lost a son, Charley, in 1865, and a daughter, Maria, and Maria's husband, in 1869. Kate Harmon outlived by many years both her husband and her son Theron.

Eliza Keyes and her two daughters, Viola and Allettie, were inveterate letter writers and savers, and so have been their descendents for four generations. The earliest letter in the collection, dated June 19, 1842, is to Eliza from her brother John Bristol in Seneca Falls, describing his visit to "Grandmother," born in 1755 and then ninety-three years old, who was "able to sit up in her chair but is not able to do the least thing even knitting." The collection ends during the Second World War, with a long series to Allettie from her nephew Ralph, stationed in the South Pacific—one hundred years of correspondence. There are letters among the Bristol brothers and sisters in the 1850s and '60s; many from the sisters Kate Harmon and Jane Freeland to Eliza; letters to Viola and Hubbel Pierce from parents and siblings on both sides; letters from Eliza to both her daughters, and from them to her; letters between the sisters, Viola and Allettie, and to and from Inez to mother, aunt, and grandmother. Especially to Allettie, there are letters from women friends left behind in Ohio and Michigan with the move to Dakota, and for two years letters to Hubbel Pierce from his army comrade Alonzo Choate. In North Dakota, Allettie and Inez married brothers,

Emmet and Elihu Mosher, whose family also contributed correspondence.

Often letters were group enterprises, as in Eliza's household,
where father and siblings added to what Viola received from her
mother. Some sheets are in pencil, on lined paper folded once,
squeezed with extra messages along margins. Family and neighborhood news—visits, work, crops, weather, disease, deaths, births,
children, journeys, prices, photographs, the writing of letters
themselves—these are staple subjects. It is also to our fortune, as we
have seen, that a large number of these correspondents happen to
be highly expressive writers, particularly Eliza and her sister Jane
Freeland, and Allettie's friends Rose Williams and Emma Watson.
Typically, as documents of family history, even so large a collection
is not a fully satisfactory source of information, for people in intimate relationships do not make a habit of recounting to each other
the obvious data a stranger wants to know. John Bristol left out the
name of his grandmother. For a reader now, it can be hard to know
who's who, where they live, what they are about, what their relationship is to the person to whom they are writing. On the other hand,
surprisingly often pieces of one letter fit with parts of another from
someone else to make unexpected sense.

A reader now also cannot help but wonder about things which few
correspondents touch on: their affection for members of their own
household, for instance (how did they regard their husband or wife,
their children); their opinions on social and political events or on the
arts. The two subjects which consistently evoke the strongest descriptive writing are correspondents' affection for the person being
written to (usually heightened by sorrow at their being apart), and
the awful deprivation of the death of someone loved. Letters like
these tell a great deal, but they do not tell us everything—after all,
they were not written for us to read.

In these pages it is Viola Keyes Pierce I want to center upon,
difficult as it may be to ravel one thread from so tangled a skein. She
was born in 1845, and when she followed her husband to Dakota
Territory she was in her mid-thirties and had been married fourteen
years. There were no children. What was her life? How much of it
can we know? Letters to her begin as early as 1862, from her parents
while she was at boarding school, and, during the years of the Civil
War, from several flirtatious young men, including Hubbel Pierce.
She and Hubbel married soon after the war and exchanged letters

with both families while they lived first with the senior Pierces on their farm in Michigan, and then by themselves near Detroit. There is a set of five letters which Hubbel wrote to Viola from Abbottsville, Dakota Territory, in the summer of 1879, when he was preparing a homestead for her arrival. Many letters between the sisters and their mother were occasioned by a trip taken by one or the other over the years; others simply because it was an easy way to communicate, even over short distances, at a time when roads were bad, there were no telephones, the weather was harsh, and there was a great deal of work to do. Viola's is one life of many, but thanks to these letters, it may also be one that we are able to approach more closely than some.

The letter that Eliza Keyes wrote to Viola on August 29, 1864, is typical of the affectionate and frank correspondence between mother and daughter over many years. Eliza's letters are humorous and intimate—Viola was a confidante as well as her child. In the late summer of 1864 Viola visited her mother's friend Lucy Prichard in Victor, New York; her older brothers Stephen and Henry had left home; Allettie was ten years old and Eddie a baby. Her parents were farming near Kelloggville, Michigan, having moved there from Detroit in the spring of 1862. Eliza's writing invites one into the family's midst, so strongly do her expressions evoke their habits.

My Dear Child, Last Saturday afternoon pa and I and the children started to go to Uncle Henry's and stopt in town and the first thing I run to the Office and there found to my joy that I had a letter and a likeness. I could hardly wait until I got back to the house. Theresa says do hurry and open it and when she looked at your picture she choked up for she sayed you looked so sober she believed you had been crying. Will looked at it and he sayed you looked as sweet as a peach and if you was there he would give you a kiss. . . . Theresa dreamed that you was dead and she thought that she and Will come to tell me and I did not seem to care much about it. She sayed I did not care as much about it as she did but thank divine providence it was nothing but a dream. . . . I asked Eddie what I should say to his sister for him. He sayd I must tell you he brought in wood and done every thing for ma. He kissed your picture when I let him take it. Lettie says you must not worry about goose for she will take good care of her. Aunt Aurora sayd if you had come and seen her before you went she was going to give you that white pelisant quilt but she would save it for you till you come home you must write to her perhaps it will be for your good if you do.

Viola's education was an important family undertaking. In 1862, for the better part of a year, she attended a "seminary" in Penfield, near Rochester, New York. Her fees, books, and clothing were paid by one of Eliza's cousins, Ezra Cornell, who subsequently founded Cornell University. He tried to see Viola as often as he could and was straightforward about money matters:

> Dear Miss, Your favor of 31st December was forwarded to me here in which you mention that you want a thicker shawl and dress to go to school & church with. Enclosed please find two dollars to use for the above uses, and write me if you received the money and if it is enough for your purposes. . . . I would be glad to learn from you what progress you are making with your studys. What you are studying etc. Yours respectfully, E. Cornell.

That was on January 8, 1862. On March 24 he wrote: "Yours of the 11th is at hand expressing your satisfaction with your school and opportunities, etc. If you desire to continue another term or two at the school and think you are improving your opportunity I shall be very glad to continue to pay your expenses. Please inform me what your next term will cost you and when the money will be required." A letter dated the same day from Stephen Keyes, Viola's father, encouraged her in a similar vein:

> You must improve every minute at school for you won't have another chance, if you want any clothes you must write Cornell. . . . Sis you must not wait too long before you write Cornell for I should think you would begin to want shoes. You must tell him what you want to use money for. Put up what things you can't use or articles of your clothing that you wear out put up so as to bring home for it may come good for the children. Take good care of your clothes.

Two weeks later Viola's mother wrote about their moving: "If you was here now how good it would be but it is for your own good to be in school so I must wait till you come. And sis how be you going to manage about coming home for I shall not dare to have you come alone. How glad I shall be when you get home. It seems as though I could not wait" (4–7–62).

Eliza showed her high regard for Viola by including her in her close friendship with Lucy Prichard, whom she had known since childhood. An undated letter from Lucy to Eliza suggests how important the two women were to each other, and also how difficult it could be to find the privacy that nurtures friendship:

O Eliza I have thought of your visit at my house so many times. I can't say as I had any visit with you at all. O if you had come alone we could of had such a nice time a talking over old times and we never had a chance to say one word alone by ourselves. But it is all gone and past now, but I hope we will live to visit one another again some time. (2–20–59 [?] Sunday)

While Viola was at the seminary in Penfield, Eliza wrote, "I am glad you are going to Lucy's to make a visit. I want you should get all their likenesses you can for it would be a great comfort to look at familiar faces once more even if it is only a picture" (3–24–62), and two weeks later she repeated requests for pictures of Lucy and her family. "Get them if you can. Tell them many is the morning I shall enjoy looking on old familiar faces." When, in August of 1864, Viola traveled to Victor, New York, to visit Lucy, her mother wrote: "How much money did you have left when you got to Lucy's. Did you get a parasol and how did your coat look and did you have a good time Sat. evening?" (8–1–64). Eliza added a long note to Lucy:

Dear Lucy I hope you and Viola are both happy. Now I hope you will both enjoy one another's company and have good times together. You say I need not worry for you will take good care of her. I do not think I shall for she has great confidence in your goodness as well as myself. All I ask is to be to her as you should want me to be to your dear little boy if he was with me. I would have liked to have had her better clothed before she went away but I could not do anything for it is hard times for us to get along for everything is so very high. You must tell your father and mother to imagine what a good time we will all have when I come down which I surely shall if I live to see another year if I keep well. . . . My dear Lucy when I am alone I wander back to friends. Friends do I say? Yes, for you have been tried and not proved false and Oh have I loved to dwell on those happy times. Always could I go to your father's house and meet with a welcome embrace all and we love you all as dear as ever. Viola said your father and mother were so good to her. I believe she loves you and your father and mother next best to her own parents. Oh how many happy hours we spent in talking about you all when V's come home from there. . . . Kiss your dear husband and baby for me for I certainly shall do it when I come. (8–11–64)

The letters Eliza sent to Viola are warm, outgoing, detailed and often funny. It is not Eliza's habit to mince words; she tells Viola just what is on her mind and what she has seen going on around her, and unhesitatingly draws her into the daily minutiae:

Oh how I wish you was here this beautiful Sabbath day. I have been taking a rest after doing up my morning work, some days I have to lay down two and three times and then again I can work all day first rate and so it goes. But Pa is real well, he has not had but two of his trembling spells this summer. He works very hard. He has got his summer fallow most ploughed, he is going to put in a piece of buck wheat. His corn and potatoes and oats looks very nice. . . . We have got 32 young chickens and Eddie has 7 ducks. He had 9 but Lettie's black cat got 2 of them then there was war you may bet. Pa catched him and gave him a tremendous whipping and he lets them alone. Our hens have done ever so well for us this summer. Our red cow has not come in but I tell you she looks fine. Our other cow does well we make more than we use. Pa's horses look first rate for the work they have done. Pa buys mill feed and cuts hay for them and then they have good pasture. We have got two splendid pigs. (6–19–70)

Since dinner I had the most beautiful bunch of flowers that you ever saw. There was 25 different kinds. One of my neighbors sent them. She called 2 months ago and I have not returned the call. She told Pa the flowers was to pay me for the call I had made her, so I guess I shall have to go over. (8–29–70)

We was all down to Kate's last Sunday and had a first rate visit. She see us coming and come up the road to meet us she said she thought Suke was with us. She says when you come we must all come down and make her a visit. I guess she sees many a lonesome hour. (8–29–70)

Lettie and I was to Aunt Julia's avisiting, and when we was drinking tea out of the little china cups Aunt Julia spoke about you they both sent their love and said God bless those two children. (nd 1869)

But Eliza Keyes was no Pollyanna. Intermixed with news of oat crops and visits are complaints and misfortunes, illnesses and deaths. So many are sick and dying that one grows in the habit of existing among them.

I grunt the most of any of us. (8–29–70)

William Strong has lost his wife and he is left with 5 children. (7–11–70)

Tomorrow we shall commence to clean house last week they buried old man Barges that hunch back. (March 1875)

Poor old Mrs. Barker is gone at last. I hope she is better off than she was here. I should think Theresa would feel as self condemned. (3–27–71)

Aunt Jane is not very well yet. She says the babe is a great talker [the child of her daughter, who had died]. She says as she is writing Lelah stands on the cabin steps a bidding some little girls on shore good night. I think you all have your share of sickness for every letter you

have written lately some one of you have been sick [to which Stephen
Keyes appends: "I would not live where everybody is sick when anybody is sick out here they die some time and that saves expense"]. (nd)

It is the Sabbath day and so nice and pleasant. Myself and the children
have just been over to the grave yard to see the new grave stones that
have been erected over the resting place of so many that have gone to
rest. There have a great many been buried in that yard since we first
came here. . . . Lettie and I was up to see Pete yesterday. She is not so
well again, she is as pale as though she was dead. She looks very bad I
sometimes think she will not live long. (nd 1874)

Eliza was not malicious, but she kept Viola current on that peren-
nially interesting subject, domestic relationships: how well or ill
people were getting along with one another. In 1871 Stephen Keyes
was working as general handyman for Eliza's sister Kate Harmon
and her husband in order to work off a debt. "Kate has bought
herself a new sewing machine. She paid 65 dollars for it, it does all
kinds of work and very nice too. Kate and Matt quarrel like everything. He finds a great deal of fault with Frank and she can't stand
that nohow, but let her take it, she would have him" (3–5–71). "I
think Maria and George ought to be ashamed to live as they do.
They had better to go to living together and behave themselves"
(7–28–71). She is decided in her judgments:

Well Alice Matson has done big things. You never wrote that she was
married. How does it set on their stomachs. If it had been one of my
girls there would have made a great talk about it. How does Henry
Keyes get along don't you go to see him Pa says you are a fool to go to
Matsons. He says they are a deceitful set and as for Maria I don't pity
her one bit. If she had behaved herself she would have a husband to
take care of her children (2–8–72)

I hope Orpha will not succeed in parting Henry and wife. If Lilly don't
do as Sarah Granger and Alice Matson has, I shall be glad because she
bears the name of Keyes, but Orph is a devil and always was. Ingram is
too good for her. I am glad we are as far from her as we are. . . . I hope
Henry will do well. I am glad he has got a good wife I should think he
would be ashamed of his mother. (nd 1874)

Pregnancies were among the statistical records she passed on: "Sis
I must tell you a bit of news. Jim Vanhouten's wife is in a delicate
way and so is Sam Vanhouten's wife and Enoch Lang's wife and old
Jasper Reet's wife—so much for so much" (7–28–71). Allettie adds
her "news":

I am going to tell you all the news this time as you said I did not tell you the news. To begin with Mrs. Reid has got a young son weighed 11½. Here is another, James Vanhouten has a young daughter also Mrs. Sam V has got a daughter, pretty well for Port Creek, and if I have told you of the births now I will tell you of the deaths. Old Mr Vanhouten is dead and Old Mr. Whipple. (1–11–72)

However matter-of-factly Eliza wrote about the many misfortunes of acquaintances all about her, she was herself far from being inured to suffering and loss. Stephen Keyes died during the winter of 1875, leaving Eliza desolated:

Oh I have moved so many times but to think that the next time I move if I live I have got to go and leave Pa behind it does seem as though I never could do it for all there is the family in the front room, and the children is both here I am alone all alone. Oh this vacancy it seems as though I can never outlive it, I miss him so much every day. (March 1875)

Letters among the family show that indeed she had much to miss, apart from his skill and hard work as a farmer. When Eliza went to New York State to visit her friends and relatives, Stephen Keyes wrote to her in a manner that suggests generous and affectionate intimacy:

You said you would do up the rest of your visiting and go to Ithaca last. You had better stay where you are till he gets home [Ezra Cornell] then come up to Penfield and then go back to Ithaca, and don't you come home till you see Cornell and visit the old place where you spent 11 years of your girlhood days of toil. I want you should have a good long visit. I wish I was there with you. We would have a good time. I wouldent put any water falls on Ma nor turn my hair black. . . . Ed Ward is purty good boy and purfictly happy when Tish don't scold him; as for Ponto he makes the most fuss, he whines and cries all the time. Emeral Whipple died about 3 o'clock in the afternoon with typhoid fever and was buried today. I can tell you ma it seems lonesome to have you gone. . . . Ma I can tell you some news our Sara is enceinte. . . . Now Ma, don't get under the cars nor to the bottom of the Lake. Write when you get this. From your husband S. S. Keyes. (4–5–69)

In the spring of 1872 Viola and Hubbel Pierce moved to a house of their own on the outskirts of Detroit, after having spent their first eight married years living with Hubbel's parents, Angela and War-

ren Pierce, on a farm. The move, by everyone's account, was trau-
matic for the couple. Hubbel's mother made of it a watery tragedy:

> My Dear Viola, I am indeed sorry to hear that you are afflicted with
> your head for surely there is no comfort, you will have to come back. I
> do not believe the water is healthy there. Ours is just as good as ever
> although there had been such a flood it is thawing a little every day and
> bids fair for good sugar weather. . . . How oft today have looked for
> what I know not but my eyes seem to wander where I saw you last and
> an unbidden tear trickles down my sunken cheek. I seem to have my
> share of sorrow but to dwell with such thoughts is truly painful. I will
> go to bed and finish another time. Hubbel it is Friday night and all day
> my mind has been wondering where you are. A solemn stillness and
> gloom is around me. . . . We are quite sorry that you went away taking
> all in consideration. Your father thinks it would be better for you here.
> There is going to be a great deal of work to be done and a good price
> for it too. Pa says if you raise ever so much there it won't bring you
> much and here is a good market always. They want Alonzo on the big
> drive and offer him $100 a month.

She signed herself "Mother to her far away children," and left room
on the sheet for Hubbel's younger brother Henry to add, "We have
got a pan of snowy corn I wish you would come home again and
Viola too. You should sit to the table and fill yourselves clear up to
your navels and furthermore we have got four little pigs and if you
come we will give you one. I will close my letter by sending my best
respects and wish you were here we are lost without you" (nd). The
Keyes family, predictably, took a less histrionic view of the change of
residence. Allettie wrote to her sister:

> We received your letter and was very sorry to hear that you and Sonney
> was so homesick. I don't think that it could have been any more
> dubious than it was the day we moved into the tin shop as the night you
> had to run with the mantille and the rain kettle. I wish I had been there
> to cheer you and Sonney about the time you were crying. Give me the
> country for all of the city. Have you left your cow and pigs and
> chickens?

And Eliza, in her note of the same day, wrote as one practiced in
distinguishing among degrees of unhappiness, well aware that some
of them—like a move to a strange city—are fairly easy to recover
from:

> I do hope by this [time] you are both more reconciled to your new

home. You can't expect to always be under your father's and mother's wing, although it was pleasant for you both. Kate said she would just like to have walked in about the time you both was *blubbering*. She said she would have cheered you both up. Pa says he is afraid you can't lay anything up and pay such rent but the Lord knows you have our best wishes for your welfare. We do so often talk of you and want to see you both ever so much and hope you will both come home this fall. (4–30–72)

But this is not to say that Eliza herself was not capable of creating a touching, dramatic scene on occasion, as in the example below where she stars as the neglected mother:

Being tired of waiting for an answer to my last letter I thought I would write and see what is the reason that you don't write. It is the hour of 11 o'clock at night. Eddie and I are alone. . . . I could not go to sleep so I got up and dressed myself and sit here alone giving my thoughts to my children that are far away and I hope both enjoying the sweet sleep of health not thinking how uneasy their poor mother is. We are all well as usual but working very hard I am so tired when night comes that I hardly know what to do with myself. . . . Well my dear children the clock has just struck 12 and now I will smoke and go to bed and try to sleep so good night to you both how I wish you was both here tonight I would clap on the tea kettle and we would have a cup of tea.

Alonzo Choate and Hubbel Pierce: A Civil War Friendship

Among the Keyes family connections, the man Viola married soon after his return from the Civil War was one of the most important. For a time, Warren Hubbel Pierce was the only adult male among the Keyses: Stephen Keyes died in 1875, Tom Battey in 1877. Allettie did not marry again until 1888, and Eliza did not remarry at all. So, although he was husband to Viola, Hubbel's temperament and actions were of concern to other women in her immediate family, as well.

During the Civil War Hubbel had been a member of Battery B of the First Michigan Light Artillery; he wrote to Viola during the march to Atlanta in May of 1864: "It is a fine sight to see a whole army on the move and to see them draw up in line for camping." They had been on the march for three weeks; he was tired, but hoping for rest. "I want you to get up a dance when we get home. Tell your mother that I will try and come home as good as I went. It is not half as bad as some say it is. This is a very pleasant country here, but I had rather be at home. Home where I can see some one that I know. Our men are following the rebels up so close that they are only 15 minutes behind them" (5–28–64). In late August Viola had a letter from her mother telling of visiting Hubbel's parents: "Sis 2 weeks ago we went up and visited Warren and Angela. They don't live very pleasant together. They had a letter from Hubbel the night before and he was well and was fat as a pig" (3–29–64). Angela Pierce's letter to Hubbel the following April shows her strong feelings and close attachment to her son, and the slow progress of vital news as well.

> What do you mean you little imp about Mr. Whitney and who ever put such nonsense in your head. I always like to go to parties as you very well know. Do you recollect the time we went down to Bowers after the girls & when you got out to open the gate you caught your feet in the lines and fell rather solid on that old stub near the gate. I never pass there but what I always think of it and am always ready for a good laugh. Why child alive didn't you know the war is about over. Maybe you will get home before this letter reaches you. Lee has surrendered himself and whole army to the man. Is not that grand. (4–13–65)

Battery B was mustered out of service in mid-June in Detroit, and Hubbel returned to his parents in Grand Rapids. Three weeks later began a three-year correspondence between Hubbel and a fellow soldier, Alonzo Choate of Gratten, Michigan. To his first letter Alonzo's sister, Hannah Joslin, added a postscript urging Hubbel to visit, and referring to Hubbel as "my brother's old woman": "When you send your Wife your picture you can send his sister one if you please" (7–9–65). The wife/husband mode of address continued throughout Alonzo's letters, and both his sister and later his wife used the terms. Hubbel seems to have kept all of Alonzo's letters— there are twenty of them—which deal with three main themes: his affection for Hubbel; his own progress toward self-betterment; and advice. These letters picture a close and unguarded friendship between two young men at a formative period in their lives.

After the war Alonzo buckled right down to a job at twenty-six dollars a month. But coming home was difficult for Hubbel; the end of the war could mean the beginning of private troubles, and Alonzo worried about Hubbel's unhappy state of mind:

> Hub I am sorry to hear that you are getting discontented and that you

talk of enlisting in the Mexican Army. Hub if you'll take my advice you will not do so for I do not believe you would ever live to get back. If you cannot live at home why strike out for yourself. There are more ways than one to make a living and the whole world lies before you. Choose your path and follow it faithfully. But above all try to live at home as long as you can, suffer a little rather than do that which may cause you misery all your life time. (8–28–65)

By October Alonzo was congratulating Hubbel on his "Lady Love" and wishing him "every prosperity and happiness on the road to Matrimony." He also strongly urged on him self-improvement.

I am glad you intend going to school this winter. Education will give you success when properly used. It serves to raise moral tone of our being to incite us to nobler and better things, in proportion as ignorance debases and renders coarse our natures. In proof of this, we have but to look at those communities where people are in a comparative state of ignorance and compare them with those that are made up mostly of well educated people. And we cannot help arriving at the conclusion that Education is ennobling, Ignorance debasing. So I say Educate and be Educated.

By the first of the year, Alonzo himself was enrolled at Eastman's Business College in Chicago, "trying to learn that which will be of use in later life," in the expectation that "by April next I shall be competent to keep books in any kind of establishment from a retail country store up to forwarding and commission business . . . if I work hard" (1–16–66). He described his full schedule which included "penmanship one hour each day," and throughout the spring urged Hubbel to attempt a similar program: "I think it would be a good plan for you to attend a commercial school if you can, as it will give you a great insight to the business world. It is something that we all need. We cannot subject ourselves to too great a discipline as regards business" (3–10–66). Hubbel Pierce was the sort of friend who required constant shoring up:

What is this I hear, discontented. Why what is the matter. This will never do Hub. You must shake off this feeling, make up your mind to do something be somebody and then go in with a will. But I wish I could see you for I could talk better than I can write. I know how to feel for you, as I have felt so a little this week. And I have made up my mind to go away. I have not made up my mind where, except first I shall go out to Oakland to see my brother which will be in about two weeks. But I hope to hear that you are all right by this time. (8–30–66)

Besides improving work, Alonzo recommended three sources of comfort: religion, the love of a good woman, and the remembrance of their friendship. Religious enthusiasm came to Alonzo at New Year's during his winter at Eastman, a holiday that "was celebrated by bringing one sinner to the feet of Christ begging for mercy, that sinner was myself." The benefits of that new knowledge, like the benefits of education, he urged also upon Hubbel.

> Suppose you will think it strange that such a wild one as I should acknowledge that there was need for a reformation of character and principle. That it was necessary to acknowledge God before man and to obey his living laws. It is so and Hub I do not feel ashamed to own it, I would sooner have this right hand cut off than deny my Savior whom I love above all else on earth. Nor do I think that your friendship for me will be weakened by it so doing. And it would be great joy for me to hear that you were striving to lead a life that will be acceptable to your God but I will not say too much for fear of offending. We should not be over zealous or we may spoil all. But for the sake of the friendship between us do not be offended at what I say. (1–16–66)

Two and a half years later his hopes were realized.

> Many times have I read your last and most precious letter to me. For it contained news over which Angels may rejoice and how my heart rejoiced within me when I learned that He who endured with me the toils and hardships of a soldier's life in defense of our country and our flag had at last determined to enlist under the banner of the cross. And my heart goes out in gratitude to God for answering my prayer in your behalf. . . . And I shall continue to pray to Him who is a prayer hearing and a prayer answering God, that you may be left by the power of his grace in the path that leadeth to life everlasting. That you may honor him both in the body and spirit which are His and become a bright and shining light so that others by you may be led to seek Christ and save their souls. . . . All the afflictions trials and troubles are for our good. And we must bear these hardships as good soldiers of the cross looking to Jesus who is the author and finisher of our faith and who had redeemed us again to God by the shedding of his own precious blood. The salvation of our souls is a life work So dear friend press onward and upward in the path you have chosen, remembering that Jesus is near you. Angels guarding and a great cloud of witnesses looking down from heaven upon you. Well Hub I don't want to weary your patience so I will tell you something about my affairs. I am working a farm this summer. . . . (7–5–68)

Alonzo's letter is very long on exhortation, but his style typically changed abruptly when he turned to sublunary matters of farm work and his plans for "going out west." He too was married by this time (summer, 1868), and Alonzo's wife, Esther, added a note:

> O how my heart was made to rejoice when Lon told me that you had found peace in believing in the Savior and while the tears of joy fell from my eyes I felt in my heart to say Bless the Lord Oh my soul. Mrs. Pierce I believe I know how you felt when your Dear Husband started in this good cause as well I remember how I felt when Lon first started yet God had not permitted us to be to each other what we are now but I don't believe I should have felt any different if we had been married but my heart was continually going out to God for his salvation. Many times in the still watches of the night have we bowed in prayer and I have asked God to give him a new heart and I felt that my prayers have been answered and may God grant that we may all live to honor God and be the means of doing much good in this world is my earnest prayer.

(There are no examples of such religious earnestness in the extant writing of Hubbel Pierce or in Keyes family letters.) Alonzo's religious embrace paralleled a year-long courtship: the views he expressed regarding God and women were similar to each other. Hubbel too had reported a "Lady Love" as early as the autumn of 1865, a cousin, Mary. Early in 1868 Alonzo congratulated him more specifically: "Hub am I to infer from your letter that you intend to join Hymens bands, and that the happy one is to be your sweet cousin Mary. Thrice happy is the man who has the love of a noble and virtuous woman" (3–10–66). But for Hubbel the course of love was not unremittingly happy, for in December of the same year, Alonzo wrote:

> First I am glad to hear that you have been so steady this summer, hoping that you are awakening to a realization of the life before you. . . . I had expected to hear of your marriage before this. But it seems that you and your lady love don't agree and that you have taken another. All I have to say is success attend your efforts if your intentions are sincere and if you are not already married that you will have to hurry up or else I shall beat you as my wedding day is appointed the 30th of this month. (12–3–66)

By the following June Hubbel was married after all, to Viola Keyes: "I am glad to hear that you are enjoying such good health and that your wife is getting better" (6–1–67).

About the prospects of happiness and prosperity in marriage Alonzo had a good deal to say. In the same letter in which he congratulated Hubbel on his intentions to wed Mary, he also cautioned him against dancing, an enjoyment Hubbel shared with his mother and which he had happily anticipated returning to after the war, as we have seen. Alonzo disapproved.

> You wanted to know whether I thought there was any harm in dancing or not. There mere act of dancing is no harm, for David you know danced with joy before the Ark of God. But the sin lies in this. When we go to a dance, we do not go for the advancement of our good or of others, but for the mere selfish enjoyment of our own worldly lusts. And besides this we are obliged to come in contact with those of loose morals. Those who fear not God or man but go there for the purpose of making others as low and degraded as themselves. And it also serves to give us a distaste for the practical duties of life. As all exciting pleasures of this kind do. . . . No pleasure is good that does not serve to fit us for that future life to come, that does not arouse in us some noble desire, to do good unto others, to be an honor to God as well as man. I shall be baptized tomorrow evening at the First Baptist Church in this City. (3–1–66)

Six weeks later Alonzo inquired, "Do you still go to as many dances as you used to. I have no desire for them any more, and hope it will be the same with you. And I feel happier and better than I did in the past" (5–1–66). A month later, and six months before his reference to Hubbel's interrupted marriage plans, Alonzo offered this counsel:

> Well Hub as the principal subject of your letter is love and marriage and seeing as you want my advice I will answer that first for fear I may not have room for it after getting through with the rest. I know something of your feelings and can sympathize with you as I have a little experience in these matters. First as to marrying, don't be in a hurry, improve every opportunity to study the character of your intended, her disposition tastes and talents for upon her depends your future happiness. Be sure you love each other as man and wife ought, not with a love caused by the passions of your lustful nature, but with a pure calm love that never dies, but grows stronger with time, a love that will intwine your hearts together as one and which no power on earth can separate. Such a love will be acceptable to God and your marriage will be registered in heaven. If you bear such a love for a young lady, I say marry her with or without your parents consent, but first try to gain them. Do nothing hasty lest you should commit an act that should mar your happiness for life. I have courted for nearly a year and my love is stronger than when I commenced. It has been the making of me for

she is a noble virtuous Christian woman, one that is beloved and respected by all around here. It was her who first tried to lead me to Christ and I thank God she was successful. And I hope one day to hear you say the same as I, Christ is my saviour, in him I trust. (6–2–66)

The path leading to love and marriage is precarious. Whereas salvation comes both by the love of Christ and that of a good woman, still one has one's lustful nature to contend with. Sexuality was not a joking matter for Hubbel and Alonzo, not in the way it was, for instance, for Viola's parents. In the same month during the war that she reported to Viola the discord between Hubbel's parents, Eliza told her that a widowed acquaintance was being courted by a widower who "owns a nice farm, nice span of horses and buggy and last though not least he has got 8 children." This Mr. Church "proposed to the old thing but she said she did not set the happy day yet." As to Stephen Keyes's opinion of the affair: "Pa says he would want a bunch of Rosemary tied under her arms and everywhere else if he had got to sleep with her" (8–11–64). Alonzo's letters altogether lack this edge of humor. Even the tone of Eliza's most cautionary letters to Viola was more relaxedly witty than any of Alonzo's: "Now sis as to that young man putting his arm around you you tell him that your mother never allowed such work when she was a girl and she did not think he was much of a gentleman and if I was there I would tell him so too but you can tell him for me. When I read that to Will and T how they laughed" (8–29–64). It was not, then, universally the habit of the age to be quite as high-minded about "love and marriage" as was Alonzo, whose attitudes were colored by his hopes for self-betterment, success, and piety, and fears of failure and poverty.

The one certain and continuing source of happiness for Alonzo was his wartime friendship with Hubbel; as the correspondence progresses he speaks increasingly strongly of his affection. On January 16, 1866, he apologized for not having written:

I can assure you with my whole heart that my friendship for you is as strong as ever. What fickleness of mind it would show if we who had shared the perils and dangers of a soldiers life, we who always had true enjoyment in each others society should now after a few months separation cease to forget one another. God forbid that I should forget you whom I love as a brother and who acted the post that a brother should when together in the Army.

Then follows his first account of courses at Eastman's Business College and his religious experience. On March 10, when he congratulated Hubbel on his engagement to Mary and advised him to avoid dancing and to attend a commercial school, Alonzo also wrote:

> Well Hub I don't know but you will have to get another old woman for I don't know when I shall ever get back [he was in Chicago]. I would like to see you very much and to have a good old chat with you. I believe it would do me good. If I should go home this spring I shall try and manage to stop and see you when I get to Grand Rapids. And I hope to see your intended also. Please to give her the best respect of your old woman, and tell her I hope she will enjoy herself with you as much as I have. For we used to have some gay old times didn't we. . . . Remember your Old Woman, as she often thinks of you.

Friendship, like the topics of religion and "love and marriage," brought out the hortatory in Alonzo:

> With pleasure did I receive your photograph. Truly it is the same old phiz. And reminding me of bygone times and bringing up past scenes before my eyes. Of camp and field, march and bivouac. In which you and I mingled together during the late struggle to put down a rebellion which strove to break and ruin the best government the world ever saw. But valued thank God. When thinking of these things I am led to use your words, such is life. . . . The forming of new ties of affection and the breaking asunder of those that have bound us to those who were near and dear to our hearts.

And on to phrases about life being a tale, a breath, a span, in the expectation of death—"May you and I and everyone be prepared to go. And to give up our account with joy and not with grief. At the Judgment Bar before our Lord, Maker and Judge" (3–26–66). A month later, when he still assumed that Hubbel was engaged to Mary, Alonzo even more strongly protested his affection.

> I hope you will forgive me and I can assure you that you have often been in my thoughts, that my mind has often reverted back to past scenes through which we passed in which you ever proved a true friend. You seem almost as dear to me as a brother, and I would be sorry to lose your friendship. I wish I could see you and have a good old talk, it would do me good. . . . Well Hub you haven't got married yet have you. I think you had better wait until you get a divorce from your Old Man, if you don't I tell your wife what times we used to have sleeping together. I like very well to do the same but I want to get an Education first. My sister (the one that you saw at the Rapids) has

jumped the Broom Stick. I still enjoy the company of the other young lady that you saw at the same time. (5–1–66)

Most of Alonzo's letters are addressed "Dear Friend Hubbel," "Dear Friend," or "Dear Hub," and he signed himself some variation of "believe me your ever true friend Alonzo." The letter of August 28, 1865, asking Hubbel not to enlist in the Mexican Army, begins "My Dear beloved Husband." ("Wife" and "Husband" roles were not assigned consistently to either.) When he wrote the first time to congratulate Hubbel on the success he had enjoyed "in seeking for a wife," he asked also to be informed of the wedding day:

It would be some consolation for the loss of my good Old Woman who stood by me through all the trials and dangers of a soldier's life. Yes Hub, I am fully aware of the affections of a good and true woman, having enjoyed them for over a year. God grant we, you and I, may always enjoy them, for then we ought surely to be happy. Dear Hub you will be no more happy to see me than I you. And I do wish you could come to see me. (9–22–66)

The following spring Alonzo was superintendent of a Sunday School and working for a Mr. Ashley, and he found another occasion to speak of his affection for his friend and its connection to the presence of his wife.

Well Hub I am sorry to say that I have lost that ring you gave me. I wore it continually till one day I was chopping, it hurt my finger so I took it off and put it in my vest pocket and it dropt out and lost. I was real sorry for it always reminds me of you and of the times we used to have together in the army. You shall be the first to have a picture of myself and wife as soon as we get some taken. She is by my side writing a letter to her brother. (4–23–67)

His affections for Hubbel blend with those for his "intended" and also with his growing piety. In the autumn of 1867 he was still working for Mr. Ashley, but making plans to go to some land he had bought in northern Michigan where he wanted eventually to build a house; in the meantime he was to "go into the lumber woods this winter." He closed with wishes for Hubbel's "future welfare and prosperity," and welfare and prosperity Alonzo still saw all about him: "The country is improving very fast up there and the land is all being taken up rapidly. When I get settled up there you must come and make me a visit and I will give you rough fare and a warm welcome." This letter had begun with apologies for a gap in his letter-writing, and a religious application to his seeming good fortune:

> For Hub I can assure you from my heart that you are still dear to me as a friend. And that I think of you very often even as I write a feeling of tenderness towards you rises in my heart. My thoughts revert to the past scenes of our acquaintance when these ties of friendship were formed which I hope will last as long as we exist in our present life. And even in the life to come that if we meet no more on earth we may meet with the redeemed hosts of heaven, around the throne of God. Where we shall see as we are seen and know as we are known. Where all is happiness, peace and love. In those be blest mansions above. This is *my* hope, is it *yours*. (10–6–67)

Alonzo next writes from the north woods, complex allegiances still on his mind.

> Oh Hub, a tender feeling rises in my heart when I think of you, and my prayer is that you may learn to love Christ and follow in his footsteps. . . . I wish you were here to go along with us up in the woods. I'll warrant we would have a good time, but I presume your wife would object to that plan and so would I if I was in her place. . . . I hardly know which end I stand on now that my wife is gone, and you may well believe I shall get where she is as soon as possible. (11–2–67)

The next summer Alonzo returned to Ashley, to work on a farm, and said he had thoughts of "going out west." He had been promising to send pictures of himself and his wife since early 1868—he finally got them off in the autumn. "Accept them as a slight token of our love and esteem for you both. They look far better than the originals, and I suppose, Hub, you will scarcely recognize the gentleman, your Old Woman and soldier companion in the army of our republic." He mentions the coming election when he intended to vote for Grant and Colfax. This letter of October 11, 1868, from Greenville, Michigan, was the last we hear of Alonzo Choate, except for one reference to him in a letter of Eliza Keyes, that he was doing farm work and someone else was caring for his children. Prosperity evidently still eluded him.

> When I last wrote we were keeping house and had rented a farm. But I made an offer and was released from my bargain. The farm has been sold and we have broken up keeping house for the present. I am

getting my wife boarded near the village of Greenville, her health is not very good. I have had another attack of my old enemy the quinzey, since that my health has been excellent. I am hard at work as usual, probably shall not do much this winter. Although we are not keeping house, yet we hope to see you all the same. Just let me know when you get to your father's and if you think you can make us a visit. If not I will try and see you as I expect to go to the Rapids soon.

He closes with more prayers and blessings, and his wife adds: "Probably I shall not see you if you come out to the Rapids as I live a good long way from there but perhaps the time will come when we can make our acquaintances more satisfactory. If not in this world may we live so as to meet in another."

There are loose ends to this correspondence, and missing details. "My health and that of my wife has not been very good this spring but I manage to keep busy to work" (7–6–68)—what were these quinzeys and vague illnesses that Alonzo, Hubbel, and both their wives were never rid of? What became of all the resolution to "educate and be educated" that spurred the energetic young soldier off to business college with commercial enterprise in his imaginings? What of his land in the north woods, and how did it happen that he seemed barely able to keep a hold on farm laboring jobs and could not maintain the rent of a farm and house? He had written two years earlier of an unfortunate comrade: "It seems to me that Will Rouse is in a bad plight and much to be pitied. Won't you ask him if he ever received my photograph and why he don't write" (12–29–66). Alonzo gave untiring effort to bolstering Hubbel from spells of being "discontented." He evidently felt these dreads himself, exaggerating pious optimism as an unsteady defense against his own steadily declining fortunes.

The quality of the affectionate friendship between Alonzo Choate and Hubbel Pierce is another puzzle. By standards of our own time, their attitudes and social aspirations were of the most conventional and conservative kind. Alonzo wanted to prosper and he assumed the same of Hubbel. His religious fervor was closely bound to economic desires, and he expressed both as well as feelings of romantic love entirely in cliché phrases. He did not say to which sect he had been persuaded, or give specific information about the background, interests, or personality of the woman he married. Spending a winter chopping wood at what he called the North Pole may show a brief streak of adventure in his temperament, or merely desperation

for a job. In any event, there are no traces of adventure in his ideas
or attitudes about anything else. In view of such conservatism and
conventionality, it may seem to some readers now unusual at least
that he was able casually to keep up the Old Woman banter with
Hubbel, and to include sister and wife in the exchange. Both men's
wives were reading the correspondence, to judge by effusive good
wishes sent to all parties.

Alonzo nowhere intimated that he saw anything unusual in his
friendship with Hubbel. It is hard to say what the tone is: innocent,
naive, off-hand—none of those words precisely fits. Yet the erotic
part of the friendship may be less unusual in their time than we
suppose. The letters are reminiscent for instance of Ishmael and
Queequeg in *Moby-Dick,* sharing a smoke in the cabin: "He seemed to
take to me quite as naturally and unbiddenly as I to him; and when
our smoke was over, he pressed his forehead against mine, clasped
me around the waist, and said that henceforth we were married;
meaning, in his country's phrase, that we were bosom friends."
Queequeg shared with Ishmael his tobacco and his thirty silver
dollars, he gave him an embalmed head, and invited him to share in
ceremonies over a wooden idol before the two went to bed.

> How it is I know not; but there is no place like a bed for confidential
> disclosures between friends. Man and wife, they say, there open the
> very bottom of their souls to each other; and some old couples often lie
> and chat over old times till nearly morning. Thus, then, in our hearts'
> honeymoon, lay I and Queequeg a cozy, loving pair.

The next chapter begins: "We had lain thus in bed, chatting and
napping at short intervals, and Queequeg now and then affectionately throwing his brown tattooed legs over mine, and then drawing
them back; so entirely sociable and free and easy were we." They are
not sleeping, so they sit up inside the bedclothes ("we felt very nice
and snug"). The men smoke and talk, "for now I liked nothing
better than to have Queequeg smoking by me, even in bed, because
he seemed to be full of such serene household joy then," and
Queequeg tells the story of his life. "His story being ended with his
pipe's last dying puff, Queequeg embraced me, pressed his forehead
against mine, and blowing out the light, we rolled over from each
other, this way and that, and very soon were sleeping." The tender
feelings which arose in Alonzo's heart when he wrote to Hubbel, the
affections he described "of a brother," his happy memories of "what
times we used to have sleeping together," these sound very similar to

the sociable and free embraces between Melville's characters. Also in the manner of Alonzo's letters, *Moby-Dick's* references to sexuality, Christianity, and work are intermixed, as in the sexually charged chapter about whale sperm, "A Squeeze of the Hand."

> As I bathed my hands among those soft, gentle globules of infiltrated tissues, woven almost within the hour; as they richly broke to my fingers, and discharged all their opulence, like fully ripe grapes their wine. . . . I declare to you, that for a time I lived as in a musky meadow . . . in that inexpressible sperm, I washed my hands and my heart in it. . . . Squeeze! squeeze! squeeze! all the morning long; I squeezed that sperm till I myself almost melted into it.

Ishmael and Queequeg's affections are protected, as it were, by the distancing of race and culture and religion, but what Melville was showing that I think is very like Alonzo's account was a climate of ordinariness about the experience of two men who loved each other more simply and directly than they did women.

Warren Hubbel Pierce was sixteen years old when he enlisted in the Grand Army of the Republic. Understandably, his closest attachments during his late teens were with other very young men, at a time not only of drastic personal change but physical danger and high emotional tension as well. Judging from Alonzo Choate's writing and what one infers about Hubbel Pierce's, both regarded women remotely, with apprehension and some fear. Alonzo writes of women only by extremes, good and noble ones who inspired him to piety and hard work, or "those of loose morals" that he was "obliged to come in contact with" on the dance floor. Mary and Eve, angel and whore were the young Alonzo's only imaginings about women, and presumably Hubbel's as well. These men had not experienced the easy friendliness between men and women that Viola, for instance, knew within her family. Little in his experience apparently prepared Hubbel to consider women as individuals. Solace from loneliness, good food, and household care were what he wanted from the women he knew—mother, wife, sisters, and inlaws. He regarded them all alike.

In the context of a study of women's private writing, the letters from Alonzo Choate to Hubbel Pierce have a place, not only because they reveal experiences of men who were important to the women we are thinking about, but also because they so markedly contrast with what we find women writing. Compilers of school manuals might not approve of some of Alonzo's grammatical infelicities, but I

would expect them to praise his efforts at sticking to elevated subjects and at attempting the florid style, and certainly they would
admire his longings for self-improvement by means of education.
Alonzo accepted and intended to perpetuate the world as he found
it. There is no radical criticism of the human condition in anything
he says, nothing as unsettling as Amy Sylvia Cory's "Phillip shot God
with his revolver." With Alonzo Choate's letters before us we can see
a little better what Eliza Keyes or Gwendoline Kinkaid or any number of other women would *not* have written.

Abbottsville, Dakota Territory, June–July 1879

Hubbel Pierce's five letters from Abbottsville to Viola back in
Michigan are both reportorial and instructional, rather like his letters from Georgia fifteen years earlier ("It is not half as bad as some
say it is. . . . I want you to get up a dance when we get home,"
(5–20–64). From the beginning of his homesteading venture, he
reported on his health, on the appearance of the land and landscape, on practical housekeeping and farming arrangements. And
he sent directives to Viola as to what to bring when she came, how to
dispose of their property in Michigan, and how to manage her
journey. Judging from other letters in the family, Hubbel and Viola
had not been separated since their marriage, and Hubbel had not
been so far away from his family for any length of time since the
Civil War. Thus the Abbottsville letters combine his plans for a move
with preoccupations about himself: health, food, and separation
from family. The letters reveal a struggle between Hubbel's efforts
to organize an ambitious venture, and his old emotional dependen-
cies.

Numbers of people came to Dakota to improve their health as well
as their fortunes, and Hubbel was one of these. On June 4, 1879, in
the earliest letter in the Abbottsville series, he wrote:

> I am feeling better than I have felt in all winter, I do not have any bad
> feeling in my stomach, and I feel hungry. Can eat anything I can get
> with a good relish, we do not have any pie or cake, no butter but plenty
> of milk. Mr. D. brought a three-year-old cow off a man for two dollars.
> She has splendid cream on the milk. . . . You must not get sick aworry-
> ing about me. I am feeling first rate. I do not have to hoe my throat out
> every morning any more. You would hardly hear me hock in all day.
> There is something worth coming here every one I have seen is as
> tough as an ox.

On June 29: "I am sorry you have the headache so much, maybe you will get rid of it out here. I have not seen any sickly looking people since I came here." When Hubbel wrote about health, he was thinking of his own, and when he reported what there was to eat, he also had his own well-being in mind. Food was something he mentioned regularly:

> I hope you will not forget to bring all of the beans that are left for I am almost starved for some. We do not have very solid food, no potatoes, no butter, gooseberry sauce and bread and milk but we will soon have plenty of potatoes. (7–6–79).
>
> They raise potatoes on sod. Turn the sod over and drop them in the furrow when they dig them they turn the sod back and press them up with hoeing or bug poison. They are worth 90 cts in Valley City. (6–4–79)
>
> Gooseberries are just splendid here. . . . But I don't think I would refuse Pie or cake or anything good. Our cook does not amount to much. We lived better when we done our own cooking. (7–19–79)

Nevertheless, in spite of his self-preoccupation, Hubbel was a good reporter when it came to descriptions of life in the territory:

> I wish you were here. You could say it could not be written, but I will try. First the land is a black clay loam from two to three feet deep, the first plowing is rather hard after one crop it is as soft as can be, any team can work it. The water in the creek is soft and as clear as crystal with a gravel bottom. . . . The river is not so clear except in winter. The timber here is box elder, not very large, some oak and elm from one to two and some nearly four feet through but not very tall. . . . They commence their work in March. There has not been much corn raised here as yet. I heard one man say he had raised 75 bushels of squaw corn per acre and we have some planted. I planted the corn that Bert gave me and in less than a week it had sprouts on over an inch long. . . . The feed is splendid you can pasture where you like and no one to say no. Mr. O has a team all he has to do when he gets through at night is to turn them out. And not this thing you have got to wear yourself out building fence. . . . The longer I am here the better I like it. (6–4–79)
>
> I went to Valley City to get me a scythe and swath and fork for we are going to be cutting hay. We came past way back in the night and I never in all my life saw so many mosquitoes. I bought a yard of net to cover my face, if I had not I could not of stood it for the wind did not blow one breath and the oxen were covered and nearly wild. The folks where we stopped said they had never seen them so bad. . . . The place where we stayed last night is a splendid farm. The man has in 500 acres of wheat and has broken 800 more of land this summer. He has a fine

herd of cattle, 20 horses and beefs, five men at work and everything I saw looks so nice it makes me feel as though I had hit upon the place to make something. (6–29–79)

There is no Indians here we saw some one day they were going to Fargo to sell some horses but they will not hurt any one. They are allowed so many days to a single family to go and trade if they are not back at the time set they can't go again. The nearest they are to us is 80 miles and they are mostly halfbreeds and own large farms there is plenty of soldiers there to look after them, so do not worry about them. I would rather see them than nobody.

Like many settlers, Hubbel wrote neutrally, though without sympathy, about Indians as individuals, and also about another group: "Do not go to Valley City for it is all filled up with people from Norway," a point of view he shared with others who were not first-generation immigrants from Europe. (Twenty years later, for instance, Emma Ladbury wrote to Allettie Mosher, Viola's sister: "The Busse place is sold and the man wants to move in the house the first of March so Mr. Kitching has to build before they can move in. I wish they weren't Norwegians that bought it" 1–22–99.)

The letters are full of elaborate instructions. The entire family was expected to be at the ready to send supplies and to complete arrangements for selling livestock and property in Michigan. Hubbel expected several of them to come west eventually, although Viola would be the first, the one he was most anxious to see, and the one he seemed to consider a full participant in the venture. Hubbel's instructions combine his shrewd and objective assessments of and knowledge about homesteading conditions with his worry about Viola's personal welfare.

I want an Oliver Chilled plow no 40 sod and a good steel cutter, straight landside if they have any of the revolving steel cutters I want one of them. That is what they use here. (6–4–79)

When you come you want to cook a good lot of meat to have cold have a bottle of tea and get a basket with a cover. You will find plenty of emigrants after you get in Milwaukee and you do not want to wear anything very nice for you will get all dirt. (6–4–79)

You had better fill the little keg with that vinegar and get some currant sprouts and save some garden seeds and be sure and bring some melon seeds. (6–15–79)

If you get me any boots get them at Kings and get no 9 with double sole and tap. These boots I bought are the best I ever had. You need a good pair of thick shoes too and a pair of those heavy rubbers at Coles you had better get the things there for you can get them cheaper and it is quite a way from the village here. You had better get some mosquito netting for it will be needed here. I never saw such large ones in my life but a little smoke will scare them away. You had better get some stocking yarn, and I want a pair of very warm gloves or mittens. Things will be nearer and cheaper here before many years.

Hubbel rebuked Viola, however, when he heard she had had a disagreement with his brother Henry over the selling of a colt.

I am afraid you were rather too hasty. I was sorry that any thing should happen to make hard feelings. I know that they are not so careful with their horses and I think Henry would of taken care the colt was not hurt. Now do not come away angry at them for you may never see them again. I do not wish to say anything to make you feel bad but come good friends with all. I have not said a word to them of what you wrote to me. (6–29–79)

In reading a collection of family letters covering a period of many years one becomes fairly adept at picking up clues about the emotional lives of the persons involved, including any nuances of intimacy and sexuality. As we have seen, the Bristol/Keyes family and their connections tended to include sexuality among life's reportable events and to be fairly open in expressing their feelings for each other. The current of sexual intimacy that runs through, for example, the jokes and fond good wishes of Stephen Keyes's letter to Eliza when she was visiting back east is very difficult to find in Hubbel Pierce's letters to Viola. To be sure, they had been married for some years, and it is also true that Hubbel expected these letters to be read by all and sundry in the family (but so, presumably, did the Keyes). Nevertheless, the letters seem oddly lacking in erotic feelings, and one infers that Viola's relationship with him was cooler than those she had experienced or observed in her parents' family.

One of the matters Hubbel gave some attention to during his months in Abbottsville was the domestic arrangements of the man with whom he initially shared a cabin.

Frank and I were getting logs out for his house he expects his wife here next week. I like him ever so much he is as good as he is big. He says he will tell you how I perform when you come. We have pretty pleasant times planning whether our wives will like it here. I am afraid she will be lonesome here without any other women. (6–4–79)

Frank is to Valley City after his wife. He will not come back until Monday. I am afraid she will be homesick the house is not roofed yet. . . . Well Viola it is Sunday night. Mrs. Abbott has got here and will

sleep in her own home. She likes it very much. . . . I shall stay with
Abbott until he gets his house ready and I shall go at my own as fast as
I can get my lumber. (6–15–79)

We have Mr. Abbott's house roofed, chinked and plastered outside. I
shall go at mine just as soon as I can but I think I shall put up a good
board shanty to do until after the warm weather and mosquitoes are
over. (7–6–79)

He does not mention the Abbotts again. The isolation of women was
a universal problem of plains settlement, and it is reassuring to read
that the two men had it on their minds. But Hubbel's response to
Mrs. Abbott herself was nowhere near as precise as his committed
concern for plows and methods of house building. It is difficult to
know how to read his praise of Frank Abbott—what did he mean by
"how I perform"? Possibly not very much, yet one is reminded of
Alonzo Choate's hi-jinks in the tent. Hubbel wrote very precisely
about objects and about relationships with men, but was nearly silent
about women or relationships between men and women.

When it comes to Hubbel's expressions of feeling for Viola herself,
these also are difficult to read. It is so easy to misinterpret gestures
which couples appear to make to one another. But putting together
Hubbel's direct addresses to Viola, as well as reflecting on the tone
of his reportings and directives, one senses that he is writing letters
to a competent worker, whose companionship was a matter of affectionate habit little encumbered by erotic feelings. The first and very
long letter of June 4 discussing his improved health, the fertile
countryside and the plow he wanted, addresses its most detailed
personal message to Angela Pierce:

Mother I wish I could call in tonight and have a smoke with you but
wait until we all get together on our farms and we will smoke some
good tobacco if you were here in a few weeks you could pick gooseber-
ries until you were crazy. Lett, I wish you were here to help they are as
large as currants and currants grow wild here. . . . Kiss Inez for me. . . .
Write a good long letter like this from your loving W. H. Pierce.

Scattered throughout are brief but nonsexual messages to Viola:

It is nearly a month since I left you. . . . I wish you were here. . . . It is
Wednesday morning, 20 minutes past 4. I take my pen to talk with you.
It is a lovely morn. Frank is asleep yet. . . . Wednesday afternoon. I will
write you a little more. I am sorry you are worried so about the colt.

Hubbel's second letter, of June 15, about boots, corn, and the arrival of Mrs. Abbott, speaks increasingly strongly about being lonely:

> Dear Wife, how I wish I could see you this rainy day instead of writing.
> I am well but lonesome. It has rained here for 3 days. Mr. D. is asleep. I
> have done everything I could think of to pass away the time. . . . Well
> Darling Wife it is the sabbath and I am seated to pen you a few lines am
> all alone. It is a splendid morning after the 3 days rain. How I would
> like to see all the Dear ones today, but as I cannot I will wait with
> patience. . . . I know you are as lonesome as I am.

His directions for her coming got rather muddled when he discovered that the Mr. Johnson he had counted on her accompanying
was not coming after all: "Now if you want to come you can but it
will be such a busy time I don't believe you can come." The letter for
June 19 discussed mosquitoes and Viola's apparent altercation over
the horse: "I suppose you are very lonesome without Lett and the
baby, but I am lonesome without you." The next two letters have
little about Viola herself except the remark "I will be glad when
Viola gets here and I think I will have something fit to eat" (7–19).
In five long letters, that is the extent of his direct addresses to Viola.
Unlike many couples (Rose and Reece Williams, Mamie and Ben
Goodwater), Viola and Hubbel Pierce were almost never separated
from each other—the summer in Abbottsville was a rare instance for
them. Certainly Hubbel was friendly, he assumed he and Viola knew
each other well, but his letters appear to withhold no secrets, no
reticences, no disappointment at things unsaid. "Lonesome" is the
strongest emotional word he uses. There were no messages to Viola
of the sort Ben Goodwater included for Mamie when she was away
for the winter, that he wished she were home, "but seeing you ant
why."

Nerves, 1904

Between mid-July and late August, 1904, when Allettie and
Emmet Mosher were traveling in Michigan and New York State
visiting Keyes relatives, Viola wrote her sister five long letters. She
reported on crop conditions—after a dry summer it had started to
rain but rust was ruining most of the grain. But what worried her
most was Hubbel's health and state of mind. He suffered increasingly from sleeplessness, stomach trouble, and "nerves," and, most
distressingly to her, he had sold the farm, apparently in haste,
without making further arrangements for either income or housing.

Viola saw the two of them now dependent upon her sister for a place to live as well as for general comfort and moral support. Her reports to Allettie reflect her worry, but they do not explain what was wrong with Hubbel. Her letter for July 14 began:

> Well Hubbel today is feeling quite well but don't know how long it will last. He got the medicine that was to quiet him and help him to sleep. He took two doses of it and he put in two hard nights it made him very nervous did not sleep at all of course the next day felt very bad. Then I had him leave off all of the Dr. medicine but the kind for his bowels and take Scramp root. Last night he rested quite good and today is feeling better if it only lasts.

Selling the farm was connected to his bad health, and both distressed her: "Our home is gone but I guess it is for the best. I don't know if he will ever be so he can work hard any more or not." There were cattle still to be sold, "then we will be glad to go in your house until we can build some thing. I think we will have time after you get home then Emmet will be there to tell us a little how to do." The next morning: "H put in a bad night again and is very nervous this morn so we are going to Edd [her youngest brother] . . . to see if it won't do him good. I can't see why he gets this way if he is to ever get well I fear he won't be any different."

Viola worried about his medicine, was relieved when he was not taking it, and sometimes sounded quite frightened at Hubbel's behavior. Her letter ten days later, begun on a Sunday, reports him no better.

> Tis after dinner and H is on the cot resting he got up this morning feeling quite good and we were most ready to go over to meeting when he looked out and saw a lot of cattle on the hill outside of the fence of course thought they were ours away he went hard as he could got up there and it was Edwards some in Lois oats so he took them back and Ralph come on the pony then went back to tell his father well when H got back he was so used up and tired we had to stay home. I was very disappointed but such is life but I will try and not complain for two nights H has slept and rested the best since he has been sick and I tell you it is a comfort to me now he is not taking any medicine only one kind for his bowels and is drinking cream but he seems to stay so weak he wishes many times you was both back but still is glad you are having a good time.
>
> We have not made any plans yet how we will do nor can until we can get rid of the cattle but don't think we will do anything about a house until Emmet is here to tell us a little how to do. . . . I tell you I put in a

bad night after selling the place. I lay on the floor and cried and said now we had no home and nowhere to go I was glad when morn came I do so hope none of the rest will ever have a nervous disease.

Well sister tis Monday afternoon washing and work done so will finish this tis quite hot. H had a very bad night so nervous it lasted until middle of forenoon now he is still but seems to be so tired I don't know how this will turn out it seems so strange when he feels better that it don't last he can't do anything only the chores that worries him a lot all I can do is hope for the best.

Tuesday 26 got up this morn so discouraged I sat right down and had a good cry then H he felt so bad he said we would go over to Elihu's [brother to Emmet and married to Allettie's daughter Inez] more settled down if he could only get better of that nervousness things would be better with us. (7–24–04)

Viola's letter two weeks later worries in addition over Allettie's illness ("I am so sorry you are having neuroligy and are so tired you won't enjoy your visit at all guess you will be glad to see home again"). Hubbel continued unwell, precipitate, and indecisive:

H is better he is not near so nervous but he don't sleep much better yet but I think if we ever know what we are going to do it will make a lot of difference with him. Our crops havent been better in a long time and it worries him to think they belong to someone else. Now he wants to buy some land on the P but he says he can't tell until you get back. I do hope we shant be as much trouble to you all as the old people there. We may live with you this winter tis a bad thing not to have a strong mind. Had a letter from Archa and of course they want us to come back there and buy but you know I don't want to do that if we had not sold out I never would sign my name to a paper to sell to anyone again. I would not worry so again for anything but I hope and trust it will be all right in the end. H mowed and raked hay all day yesterday for Edd and next week they are coming to stack for him he can't stand to pitch much.

Viola was haunted by the prospect of being dependent on her sister. Her letters contain several references to very old people who are ill and a burden to their families:

The man that lived on Sid's place last year had the Grippe then rheumatism so he could do nothing at all now has gone to the Hot Springs so you see it takes the best of them. You know what a well looking man he was what do you suppose will be done with the old people. I do hope I shan't be spared to be such trouble but we little know what is in store for any of us but I will try hard to clean my own dirt and filth. (7–24–04)

I am real sorry for Elmer's folks those old people will spoil their lives
the old lady wrote Maggie it was getting hard on her to wait on Obed so
much and Miller said she is just the one to do it. Oh my how he does
despise her. Phila says she don't know what will be done with them.
Well tis a pity one can't take the long journey when they get like that.
(8–6–04)

A letter from Inez Mosher, Allettie's daughter, confirms the muddled state of things in the Pierce household:

I don't believe Uncle Hubbels will do a thing until you get back. They
mourn all the time because they sold their place. Now they have got rid
of their cattle we want them to sell two of their hogs and bring the
other one here and turn it in our hog pasture and then go over to your
place and build their coop and barn and then build their house when
you come back. We thought they could leave their chickens and only be
gone three or four days to a time but I dident know I don't suppose
they will. (8–9–04)

It sounds as though Inez as well as her mother was used to looking
after Viola and Hubbel.
    Viola's next letter, dated August 18, reported harvesting wheat
and barley and was still vague about plans ("Now I suppose you
wonder what we are going to do well we don't know yet he is waiting
for Emmet to get home"). They had considered buying another
place, or returning to Hubbel's parents in Michigan, but rejected
both ideas ("We could go home for the winter perhaps that might
help him but I don't want to go back to live and leave the rest here").
The likeliest idea was the chicken coop at the Moshers; clearly both
were impatient for the travelers' return:

H said yesterday if we could find you in Dazey how glad he would be
he never made such a fuss about any one's being gone. Its after dinner
and he is laying down. I expect you will see us soon as you get here for
H can hardly wait for you to come last night he did not sleep a bit after
12 o'clock it does seem so strange he can't get better.

The last letter in this series to Allettie on her travels, dated August
31, 1904, reports rain after the long dry summer, but no change in
Hubbel's condition:

It can't do any good only freshen up the air and give us rain weather. . . .
Hubbel is some better but don't sleep yet not all night but I think if he
ever makes up his mind what he is going to do that will help him some

but he can't do anything very hard but am in hopes he will be different some time.

His inability to make up his mind left Viola increasingly disoriented; she was glad Allettie had gone to a fair: "The year we was there I enjoyed such things but still I would sooner be here strange aint it how one gets used to a place but if I ever get another home of our own I shall be very thankful." The rain continued over the several days taken up by the writing of the letter, and she reports accumulated misfortunes among acquaintances (dropsy, a sick baby, a dead husband, crop losses—"but such is this life made up of much sorrow for some"). She passed on a lugubrious report from Emmet's sister Phila:

Phila had a very sorryfull letter from the old lady Mosher she says they have enough to eat such as it is could have as good in state prison and nothing to wear said you and Emmet ought to give them the money to live on. That you was buying out for fine clothes and running around having a good time she said the Lord help your father for his boys don't. Now I tell you if I was Emmet I would give her an awful talking to, Phila said Edd read the letter and he never slept hardly bit all night he looks very bad I fear they will make you all a lot of trouble but such is life.

And she ends with the major refrain of all her letters, "Oh come home come home."

Viola and Hubbel Pierce died during the influenza epidemic of 1918–1919, having lived, for all their ailments, into their seventies.

What of Viola from all of these letters? Who was she, Viola Rosalia Pierce as her sister once addressed her, signing herself elaborately Allettie Jane Keyes? Viola's youth began in some exuberance. For a year she attended Penfield "seminary"; she excited warmth in new acquaintances. Lucy Pritchard after the visit in 1864 wrote: "Viola it will not do for you to come to Victor again for all the young men fell in love with you. Mary sends her love to you and says she would like to see you once more for she liked you so well. She thinks I had better take you and always keep you" (5–16–64). Viola kept an unsigned letter, dated December 13, 1863, from a young man in Pontiac, Michigan: "Miss Viola, Two weeks ago this Sabbath Evening it was my good fortune to first become acquainted and enjoy for a brief space of time the pleasure of your agreeable murmur and conversation," an event he attributed to her good manners rather than to "superior enjoyment founded on person, murmurs, or conversation." He was thereby encouraged to address her "by the pen, which is called the tongue of the absent." Viola kept a second letter from one Eugene Covey, of Rochester, an acquaintance from her days in Penfield, who took the liberty, he said, of addressing her "through the formal agents of pen and paper. . . . Do you have any sleighrides out where you live? If so do you ever get so sleepy? I often think of those days that have passed and those splendid rides we used to have when you were attending school at the Sem." He asked that she "grant one the pleasure of continuing the correspondence merely for social friendship and improvement" (3–15–64). Whether inspiring "murmurs" or improvement, Viola would appear to have had a not unpleasant youthful social life.

How did she become "poor Auntie"? How was it that, when she moved for the first time to a house of her own, in her mid-twenties, after eight years of marriage, she was "blubbering"? Her mother's earliest letters would make it appear that Viola was expected to look after herself—in making travel arrangements, in negotiating funds with Ezra Cornell—and to be able also to withstand general human vicissitudes, judging from her mother's detailed reports of "news." Yet as the years went by, Viola became more a source of concern than comfort. Viola often complained of being unwell (and her mother told her "now don't forget to see Orpha and ask her about that ammonia for the head ache, for I believe it will help you," 4–30–72). At the time of the move to Detroit, her mother wrote, "If you move in town to keep boarders I hope you will do well but sis you are so fat I am afraid the hot weather will be too much for you" (2–8–72), and again the same year (nd): "Now you say you are getting so fat. Mrs. Sutton the Post master's wife wants to know if your fat is going to fall into your arms. Sonny I think you will soon have to pack up and leave Suke [Viola] for she will soon be as fat as aunt Salome." From her mother's letters Viola received advice and encouragement, from her husband's, directives. When in her fifties, she wanted her sister virtually to manage her life. "Lonesome" is a word Viola and Hubbel both use—it casts them adrift. But it was not so for Viola always. Not long after the move to Dakota, Viola, on a visit with Hubbel to Michigan, wrote to her mother, resolute but appalled at his family's state of affairs:

Well Ma we went to see Aunt Orpha and I could not keep the tears back when I see her. Her mind is fast going but when I made her know who we was she was so glad to see us. Burt was there but we never noticed him nor even spoke to him. I told her to sell out and put the money out and go to some of the homes and live as she ought to and let the rest go to the devile or do the best and you ought to of heard that snipe of a boy but I told him about what I thought. . . . She said she prayed every day to die I had rather you would always stay in Dakota than live as she does.

Certainly Viola's life was complicated by Hubbel's, so different was his family from hers: less witty, more self-absorbed, and more earnestly quarrelsome. For Hubbel the years spent in the Civil War were crucial to his health and to his emotional attachments. His friendship with Alonzo would appear to have become for him the model of all personal attachments, and the chronic deterioration of his lungs and intestines was likewise well set by 1865. His and his mother's letters described Angela Pierce as the person most important to him; he wanted to be taken care of. Hubbel Pierce wrote as a hard-working and earnest man, whose greatest adventure after the war was the venture to Abbottsville for health and wealth. His writing does not show him to have been an imaginative or witty man. He appears never to have imagined Viola's desires in the way Stephen Keyes had Eliza's ("don't come home till you see Cornell and visit the old place where you spent 11 years of your girlhood days of toil" 4–5–69); or as Viola had Allettie's ("I thought perhaps last Sunday you was to meeting on Fort Creek where you used to take so much comfort when a girl and had Pa and Ma. Oh for some happy days once more" 7–18–04). Hubbel did not write that far outside of himself.

Viola lost the exuberance and resolution of her youth and did not match her mother's long-lived resilience. Her family wrote as though they worried about her more and more, yet all regarded her consistently with affection. She was Hubbel's second choice for a wife; even so, their troubles were not for lack of each other's companionship, though sexuality between the two apparently was minimal. Viola always tried her best and always was discouraged—by headaches, by the weight she gained, by Hubbel's sickly stomach, unhappiness, and sometimes disturbingly volatile relatives, and by the harsh and unsettled Dakota weather. No wonder she and Hubbel were nervous.

Yet the intimate family network never excluded her. She was privy to "news" and passed it on, whether sad, or ridiculous, or—occasionally—joyful.

VI

Two Lives

Julia Gage Carpenter, "Frantically Lonely"

"This is *awful country*, and I want to live East," Julia Gage Carpenter wrote in her diary in early January of 1884, during a week when the temperature had been 48° below zero at noon (1–4–84). Between April 7 and 16 the same year:

> Frank did *not* come. I stayed in the house *all alone* over night. . . . Frank went to Fargo to see about his 'Sue Claim.' I stayed alone all day and over night. . . . Alone all day and night again. *Dreadfully, dreadfully* forlorn. Can't stand being alone so much. . . . Frank came home this morning. . . . Frank and I took tea with Dave and Ina and stayed overnight. Frank gone to Gardner, 25 miles, expected to be home tomorrow but it has rained all day and I fear the roads are impassable. I have been alone all day and must be here alone all night. (I am *frantically* lonely. Can hardly endure it.)[1]

This woman wrote of herself as a wholly reluctant pioneer in the diary she began on February 9, 1882, the day she and Frank Carpenter (his legal name was James D. Carpenter) were married, and continued to the early 1900s. The diary describes some events at considerable length and leaves sketchy or unrecorded other periods of her life; taking what is written with what is not, we can glimpse the way she saw things, if not presume to know her life.

"The last of January the following invitations were sent." So the diary opens, reproducing one of the invitations on the page, followed by an account of the ceremony, a list of guests and wedding presents ("the wedding passed off very pleasantly with the exception

187

that Mother had a bad attack from the warm rooms and close air"). After a month with her family in Syracuse, New York, Julia and Frank boarded the train for their homestead claim in Lamoure County, Dakota Territory (now southeastern North Dakota), and began what was, for Julia at least, a misguided venture. The railroad took them as far as Jamestown; the last twenty-two mosquito-infested miles due south they traveled by prairie schooner ("a heavy farm wagon drawn by four mules"). Edgeley, the nearest town, to the south, had seventy buildings and was six weeks old, according to Julia. The scene of their arrival had all the makings of a pioneering romance—one wants only to add indomitable spirit, derring-do, and like cinematic virtues. But Julia Carpenter was miscast. She had no yen for the unexplored, she lacked humor, imagination, and stamina to transcend physical discomfort, and she was unwilling to travel light, to leave behind her past as well as luggage.

"I want to live East" meant Syracuse, her parents, two sisters and a brother (although the brother and one sister were to move to Aberdeen, South Dakota, only a night's train ride away). The East also meant an urban upper middle class way of living: calls, parties, good food, furniture, stylish clothing, and a mild climate. Julia was homesick for Syracuse as long as her parents were alive, and she did all she could to superimpose the Syracuse way of living on that of Dakota Territory, beginning with the croquet set she and Frank bought in Ellendale and played with outside the shanty door. She expressed deep resistance to virtually all the harsher aspects of the settlement experience—dirt, cold, heat, mosquitoes, exhaustion, inconvenience, loneliness, illness, all the deprivations of rural living—by going home whenever she could, and by accumulating luxuries and seeking out such nonrural pastimes as rollerskating, paying calls, and going to masquerade balls. Although the diary occasionally reports a ploughing or threshing, the land, scenery, plants and animals, and farming seldom capture her attention. She did not enjoy herself in the country. Her manner of writing confirms this alienation, for all she writes about homesteading is as from the outside, with journalistic detachment. She was in a foreign country.

In North Dakota Julia Carpenter mixed suburban habits with frontier exigencies, hardly ever adapting the one to the other with much comfort. The fine china, glassware, furnishings, and clothes she brought with her as wedding presents and that her family continued to send her for Christmas and birthdays fitted incongruously with the twelve-foot-square claim shanty home she describes. While Frank Carpenter was trying to plant, harvest, and maintain farm lands, she traveled a good deal: to Aberdeen, South Dakota, to see her brother and sister, and to Chicago and Syracuse to be with her other sister and her parents. When she was in Dakota those first years, she lived for weeks at a time in hotels or boarding houses while Frank and King, their hired man, did the farm work.

The diary is fullest during the first three or four years of her marriage and Dakota venture, between February 1882 and the autumn of 1885. Then her child, Harry, was born January 7, 1886; Magdalena on April 2, 1887; James on July 14, 1888, and the entries diminish. The earlier writings, however, occur often and in detail, and they emphasize how unsettled and roving, for her, homesteading and "settlement" turned out to be. Thus, after the wedding on February 9, 1882, it took about six weeks of visiting in the East before Julia and Frank Carpenter arrived in Casselton, North Dakota, (about seventy-five miles east of Jamestown and twenty miles west of Fargo) where they spent four weeks with the Dalrymple family, owners of a very large "bonanza" farm where Frank was later to be engaged as bookkeeper.[2] Then they boarded three weeks in Wheatland (five miles west of Casselton), and on June 1 traveled another seventy miles west to Jamestown by prairie schooner and stayed at the Dakota House, Frank by this time having picked the land he wanted. On June 15 Frank, King, and Julia traveled by farm wagon drawn by 4 mules to see the land, a trip south from Jamestown of about forty miles, and then another thirty miles farther south to Ellendale, where the men bought lumber to take back to the claim and start building the shanty, and Julia traveled by train to Aberdeen, South Dakota, where she boarded two weeks at the Park Plaza Hotel and visited her brother.

On June 30 Frank arrived by train to pick her up and they returned to Ellendale staying in a hotel, the next day going by wagon and mules with a load of lumber back to the claim shack. Julia remained there a month, boarded at Wheatland on August 2 for a month, then moved to the farm of Frank's brother Will to live until November 2, when she left for her parents' home in Fayetteville, a suburb of Syracuse, for the wedding of her sister Maud to L. Frank Baum (author of the *Wizard of Oz* books—the Baums later moved to Aberdeen and lived sometimes also in Chicago). Frank Carpenter joined her in Fayetteville for Thanksgiving and Christmas, and she returned to Casselton May 11, where both stayed until June 8 when they went again to the homestead claim. On July 15, 1883, Julia's mother and brother T.C. visited on the claim; on July 17 all went by wagon and mules to Jamestown where her mother and brother took a train to Bismarck (Matilda Gage may have been on a speaking tour, although Julia's diary does not say so). In August the Carpenters left the claim and moved again to Casselton and Frank went to work for S. C. Dalrymple as bookkeeper. On September 8, 1884, Julia left Casselton for Fayetteville again because her father was ill; he died on September 16 but she did not return to Casselton until February 7, 1885. Starting April 6, she boarded for three weeks in the town of Lamoure at the Windsor Hotel while Frank seeded for his brother Will, and on May 1 she moved to the claim again, now very near the townsite of St. George. On May 31 she went to Ellendale and by train to Aberdeen for T. C.'s wedding, returning to St. George on June 4 for the rest of the summer on the claim. On September 14 she left again, by way of Aberdeen, for Chicago to visit her sister Maud and to Syracuse on October 13. Her first child was born there on January 7, and she returned to Casselton July 9, 1886.

Subsequent years are much sketchier in the diary. She reports a trip to Aberdeen for Christmas 1887, her mother's death on March 18, 1898, and the move to Fargo September 14, 1901. The diary is peppered with names: names of towns barely starting at the time the Carpenters arrived: Ellendale, Grand Rapids, Wheatland, St. George, Yorktown, Lamoure; names of her husband's brothers, Will and Homer, who farmed in the region, and Emma, wife of one of them; names of her sisters' children, Bunting, Leslie, and Robin. Julia writes partly, one infers, especially in the earlier pages, to record events she thought were important; and, later, to reassure herself as she realizes the venture was much harder on her than ever she had supposed it would be.

There are a number of characteristics that mark Julia Carpenter's diary as a "book" and different from the productions of most diary writers. There are rather formal essaylike pieces with titles ("Pioneer Shanty," "My First Washing") and long entries about family calamities—the deaths of her father, her mother, her third child. There are lists: of wedding and Christmas presents, both given and received; of her children's teeth as they came in; of menus, funeral flowers, and, in the last pages, lists of her ancestors and family members. There are consistent omissions: husband, pregnancies and children, her mother's feminist politics. The mentions of Frank Carpenter are sketchy after the initial pioneer shanty adventuring, and there is even less written about her children, their interests and personalities. She often says that she is ill, but never mentions being pregnant, her three childbirths being announced without preliminaries. Her mother, Matilda Gage, active among the Syracuse suffragettes, was a contributing author to *History of Woman's Suffrage*, and she wrote *Women and the Church*. Julia listed the history among her wedding presents, and once wrote that her mother had gone to Washington "to attend WS Convention," but does not elaborate on Matilda Gage's professional life. It is hard to know what to make of these omissions, except to wonder whether, like the repeated cries of loneliness and the list-making, they originate in self-absorption and progressive despondency.

To an outside reader, a particularly attractive aspect of Julia Carpenter's diary is her objective reporting of miscellaneous facts that interest her; she has a good eye and writes as though she enjoys describing these curiosities. Writing is something she can do, even though she may not be adept at coping with the conditions she writes about. In fact, if it is difficult to keep track of the diary's sequence of events—all the comings and goings—her entries are clear and informative when read more thematically. During the few days of rushed packing in mid-August of 1883 when the Carpenters moved from the homestead to Casselton ("One day's notice to break up house-keeping is *rather* short"), Julia developed dysentery, their trip was delayed a day in starting, and they spent several more days in Grand Rapids.

In the evening we had the worst hail storm I ever saw. Hail as large as hen's eggs, one was measured 5½ inches in circumference. Frank brought one the size of a small egg to show me. In the hotel we were stopping at, 129 panes of glass were broken. The windows each had four large panes. The lower panes were protected by wire mosquito screen, the upper panes in our room were broken with a crash. The hail on the roof sounded like large stones being dumped out of a wagon. Fortunately there was no wind with this storm. The crops around were entirely ruined. Sunday morning not a spear of wheat could be seen. All was cut off and sent into the ground. After the storm we found poor little Snip clinging to the wires of the cage, frightened almost to death. (8–18–83)

(Poor Snip, whom they had brought in his cage from Syracuse, a wedding present from Julia's sister Maud, died on the next stage of the journey when he flew out of his cage and was caught in a wheel of the buckboard.) The description of the hail storm, written in the midst of a difficult journey and her illness, would need only minor revision for a wider audience. Frank had an attack of malarial fever in the midst of beginning his work for S. C. Dalrymple, and the remainder of the previous venture was just as unfortunate. She consistently refers to the homestead property by section number.

> When King and Homer came from 64–134–32 they dropped two mahogany chairs off from the wagon breaking one in splinters by running over it. Also dropped off the tea pot and ran over it. In a wheat sack we had a quantity of soiled clothes which they either lost or had stolen. (9–10–83)

A few days later the opportunity to describe the Northern Lights cheers her:

> Brilliant aurora borealis tonight. Could be seen in all parts of the sky: north, south, east, west and overhead. The color was mostly a bright green; in the north this green was bordered with a rose color. These lights were constantly changing and flickering. Frank is getting better. (9–16–83)

On cobwebs:

> Emma and I made a dozen calls this afternoon. It was so warm that we wore nothing around us. When riding today I saw more cobwebs than ever before and very heavy ones. If we got out of the wagon for five minutes they would form around the ship, across the seat &c. They were strung from the roofs of houses to piazzas and then to the ground and so on. Even in riding along one drove through many. Emma says in Wisconsin the people had a day they called "Cobweb Day." I think this must have been the same. (10–9–83)

On tramps:

> The town is filling up with laboring men and tramps. Fifteen hundred men looking for work. More asking for food at your door all times of day. We have had all of our wood sawed and chopped, yard cleared up, garden hoed, &c &c by these men for their board. We boarded one man, Pete, for two weeks and another, Frank, for two days this week. (8–nd–83)

On April 1, 1885, Julia Carpenter was packing again to return from Casselton to the claim, and again on the day of departure she fell ill—"awakened with a *terrible* sick headache. Was very sick all day"—but by the eighth they reached Lamoure where she spent three weeks in a hotel while Frank seeded for his brother Will. On Sunday the 26th: "reached St. George. . . . Everything looked so dirty and poverty stricken that I had a good crying spell." She had brought with her a six-month-old kitten: "She is my *greatest* comfort. I have named her Peter after the dear old Peter of *home days*," but on June 14: "Peter was eaten by Thomas Cat last night." The first week of May she had hail and frost to write about:

> Freezing cold. Milk froze in cupboard, water in the pails. Water froze by our bed side. We suffered with cold all day. I sat with my feet in the oven most of the day and bowed over the stove. Although we had a hot fire the storm was so cold that my breath came out like smoke as often seen out of doors on cold winter mornings. Such is the life in a Claim Shanty of the far west. (5–6–85)

She describes a particularly violent form of transportation:

> Coming home from Mrs. Campbell's I was thrown off from the "Go Bang," a sort of stone boat, some four inches high. We were sitting on chairs. Had two mules on the "Go Bang." It coming around a corner too fast was thrown off. Stretched out full length on the ground. (7–5–85)

A blizzard the winter of 1888:

> January 12: The blizzard of this date was a most disastrous storm. Some 200 or 300 lives lost. The storm raged from Manitoba to Texas, especially severe in Dakota, Nebraska, and Kansas. It was the only day during the winter so far that Frank did not water his stock. Many could not get to the barns to feed the stock, or died in the attempt. Frank could not see the house when only a few feet from it. Some think it the worst storm of the century, others think one about as severe occured fifteen years ago. The loss of life was greater in South Dakota than in other parts, as the morning there was bright and warm, the blizzard coming on suddenly. The greatest loss of life was men feeding their stock, teachers, and school children. There was a great deal of electricity in the air. Frank went to put up the draft in the stove when his fingers snapped and fire came from them. He tried this again and again putting first one finger and then another near the stove, always with the same effect. I did not try it. When Frank was out of the room there was still a snapping.

An entry like this one is more ambitious, more self-conscious than personal writing, meant only to record daily events for the satisfaction of the writer, needs to be.

Her most consistent writing comes in the early pages of the diary, when, presumably, Julia Carpenter's powers of observation were most strongly stimulated by shock. Just before setting out from Ellendale after her trip to Aberdeen, she and Frank spent the night in a hotel, which produces a concise description of frontier accommodations:

> The landlord showed us up stairs to a small room just large enough to contain two beds, one at the foot of the other. The foot bed contained a man, we were to occupy the other. The next room to ours was separated simply by studding, no lath, plaster or anything to shield us from the view of the man in that bed. So on through the house we could see the different occupants of the rooms. The windows in our room were broken, the door was minus. The landlord set the lamp on the floor (as there was no stand, chair, nothing but two beds). I asked him to take it down and we undressed in the dark, I simply taking off my dress and shoes and putting on my ulster. In the room the air was stifling. In the morning the man in the bed at the foot of ours and the one in the room adjoining seemed afraid to get up knowing a woman was so near. So I made the first move, slipping off my ulster and putting on my dress. There were no bathing arrangements in our room, each person washed in the office out of a tin wash dish, and *one* towel served for all. Soon after entering the dining room, a man, evidently the one who occupied the bed at the foot of ours, and who lay with his head covered with the bedding, entered the room. (7–1–82)

On the very muddy road between Ellendale and the claim they encountered mosquitoes.

> With all the pain I ever suffered, I never endured such agony as I did that night. The mosquitoes numbered millions. The coulies were full of them. I wore a broad brimmed hat with the lower part tucked in the ulster, but it seemed hardly the least protection. I was bitten over my whole body not only through my gloves but through three thicknesses, ulster, dress, and wrapper sleeves; the miserable insects even found a small hole in the side of my shoes. . . . But what I endured was nothing in comparison to what Frank went through, he having neither gloves, netting or any protection. Every few minutes he would jump out of the wagon, slapping the mosquitoes off from the mules, whose sides were so covered with them that their color could not have been told. . . . Could we have driven fast, the little breeze thus produced would have made away with some of them. . . . At last we reached our home. . . .

Frank had borrowed a tent, and as we entered it I sunk to the ground
in exhaustion and immediately fell into a heavy sleep. Tired as Frank
was he made a fire, boiled the tea kettle and steeped a strong cup of
tea. He awakened me and after drinking a cup of tea, I again sunk into
a heavy sleep, and there I lay until morning, with hat, dress, gloves &c
all on. (7–2–82)

For the first year or so Julia Carpenter wrote in this particularly
clear expository manner, when all was new, marriage as well as the
Territory, and everything foreign to what she had known. She had
much to tell. As the years went by there were fewer such explanatory
entries, more lists of presents and meals, brief notations of illnesses,
weather, crop seedings and harvests, trips. But not everything was
grim and alien. She also reported what sound like happy and peaceful moments, although they are rare. The one time she writes that
she actively participated in farm work out of doors was during the
months on the farm of Frank's brother Will.

We kept house and I was very happy. During harvest I had five men to
cook for including Frank. I quite overdid. After harvest we let King go
and Frank and I lived alone very happily. I used to plough nearly every
day with the Gang plough, while Frank did the scrubbing, chopped the
wood, did the barn work &c. (8–4–82)

Another pleasant interlude occurred on a trip back from Jamestown,
July 18, 1883.

Stayed overnight in a cabin barn without a floor, except that provided
by nature. The mules occupied two thirds of the barn, we the remaining third. I slept on the one blanket we had with us, and Frank on the
grass. He is always so wholly unselfish. The mosquitoes troubled us
somewhat at first, but a smudge soon made way with them. Oh how we
both longed for water, but the sloughs were all dry, and there were no
wells within 6 or 8 miles. I slept but little I was so thirsty.

However, more often, pleasant associations are mixed with grimmer
ones. Four days later, when the Carpenters were traveling to Ellendale with Julia's mother and brother who had been visiting, they
stopped for water at a shanty where one man had just shot another
for being "too intimate" with his wife. "He burst open a wire screen
window with an ax and shot Lynnes while in bed three times. The
man was just alive when we called there." A week later she is alone in
the house and the temperature is 93:

Snip has been moulting for a week. Buffalo birds have come in quantities in the last several weeks, also a few meadow larks. Buffalo birds are brown, and nearly the size of a robin. They are very tame, sometimes light on the mules backs and ears, occasionally come into the house. Mr. Lee, one of our neighbors, saw two antelope a mile or two from here last week. When King came from Lamoure he said Mr Lynne the man shot on the 22nd was at Grand Rapids doing well, would get along if inflamation did not set in. The man Oatenbarg who shot him was in the hands of the sheriff at the same place and his wife working there for some one. I am having a great deal of back ache.

This entry typifies, I think, Julia Carpenter's way of writing about her life and state of mind. She really is a good observer, and she appreciates what she sees, but so much of it is on the edge of violence and disaster, in this case the attempted murder and heat wave, that she treasured sights of antelope and trespassing buffalo birds. The backaches, the attacks of "La Grippe," sick headaches, and other ailments were almost always with her, but in between she did acknowledge more peaceable moments. Another came years later.

July 1898. Frank and Robert Baum [husband and son of her sister Maud in Aberdeen, Frank the author of the Wizard of Oz books] came early in July to spend the summer with us. During August we camped out in the hills where Frank was putting up hay. We slept in a tent and had a cook shanty on wheels for our kitchen. We also had two portable rooms and a portable bain.

I cannot help supposing, as I pass the skipped-over months of no record and read of punishingly detailed pains and deaths, that there was in Julia Carpenter's life a relentless sadness she could not shake off. She loved her husband and children, she had friends and supportive relatives nearby, and although they began frugally enough—"picked up about 500 lbs of buffalo bones. These bring $10 or $12 a ton at Ellendale. They are sent East and ground for fertilizer"—they seem not to have been uncomfortably poor. And yet she inevitably expected the worst, barely fending off collapse, anticipating exhaustion, the headaches and backaches the price of boredom and fright. Once, after recounting a masquerade party in Casselton, she wrote and underlined the phrase: "*To Remember What I Read. Discuss and talk with Frank. Think it over the last thing at night. Think of some one point and connect with some other*" (2–2–84). Books and ideas are not the subjects of her diary, yet one

wants to credit the descriptive flashes with her trying to connect one
difficult point with some other in her experience.

Even more than other upper middle class women, Julia Carpenter
expected to be protected, but she was never protected enough.
There was a thinner line of safety between herself and brutality than
was the case with, say, Johanna Kildahl or Fannie Quain. There were
difficulties enough for intellectual women like Fannie Quain and
Johanna Kildahl; nevertheless, their professional aspirations offered
them enough emotional protection not to be irrevocably discouraged
by the mud trickling inside sodtown walls. Julia Carpenter, however,
writes as though she expected someone else to cope, and her diary is
full of incongruous anecdotes: "When I came home yesterday the
mud was so bad that I got in to my ankles, lost off both my shoes,
ruined a nice pair of French kid shoes. Covered my hands &c. It
beats all how sticky the mud is" (4–7–84).

Except for repeating how lonely she is without him, or how disappointed that he has not returned when he promised to, Julia writes
no word of complaint about Frank Carpenter. But if there is no fault
finding, neither is there any reflection about him. What his aspirations might have been, whether his reported great solicitude for her
came from dismay at having brought her to this place, is hard to tell.
She appeared to know that she was a worry to him, and also possibly
an impediment, her unhappiness making necessary the successive
moves to Casselton and Fargo, away from farming to his eventual
career as a traveling insurance salesman.

When Julia did write about Frank, it was to say how hard he was
working, how solicitous he had been toward her, or how long he had
been away. *Her* trips to Syracuse and Aberdeen were for weeks and
months at a time; his, though frequent, of short distances for a few
days. Julia wrote as though the two of them were apart more often
than not; indeed, she made note of his presence. Certainly it was
Frank who coped with the daily vicissitudes. He did what he could to
fend off mosquitoes and protect her comforts on the trip out as we
have seen, and that was the pattern for the way they managed.
Though she did not say so, Julia was in her third month of pregnancy with her first child when she wrote this:

Frank commenced the 10th to put up hay for Sykes-Hughes farm. Has
put up hay for himself during the last two weeks. Dear Frank is so kind
to me. I have been extremely poorly all summer but that dear boy has
done his *own* work, *much* of mine and taken care of me all without a

murmur. It's after eleven and twelve o'clock before he gets to bed and then perhaps up with me in the night and up to work early in the morning again. *Dear* Husband. (7–21–85)

In November of their first year, Julia returned to Syracuse for the rest of the winter and spring: "I started for home, Fayetteville, NY, leaving Frank and Snip behind, little knowing when I would see them again," and she was not back in Casselton until the 11th of May. On the 8th of June when they went to the homestead: "Frank and I came through to 64–134–32 the same day reaching the shanty between 9 and 10 pm. Things looked pretty *blue* to me. The house was so *dirty* too." But two years later things were more in hand; when she returned from the east, homecoming was pleasant: "I reached Casselton 7th at 7 am, train being nearly three hours late. The house looked very cozy. Frank had swept the whole house, even the attic, scrubbed kitchen and cellar floors, blacked stoves, cleaned paint &c. He tried to make bread but scalded the yeast and bread would not rise" (2–5–85). A week later, "Frank did quite a large washing" (2–16–85), and the next week, "I ironed my first starched shirts and collars. Looked very fair" (2–27–85).

The tone of her writing about Frank is consistently kindly and solicitous (if sometimes condescending—"dear boy"): "Dear Husband's birthday" (8–2–85); "Commenced cutting our grain this pm. Poor husband works so hard. I fear he will overdo. Thermometer 100° at three pm in coolest place on north side" (8–15–85). She thought of him while she was in Syracuse at Thanksgiving, 1885: "My dear husband took his Thanksgiving dinner on a load of stone on the road. Poor boy." Julia mourned his absence when she was in Dakota and he was away from her, not when she was away, yet on one occasion she records that her being away left him unhappy, and she describes her return with more details than usual about the family, possibly with a twinge of guilt:

Harry, Magdalena and I went to Aberdeen to spend the holidays with dear Helen and family. T. C. met us on the train (12–21–87). . . . Children and I came home. Frank met us at Edgeley. He had been *terribly* lonely. We had a fearful ride home. No track. Horses walked every step (1–5–88). Frank went to town for my trunk. Stuck on road. Was obliged to leave wagon, trunk, and all on prairie all night (1–7–88). Frank and I did a big washing. Harry caught his right thumb in whirls at side of wringer, cutting into the root of the nail tearing nail out by the roots. (1–10–88)

Christmas and birthdays were important days for Julia Carpenter (not to overstate the case, the exhaustive lists she made of everyone's presents may well have partly been intended to help her remember whom to thank for what). "Rained all day. Nice birthday letter from dear Helen. Frank gave me $15 and a new kitchen stove and wrote me such a nice letter" (5–21–84). Frank's birthday bestirs her ingenuity as well as her affection.

> Frank's birthday. Harry gave him a dark colored cotton shirt. Magdalena gave him a tooth brush. Leslie gave him a bouquet and I made him a chocolate cake, decorating the same with natural flowers. (8–2–87)

> Frank's birthday. I had invited Mr. and Mrs. Campbell and Rev. and Mrs. Hobart to tea. For tea raised biscuits and butter, pressed turkey, cabbage salad, fresh whortle berries, chocolate cake, pink layer cake, grapes. In the evening we had fire works given the children by Helen when we came from Aberdeen. (8–2–89)

Christmasses were evidently events that required courage, heightening as they did the contrast between life in the East and life out West. The Carpenters' first Christmas together was celebrated in 1883, after nearly two years of marriage.

> Frank and I spent Christmas day alone. I stuffed and roasted my first turkey. For dinner we had roast turkey, potatoes, cranberry sauce, bread brown and white, cranberry pie, chocolate cake, candies, nuts, raisins and oranges. We spent the evening with Emma. It was a very stormy night. My presents were as follows. From Mother, a silver fox fur collar for cloak, a pair of brown kid gloves, a pair of grey silk mittens lined with wool, two skeins of Germantown, 2nd volume of National Woman Suffrage History; from Pa a lovely pair of soft kid shoes; from husband Frank a pair of high over shoes, a big turkey, a pail of honey, a box of sardines, a bag of oranges and chocolate drops. (12–25–83)

There are many other presents from her relatives, and one notes the contrast between the mostly luxurious gifts that her parents sent her and the practical ones from Frank. Christmas 1884 she was with her mother and sisters in Syracuse, following her father's death in mid-September. "I missed dear Pa" is about all she says, except for listing the presents. Christmas of 1885 also was in Syracuse; she returned in July after Harry's birth. In 1886 she was in Casselton and, except for listing presents, had little to say except that the weather was cold, "probably 50° below zero," and so was New Year's: "Frank, Harry and I took dinner alone. We were frightfully lonely." Christmas of 1887 she was with her mother, brother, and sister in Aberdeen. 1888's was a subdued Christmas because the third infant, Jamie, was ill (he died in March); the Carpenters missed the family gathering in Aberdeen, although her mother visited shortly after Christmas. 1889's was also a quiet day: "Our Christmas dinner we ate alone. Frank dressed a chicken and we had a bowl of Sophie's jelly. I sat up for the first time," having "taken sick" two weeks earlier. "Dear Mother came" on the 26th, the last time she speaks of being with her mother, and there are no more entries until the fall of 1897 and her mother's death, on March 18, 1898, in Chicago. The next Christmas Julia writes about is in 1900, their last before moving to Fargo where Frank went "to travel with the Deering people." "Oh we had so many fine presents this Christmas as we always do, but I always miss dear Mother's presents." Her brother and sisters sent "French flannel for waist with gold braid for trimming, hook and eyes, linings silk &c, two fine wool underwrappers," a tablecloth, kid gloves, jewelry. "From Frank C. box of honey, broom."

The move to Fargo came in mid-September: "Settled at 409 7th Avenue North. I am so terribly lonely that I am sick. Frank is at Lidgerwood, ND. Children entered High School." Her sister Helen came from Aberdeen to spend the winter with her. "Frank came home Xmas eve. from Lidgerwood. We all had many presents." For Julia finery from relatives: a "new black silk waist, all made," black satin hair bow, golf gloves; and from Frank "$20, turkey." The next year was similar, though without Helen.

> Christmas 1902. Magdalena is spending her vacation in Aberdeen. Frank came home Wednesday eve night before Christmas. I was sick in bed all the week with La Grippe. My presents were: from Maud lovely Morris chair, ring formerly Mother's, bolt of battenberg braid, pretty collar, candy. . . . from Frank $5.00 and two pair drawers. . . . Papa from Mama and children, solid oak rocker, three neck ties, three pair socks, suspenders, box tooth picks.

1903 sounds more prosperous: "Julia from Frank, fifteen yards of silk, dark blue, for dress. Bedroom set for wash stand, 12 pieces." But Frank was "out on insurance business" New Year's day, and there the diary ends.

For all her saying that she was "desperately lonely" on the claim, and in Edgeley, Casselton, and Fargo during Frank's absences, Julia also wrote of being lonely when he was there if there was no one else as well, at least after the first year or two. Only when she was in the company of her mother and sisters did she record no complaints; even her illnesses seem fewer. Her writing about these women is more emotionally colored than her writing about any other subject, including her own children. She is also cheered by Emma Carpenter, wife of one of Frank's brothers. The two sometimes spent the night together when Frank was away, and they made calls, once twenty-one in a single day. Repeatedly, Julia's well-being improved in the company of these women, and declined when there were only men with her.

> We still cook, eat, sit and sleep in the one room. King is at work making a lean-to addition. I am so weak every day that I hardly feel able to do anything. When in Casselton, Emma and I had a foot race, I coming out ahead (7–11–83)

> Quite warm and pleasant. I am not feeling very well. For birthday presents, from Mother $1, from Helen two handkerchiefs, from T.C. ticket from Ellendale to Aberdeen and return [to attend his wedding the following week]; from Frank, a pair of French kid shoes, apples and maple sugar. We have but one room in this shanty, oh it is so trying living here. (5–21–85)

Julia worried particularly about her sister Maud, whose wedding she went home for in November 1882, nine months after her own. A year later: "Received telegram from brother Frank Baum saying 'It's a nine lb. boy, all doing well.' I was terribly frightened, could scarcely open the envelope fearing it was unfavorable news from Maud. I heard afterwards that the baby came at 20 minutes of one, December 4" (12–4–83). Julia visited Maud in Chicago after her trip home for their father's death in 1884: "found her sick in bed. I stayed two weeks taking care of her and baby" (11–22–84). In 1886 Julia returned to Dakota with her own first baby: "Have been home a month today, and am almost crazy with homesickness. . . . Poor Harry, poor Mama. Dear dear Maud has been sick in bed over six months. Poor, poor child. I am almost wild over her, over baby, darling sister. Poor little Robin took all her strength" (8–9–86). And later: "Dear Maudie came from the sanitarium much improved. For several weeks was around the house although very lame. During the first of November I received a letter saying she was again in bed utterly discouraged with an abcess in her side" (nd 1886). Maud's

sufferings were similar to her own: "Am better this morning though
still in bed. Haven't the least appetite. Mrs. Seeler and Mrs.
Campbell have been extremely kind but oh how I miss mother. I am
so low spirited that life seems unendurable. I long to live near my
only people" (7–13–85). When the Aberdeen contingent had left
after a long autumn visit, she wrote again, "I am frantically lonely"
(10–14–87). She uses the last eight pages of her diary to copy letters
from Maud written during the winter of 1904 when she and Frank
Baum were traveling in the southwest. From her writing, it would
seem that Julia worried about Maud, considered Maud's plight at
least as precarious as her own, and also cherished her as the surest
hedge against loneliness.

Much of Julia Carpenter's diary gives the impression of information, but we read by inference, for there are few declarative statements. Julia does not explain how she came to be persuaded to the
Dakota venture in the first place. Her own and Frank's grandmothers were cousins, and there is one elusive reference, as her
father was dying, to family interests in Dakota: "A letter came from
T. C. sending a sample of wheat from Pa's farm. Mother said he did
not even look, take it into his hand, although he had always been so
much interested in Dakota" (9–2–84). It is even difficult to tell how
well the Edgeley homestead prospered. The diary records children's
births, teethings, their going to high school and summer visits to
Helen and Maud, but not a word about what Harry and Magdalena
were like. There is a single entry about Magdalena at age ten,
without comment or interpretation:

> During the night of October 13, Magdalena awakened me in the night
> by coming down stairs and speaking to me saying, 'Mamma I am afraid.
> I was awake in the night and saw someone standing in the door,
> dressed in white, looked like a night dress.' She at first thought it was
> Harry although it seemed taller. She hollered to me and jumped out of
> bed, lighted a match and when she looked again it was gone. She saw it
> twice before getting out of bed. It seemed to be coming toward her.
> (10–13–97)

It would be interesting to know whether the apparition became, in
Julia's mind, connected to her own mother's death the following
March.

There are two notations on churchgoing, and two on visits from
clergymen, but virtually no reflections on religion. Pasted to the

inside front cover of the volume is a newspaper photograph of Mary Baker Eddy's house in Syracuse, but there is not a single reference to Christian Science. Not even family burials reveal much more than conventional piety and sentimentality. The funerals of her father and of his mother three weeks later took place at their homes: "At the grave we children carried two large baskets of flowers and strewed them in the grave on the coffin" (9–19–84). Her mother's funeral was held in the parlor of Maud's house in Chicago, where Mrs. Gage had been visiting, and her body was cremated. The funeral of Jamie Carpenter was conducted by a Presbyterian minister named Mr. Langue and the eight-month-old buried "in the yard north of the house." "We had a little dark coffin with silver mountings and a silver plate which said 'Suffer little children to come unto me.'" What Julia Carpenter's church allegiances were, or how strong they were, is difficult to conjecture from her writing in the diary.

The diary stands as a rather graphic illustration of Ann Douglas's observation concerning the alliance between women and Protestant clergymen in nineteenth-century America: if women were not allowed to express themselves on the subject of sexuality, they were permitted to do so about death.

> Barred by external taboos and internal anxieties from elaboration on the overtly sexual acts of impregnation and childbirth, women and ministers concentrated on illness and death: they were more interested in the moments at which crude energy failed than in those at which it accelerated. . . . The tombstone is the sacred emblem in the cult of the overlooked.[3]

Julia Carpenter lavished on the three deaths nearest to her an all but morbid preoccupation, with ugly details that her writing otherwise lacks. For instance, for all the close documentation of furnishings and construction of the claim shanty, she had nothing to say about sanitation—outhouse or garbage—yet when her mother died, she reported (at second hand because she was not there): "Maud was awakened out of a sound sleep by a fall in the bath room. She jumped out of bed and ran, finding mother lying on the bathroom floor and Maud knew immediately Mother was paralyzed. Mother had evidently been taking an injection. . . . They were obliged to change Mother's night dress" (3–18–98). This goes farther, it seems to me, than the "concentration" Ann Douglas speaks of among women and clergymen on illness and death. Julia wrote many times about Frank's asthma, her own headaches, "stomach attack," dysentery, bowel complaints, but nowhere else mentions an enema. When it comes to the laying out of the body and the funeral itself, Julia's writing is probably more in keeping with the funerary style Douglas describes:

> When I first saw Mother she lay under a little canopy of white. Later the undertakers came and laid Mother on a black leather couch. She was dressed in a dark blue tea gown, a pattern dress. This was a favorite dress of Mother, one that I had helped give her one Christmas. We sat in her room the most of the time. The funeral took place Monday afternoon, the undertakers laying her in the casket in the parlor. The casket and room were filled with flowers. She lay in a *bed of flowers.*

Henry Gage died on September 16, 1884, at the age of 66, and Julia dwelt almost punishingly on very distressing details, some told to her, some observed. Her father evidently suffered a paralytic stroke the first of the month and was being cared for by Mrs. Gage, Helen, and Maud.

> In the morning Mother was in Pa's bedroom talking with him while Helen was sweeping the sitting room. Mother went out of the room, Pa was still in bed, was gone not to exceed ten minutes, if five. In the meantime Helen going on with sweeping. When Mother returned, she found Pa laughing wildly. He laughed so long and loud that it was sympathetic. When Mother returned she spoke to Pa, he did not reply. She spoke again and again with no answer. Then Helen went in to see what it meant, then Pa commenced to cry, then to laugh. She realized he had become paralyzed and was becoming hysterical. (9–4–84)

Her writing also stretched out his last moments:

> Pa ate some Delaware grapes, about the last thing before passing into an unconscious state. All that day we looked for his death. His breathing was horrible. To labor to try to breath like him would tire one out in less than half a minute. His cheeks would puff in and out, his lips make dreadful noise, his head shake with the hard breathing. Then all of a sudden all would be quiet, he seemed to have stopped breathing, we would think all was over then this struggle would recommence. . . . It was a fearful night. The wind blew through the trees, the night was dark and no passing in the street as usual. . . . After he had entirely stopped breathing, his right hand slowly raised and laid on his breast. . . . The pain in his head was discovered by his putting his left hand to his head while there was strength. (9–16–84)

After such a watch, the lighter sentimentality about the funeral reads in a different key: "Dear Pa was laid in his last resting place. It was a bright, beautiful day, warm." There were masses of flowers and kind neighbors, "all showing love for our dear, dear father. May we all meet him again." His children strewed flowers on the grave. "How I miss Pa in our little western home where he always longed so to come." That was not how she spoke of the shanty when she was in Dakota.

The dying of the Carpenter's third child, Jamie, in his eighth month, also ended, mercifully, on a bed of flowers: Julia made a list of them after eight torturous pages on his sickness. It is difficult to tell just what went wrong. She was persuaded not to nurse him and never found satisfactory substitute nourishment, although when he was for a few weeks given to a wet nurse he improved. His birth had not been auspicious, though Helen had come with her from Aberdeen; only she, Frank, and a hired girl attended the birth; a nurse arrived later, but there is no mention of a doctor. "I was only hard sick about 1½ hours, but torn all to pieces" (7–14–88). Every so often the baby had terrible attacks of "bowel complaint": "The baby lay perfectly lifeless, hands and arms stretched out, palms turned up, chin dropped, eyes half opened and every sign of approaching death." He did not die that time, but no food they tried worked, so Julia took all the children to Aberdeen: "We were gone nearly two months. I had a *very* hard time, all the children sick nearly all the time I was there." Times got progressively harder until the eleventh of March. Her guilt and fear, bafflement and exhaustion, her longing to believe that she could not possibly have done to him any wilful harm, all the while trying to keep a rhythm to the rest of the household, all these nuances weave among her nearly total recall of what happened at Jamie's end, as though she chiefly had her own words to make him exist at all. Her words will not let go. I want to include her final four pages.

Monday evening he seemed unusually wakeful but I thought it owing to Mr. and Mrs. Campbell coming in to spend the evening with us. I usually kept it very still evenings sitting by his side, rocking him when necessary. He was extremely wakeful or restless evenings, seemed to settle down somewhat after all were in bed. This Monday evening we fed him at six o'clock and not again until twelve as the MD had given strict orders that baby should have very little or nothing to eat nights. After 12 he had a pretty good night. He had seemed so comfortable both Monday and Tuesday that I had dessert for dinner (an uncommon thing during Jamie's illness), and on Tuesday I made a loaf of bread. Between four and six o'clock Tuesday afternoon he took a bit of red calico and looked at it, took several different spools of thread and tasted of them, held his rattle for awhile &c. I did not see the least sign of his being worse.

Tuesday evening he was very restless again but I thought him restless from Harry and Magdalena being up until after nine o'clock. They usually went to bed at seven, and Jamie would not rest while they were up. He was fed at six o'clock then went to sleep on my shoulder after being undressed. He did not worry much when undressed and was quite good during his bath in the morning. Although both this morning and the previous morning I had noticed his arms were especially cold. About 12 o'clock Frank came in from the kitchen. Jamie would worry if I stopped rocking him a minute as I had not yet made my cot (I slept on a cot in the sitting room with Jamie in his cradle). About 12 o'clock I had fed him and when I got into my cot, looked at Jamie boy, he had his food, his eyes were open and his bottle still in his mouth. He was perfectly quiet and did not worry to be rocked as he often did. I went right off to sleep supposing of course that my darling was going off to sleep all night, but whether he did or not I never knew. He usually awakened somewhere between two and four o'clock waking me immediately.

This night I slept from 12 until 6 AM when I was awakened by him. He seemed to breathe funny yet I warmed his dinner and gave him but he did not take it although I had thought he took the wine. He kept gasping. I ran into the bed room and told Frank that Jamie was dying yet I had so little thought that he was that I covered up Harry. Frank and I ran into the sitting room. Jamie was still gasping, I took him in my arms calling Jamie, Jamie, he did not look at me, but his eye gradually closed, he gasped a few times and was *dead, my* baby, *my* darling, *my* boy Jamie all without a moments warning. When Frank got up we had given him a second dose of wine which we thought he swallowed but later so much came from his mouth that he could not have swallowed it and he was too far gone. We sent for Mrs. F. Campbell, she came very soon. We put Jamie in a warm bath, rubbed some brandy on him, but my boy was gone beyond help. Mrs. Campbell laid him out for some time one side of him was warm. He never stiffened, was as limber when buried as in life. I put his dear precious body into the coffin. We had a little dark coffin with silver mountings and a silver plate which said "Suffer little children to come unto me." The coffin was lined with white. Jamie my boy wore a little linen shirt, a flannel pinned over his sheet as in life, a flannel band, flannel waist and skirt, two large diapers, red woolen stockings, a fine white dress (one of Harry's first long dresses made by Maud) made with a number of fine tucks with fine embroidery on the bottom, the yoke of fine embroidery and [line unreadable].

Mr. F & E Campbell brought vines and flowers. Helen and Mother also brought flowers from Aberdeen. His head was turned a little on his right side. He looked very sweet and peaceful but oh so poor and thin. The vines were Ivy (English), Kenilworth Ivy, Variegated Wandering Jew and Smilax with Rose Geranium leaves and Geranium leaves with white edges. The flowers were Oxalis, Jimson, Geranium, Nicotiana (resembles white petunias) and sweet Alyssum Royal Geranium. Mother and Helen came from Aberdeen on Thursday. The funeral was to have been at 4 PM but owing to the NP train being late we postponed until 5:30 thinking Will might come. His grave was lined entirely with white cloth. He was buried in the yard north of the house. Mr. Langue the Presbyterian minister conducted the services. The song sung was "Gone to the grave is our Loved One." The Bearers were Charles Hull, Charles West, F. F. Woolly and Marshall Sanderson.

Jamie had blue eyes, darker than Harry's lighter than Magdalena's a round nose. He had pretty features and would have made a pretty baby. His hair was about the color of mine, medium shade of brown. Sunday March 10th one upper molar came through. He was a very patient baby, wonderfully so for one that suffered so. Besides the terrible stomach trouble he had chronic catarrh of the bowels, and a rupture.

Died. James Lucien Carpenter, March 13th, 1889, aged 8 months. Youngest child of James D. and Julia L. Gage Carpenter. Edgeley, Lamoure County, North Dakota.

What went wrong? How did the American dream elude her, and the "little western home" turn into a prison of dirt and sadness? After the first year or so, Julia Carpenter almost never wrote of looking forward to anything, or imagining any other life for herself than living "East." Neither better houses nor increased sociability made her any less "frantically lonely." Only during the first months of her marriage did she write about being happy to be with Frank and no one else, when her living conditions were crowded and not much better than camping. And the work she performed in the fields that October, while Frank "scrubbed" and did the barn chores, was the only field work she ever mentioned doing. Her happiness that time, I strongly suspect, was connected to her participation in the major work of the farm. Had she kept that up, she might have had more hope for herself, she might have discovered a way to live peaceably in North Dakota, a citizen and not an exile. As it was, her unhappiness was chronic and nearly disease-making, for which I think there is an applicable term in public health nursing: *failure to thrive*. There was no "cause" whose removal would cure her, she was unable to live well.

Julia's account of herself in the diary, and I read it as that, not an inclusive autobiography, makes me wonder how widespread was her frantic loneliness, the more so as she did not appear to consider herself out of the ordinary. She did not pick out other, happier, women to compare herself to. She says very little, in fact, of other women she knows, which makes me think she thought they and she were much alike. Julia had everything a woman is supposed to: loving husband and family, including some moderately distinguished members, whom she loved in return; friends; interesting times to be living in; and eventually relative prosperity. But she did not find room for herself. She waited in hotel rooms during harvests and plantings, she waited out the winter months in Syracuse and Aberdeen, and she waited nights through for Frank to come home. It was not so much that the cold and primitive living were too much for her, or that the first several years were economically difficult, though these were so, as that Julia failed to discover an active contribution she might make. She failed to thrive. "Poor Harry, poor Mama." But Harry married Philadelphia Shapiro, the daughter of a judge, became president of an investment company in Fargo, moved to New York City in 1935, and died at the age of 74, by all accounts a wealthy and successful man. Frank Carpenter died in 1920, and Julia joined the household of her daughter Magdalena, who had married Albert Birch. Julia Carpenter died in 1931.

Emma Mott, "Lady Instructor"

There are virtually no examples during the settlement period in North Dakota of women who entered professional and public life and continued these careers until retirement age, this in spite of the fact that the decades at the turn of the twentieth century were rather promising for women's education, years that saw the founding of women's colleges and increasing admittance of women at universities. Various North Dakota women, as we have seen, took advantage of these opportunities in education: Fannie Dunn Quain, born in Bismarck, attended normal school in St. Cloud, Minnesota, and graduated in 1898 with an M.D. from the University of Michigan; Elsie Hadley White, born in Indiana, earned an A.B. at Earlham College and was the first woman to earn an M.A. in mathematics at the University of Michigan. But their careers came to an early stop, Fannie Quain's when her children were born, after several years'

practice in eye and ear in Bismarck, and Elsie White's after a single
year teaching mathematics at Valley City College when she married
Frank White who in 1901 was elected governor. A few women began
careers in North Dakota and continued them elsewhere, like Cora
Smith of Grand Forks, who returned after medical school to practice
a few years, then moved to Seattle. It is difficult to explain why
women who spent their adult lives in North Dakota consistently did
not practice their professions. Whether they were professional
women who came to the region already qualified, or grew up here
and were educated in the state and elsewhere, appears not to have
made any difference. In either case, North Dakota in its early history
resisted including them in public life.

It may be suggestive to examine the life of one woman with
professional training: Emma Mott.* Very little information about
her survived. Four volumes of her husband's diaries were the only
papers saved when her house in Grafton burned. These and reports
of her in records of the University of North Dakota where she
taught in its first year, a WPA Historical Data Project interview a
year before she died, and the recollections of her grandson, Henry
Mott of Fargo, are all one has available to recover her very interesting life.[4] Henry Mott remembers her as strong, healthy, and
domineering: she "had her ideas, and that's how things were" (1–
22–1979). Active in WCTU, Emma Mott with her husband broke up
all twenty-seven saloons in Grafton, after which she carried their
keys at her belt. One senses the mettle of the woman in a letter she
wrote to the parents of a student in her charge.

February 23, 1885

Ms. E. A. Thorp,

Yours at hand. I am very glad Nellie has told you. This I wanted to do
long ago but she feared the effect on her mamma and promised to deal
justly with me. This she has by no means done. I feel now that the true
turning point in her character has come and if rightly dealt with she
may be broken of a fault which otherwise may bring you untold trouble
and disgrace. I do not know how much she may have told you but the
thefts to which she has owned and the articles returned are many. That
this is not the beginning of this fault possibly you know. The shock to
me was very great. You know I had unlimited confidence in her or I

---

*Portions of this section have appeared, in a slightly different form, in *Plainswoman*,
vol IV, no. 5 (September 1981).

would never have offered to assist her through the University or left
the key to my room in her possession. She dashed it all away with her
own hand and free will. I have been *poorly paid*. Now as I said before if
rightly handled you may yet save her, but she *must be made to see* the
enormity of her fault and its *probable consequences* if she does not correct
it. To condone it *now* without attaching some penality is to ruin her.
The way in which *she calls on God to witness her innocence* and then have
to own and restore property is of itself *shocking*. To stir it publicly is
only to brand her among thousands who otherwise would never know
anything about it. It has all died out here now and a revival of it is not
to be desired but, that I leave with you tho I would rather help Nellie
up than *down*. *Nellie was dearer to me than any pupil I ever had*, and I
sincerely hope that *being so young* she may outlive this *grievous fault*.

Sincerely yours,
E. S. Mott

Before establishing herself in Grafton, Emma Mott had had a varied
career. She was born January 7, 1849, in Branchville, New Jersey.
Her father, Henry Schoenmacher, of German descent, was a lawyer
by profession; her mother, Drucilla Price, was of Scottish ancestry.
Emma began teaching school at age 15 in Pennsylvania (New Jersey
having refused to consider her because she was too young to certify),
and over the years alternately earned money by teaching and took
college courses. She studied at the normal school in Trenton, the
Collegiate Institute at Newton, New Jersey, at the Philadelphia Conservatory of Elocution and Oratory, and at Bryant and Stratton
Business College. Music was a part of her professional life as well.
She played the organ in Chicago, sang an oratorio in New York City
(under the direction of Leopold Damrosch at the time she was on
her wedding trip), and she taught music in Grafton. In 1873 she
traveled to Oklahoma to visit a cousin, writing up an account of her
journey.

Emma Mott was in her mid-thirties by the time she ventured to
North Dakota. Accounts of this journey vary. Henry Mott thinks his
grandmother traveled by steamer to Minto, homesteaded a half
section, spent a year by herself in a sod shanty, started the first
school in Minto, and only married shortly before beginning to teach
at the university in Grand Forks in the fall of 1884. Henry Mott's
mother, the wife of Emma's only son, Valentine, wrote a slightly
different version of her life in an article published in the *Walsh
County Record* on July 25, 1940. Mrs. Valentine Mott was interviewed

in behalf of Emma Mott for the Historical Data Project by Ban-
jamine Rinde on August 19, 1940, who gave reasons for relying on
her and on her article: "Mrs. Mott is 93 years old [actually she was
91] and her memory is blank on most things."

His field worker's form gives some interesting details. It reports
Emma Mott as coming with her husband in 1882 from Cortland,
Ohio, traveling by steamboat to Duluth, and from there to Grafton
by rail, bringing with them "some furniture, chickens, and books."
The Motts resided in Grafton from the beginning: "Mrs. Mott filed
on a farm south of Edinburg but did not comply with the requirements for proving up, another wanted it, fired a bullet through
house and they had to leave it." The report cites her as teacher of
the first school in Grafton in 1882 at a salary of $40. She "brought
own" textbooks, taught seventy pupils in a building 50 by 30 feet
with six windows and two doors, and was supplied with desks but no
blackboard. The schoolhouse later served as city warehouse.

Emma Mott's husband was Henry Harrison Mott, born in
Courtland, Ohio, in 1852 (and three years younger than she). He
died in 1909, age 56. His parents' families were English. His father,
Valentine Mott, was a lawyer, and his mother, Lucinda Carbore, a
teacher. Henry Mott started out as a lawyer also, but, few being
needed in Grafton, he found it more profitable to become a surveyor (a profession continued by his son and grandson), and was
responsible for constructing field drains in Walsh and Pembina
Counties. He also kept weather reports for the Grafton newspaper.
He was first cousin to the suffrage leader Lucretia Mott, a connection that may be reflected in an astonishing entry in his journal:

> March 15, 1906. Equality before the law. I lived too early to see it. One
> half of the race disfranchised, and we call ourselves enlightened. Bah!
> We are half barbarians yet. The right to say who and what shall govern
> our lives resting on no other foundation than the form of the procrea-
> tive organs. I am heartily ashamed and humiliated to be thus forced to
> be classed among the usurpers.

It is of course difficult to reconstruct in an accurate and fair
manner someone's life at two removes, yet it seems safe to assume
that Emma Mott's was a strong personality. She was alone as well as
economically independent between the ages of sixteen and thirty-
four, and even when full-time teaching tapered off into private
music lessons, church, and WCTU work after her son was born in

1890, she behaved independently. Henry Mott's diary suggests that she considered some income to be her own, for he speaks of exchanging small loans with her. Before marrying she had established herself in two professions, music and teaching, and had lived in several locations: Philadelphia, Chicago, and at two colleges she mentions, Ripon in Wisconsin, and Oberlin in Ohio. Her undertaking university teaching indicates a certain forbearance on the part of both herself and Henry Mott, for she lived in rooms on campus, Grafton being forty miles from Grand Forks. That the venture turned out to be a disaster can be partly attributed to the new institution's inability to endure her strongmindedness.

The University of North Dakota opened in the autumn of 1884 in an unfinished four-story brick building, with not a tree or shrub in sight. Broadway (now University Avenue) was a plowed strip to Grand Forks a mile away, but most people walked along the railroad track, and classes did not begin until early afternoon to give them time to get there. Drinking water came in barrels from Grand Forks, and sewage was emptied into the coulee. The cistern leaked, and there was inadequate heating and a desperate need for a plank walk to the railroad flag stop. As for students, none of the seventy-nine enrolled during 1884–85 actually took college courses. Ten were in the senior preparatory class (fourth-year high school level), eighteen in the junior preparatory, and the fifty-one not up to high school work were in the "sub-preparatory" class. About twenty-six students completed the year; none came from more than fifty miles away and none had been born in North Dakota.[5]

It is truly amazing that a university should have been imagined, let alone built, in such unlikely circumstances, but 1883 was a boom year in Grand Forks and there was apprehension that all patronage would go to the southern part of the territory if the north did not act quickly. Even more critical than the problems of difficult physical conditions and undereducated and scanty student body was the founders' ambivalence about educational objectives. Though a Normal department was soon established to provide teachers for elementary and high schools, every effort was made to model the school upon the classical curriculum and architecture of New England colleges, even though many of them by the 1880s were favoring science and applied subjects over Greek and Latin. Webster Merrifield when he became president decreed that a row of Russian olive trees be planted along the coulee (a natural drainage ditch) in imitation of the "Scholars' Walk" at Yale. But early detractors of the university protested that the curriculum did not reflect the region's agricultural society, and were angered when some students admitted that escaping work on the family farm was their sole motive for attending.

There were clashes of temperament as well as of vision, and many of the difficulties of that first year came to melodramatic crisis about the person of Emma Mott, who resigned from the teaching staff in mid-May and summarily left. The minutes of the Board of Regents record as early as February 17: "Resignation of Mrs. Mott presented. No action taken," but drastic action was taken at the Board's meeting of May 12 when it was "Moved that the Secretary be instructed to notify Mrs. Mott that her services will not be required the coming year, present term to close with the school year." Here is her replying letter of May 18 as it was copied into the Board minutes of June 15, 1885.

To the Board of Regents, UND, Grand Forks, Dakota Territory. Gentlemen: I return the enclosed notice to you as an "estray." It has been long known to a majority of the Board of Regents and to the public that I have remained here contrary to my own desires in the matter for months, even before I sent in my resignation, and also that nothing could induce me to be a candidate for further University honors. You refused to accept my resignation tendered to you, and then sent to me a notice of preparation of which you know is but a waste of Territorial time, talent and money. Under the circumstances I can construe this movement into nothing less than intended insult and harm to me, and since another resignation might not ensure my present release from the general melee, I act for myself in declaring my position as "Lady Supervisor and Instructor" vacant from this date, May 18th, 1885. Yours truly, E. S. Mott. Allow me to propound one question, viz:

if, in the light of your recent by-laws the term of office of the instructors in the University terminate with one year, by what authority or rule of diplomacy do you presume to draw a boundary line for that which never has been and never will be subject to your disposal, my future time. E. S. Mott.

(About the *estray* she was correct if not complimentary: it is a term in law for a stray domestic animal.)

How did matters come to such a pass? Emma Mott was not the only casualty that first year—the president and the janitor lost their jobs as well—but the irritations she stirred up called attention to fundamental anomalies, among them the delusion that another Yale could be founded upon the plains. And this ideal envisioned a male institution. Although women students were admitted from the beginning—in fact five of the first seven graduates were women—the board of regents were all men, and all faculty applicants were men. (As to students, it is likely that families who could afford to preferred to send their sons away to college, and considered the local university good enough for the daughters.) Among the three appointed to the faculty by the Board at its meeting of July 2, 1884 was the Reverend William Maxwell Blackburn, president. A graduate in 1850 of Hanover College and former pastor of the Central Presbyterian Church in Cincinnati, Blackburn had been professor of biblical and ecclesiastical history at the Presbyterian Theological Seminary of the Northwest, and in 1879 had published *The History of the Christian Church from Its Origin to the Present Time*. He had a wife and two daughters.

The second appointment went to Henry Montgomery (A.B. University College, Toronto, B.Sc. Victoria College) to be Vice President and professor of natural science. Montgomery helped in the planning of the building and argued strongly but futilely against boarding students. He wanted to be president, but was turned down, though during the two following years, he served as acting president. Hired as professor of Greek and Latin languages and literature was Webster Merrifield, who was also to teach algebra and geometry. Merrifield had visited Grand Forks in the summer of 1879, having taken the train as far as Fargo and walked the rest of the way. He was 34 years old, A.B. Yale 1878, had taught at a boys' school in New York State and tutored Greek and Latin at Yale for four years, before resigning because of ill health. Blackburn's salary was $2,500, Montgomery's $2,000, and Merrifield's $1,500. In addition, the Board budgeted $1000 for a "lady instructor" and $60 a month for a janitor. And, at its meeting of July 10, the Board accepted the recommendation of President-elect Blackburn for "the employment of Mrs. E. S. Mott of Grafton as an Instructor who should also have oversight of the young ladies of the University as an advisor." She was not considered to have faculty status and attended meetings only by invitation of the men.

As we have seen, there were no students ready for Caesar and Xenophon, Merrifield's specialties. By far the largest enrollment was in what was euphemistically named the "sub-junior preparatory class," under the direction of Mrs. Mott, and this was the program that gave the most trouble. As early as mid-September the faculty was meeting "in full" (a way of saying that Mrs. Mott was also present) in order to discuss ways to lighten her load and, presumably, give the men something to teach. The president took the "B" class in English grammar. But Mrs. Mott's sub-junior preparatory class was still so large that she was assigned a part-time assistant, Cora Smith, then a senior at Grand Forks High School. (Cora Smith became one of the five women in the university's first graduating class of 1890, the same year in which she also taught girls' calisthenics. She then took a degree in medicine in Boston University and returned to Grand Forks in 1893, setting up a medical practice, but continued to teach women's physical education—calisthenics, drill, and marching. In 1895, a year in which there were insufficient state funds to pay faculty salaries, Cora Smith staged a student entertainment at the Metropolitan Theater in order to raise money to keep the university open. She subsequently lived in Seattle and Los Angeles, where she continued to practice medicine and became prominent in the suffrage movement.)

Clearly Mrs. Mott was swamped with work, and yet, in the midst of trying to cope with an entire non-college student body, the faculty was "given notice" by President Blackburn "of his intention, at an early meeting, to move the adoption of courses of study in the following subjects: History, mental and moral philosophy, natural theology and evidences of Christianity, Logic, Civil Policy and Political Economy." That was on September 26. Four days later, with "Mr. Blackburn in the chair" and Mrs. Mott again in attendance, the faculty met to request that she make "a special and brief" report about her department, "omitting wants and recommendations." Montgomery and Merrifield were assigned as a committee to reorganize the sub-junior preparatory class. It would appear that by late September Emma Mott was doing most of the teaching and was having taken away from her what little authority might accrue in the classroom.

The next mention of Mrs. Mott in minute books was in February when the Board received, but did not act upon, her initial resignation. On the 18th the Board met to "investigate certain reported clashing of authority of the Faculty and Mrs. Mott," and she was asked to be present. The minutes continue:

On motion the Board listened to President Blackburn who among other things charged Mrs. Mott with being a tale bearer and not using

proper discretion in case of misdemeanors of the students and advised
the Board that Mrs. Mott be dismissed from the corps of teachers but
not establishing the facts after which Mrs. Mott who denied the charges
was heard.

Some of the clashing of authority was aggravated by the housing
arrangements, whereby the Blackburn family and Mrs. Mott had
quarters on the first floor of the university building, Mrs. Mott
having assigned to her, according to Board minutes of September 3,
the large bedroom facing the hall, a study, and classrooms on the
northwest side. In his history of the University of North Dakota,
Louis Geiger writes that, according to Blackburn, "she deliberately
and regularly began eating while he was asking the blessing. Her
heated retort that the food was equally poor before or after the
blessing hardly illuminated the enquiry." Be that as it may, when the
Board reconvened their February 18 meeting at three in the afternoon, they "moved and carried that the family of Dr. Blackburn
occupy a separate dining-room and that his daughters be requested
not to mingle with the students except in the parlor in the same
manner as visitors."

Whatever easing of domestic tensions may have resulted from
separate dining arrangements, clashes continued for Emma Mott in
professional matters. The minutes of the "full" faculty meeting of
March 12 record three resolutions:

That Mrs. Mott be invited to attend this meeting.

That the following notice be posted on the bulletin board: "The halls
and stair cases of this building are not intended to be places for
congregating unnecessarily nor for long conversations." By order of the
faculty.

That in as much as Mrs. Mott has not responded to the invitation of the
Faculty, the Secretary of the Faculty [Webster Merrifield] be instructed
to communicate with her with a view to ascertaining whether she meets
the class in Elocution oftener than twice a week.

Five days later Merrifield was instructed to investigate more specifically the elocution class, and as a result of his report the following
day, he was "instructed to inform Mrs. Mott 'that it is the wish of the
Faculty that the class in Elocution shall meet for teaching or practice,
or both, only twice per week, and one hour at each session.' Moved
and carried."

Geiger refers to Mrs. Mott as being "remembered less for her erudition than her exaggeratedly eloquent rendition of 'Curfew Shall Not Ring Tonight.'" For that matter, every reference he makes to her is condescending—he calls her a "strong-minded little woman with a sharp tongue."

Undoubtedly there were scores of other entertaining stories about Emma Mott if one only knew them; there always are. The word *elocution* in our day has a silly ring to it, yet what Emma Mott was trying to do with her unschooled pupils for more than two hours a week (variations of 'oral interpretation' or public speaking) may well have been useful to them. When President Blackburn presented to the Board Mrs. Mott's year-end class report, he explained that although she had included in that report the hours and numbers of pupils whom she supervised in study hall, he could not allow her to count them among her duties, even though, he admitted, the study hall had to be supervised by someone. Blackburn made a large wavy line crossing out that part of her neat handwritten chart. The men's harrassment of her seems petty, constant, and slightly comic. Emma Mott was assigned to unrelieved remedial teaching, and when it turned out that remedial teaching was virtually all that was being done for the year, she was not allowed to make known her "wants and recommendations." There is a comic-strip aura to the scenes: three men formally meeting, one in "the chair," another keeping all those minutes in an impeccable hand, recording unanimous votes and committee assignments; the long discussions of course contents: "Moved and carried that from Monday next the classes in Algebra and 'A' Arithmetic be put together and continue through Ratio and Proportion in Arithmetic, after which the entire class shall resume Algebra at the subject of Fractions. Adjourned." (3–18–85)

The status of female instructors did not improve with Mrs. Mott's departure. At the Board meeting of May 12 when the secretary was instructed to inform Mrs. Mott that her services would not be required the coming year, it was also "moved and lost to retain Blackburn as president at $2500." The two other men were allowed suitable raises: $500 for Merrifield and $250 for Montgomery. In regard to the position of lady instructor, the Board asked advice from the faculty who, in minutes for June 27,

> Resolved that the Faculty respectfully recommend to the Board of Regents the appointment, at a salary not to exceed Seven-hundred and fifty dollars for the first year, of a lady whose duties shall be to superintend the young ladies residing in the building and to give

instruction in Elementary branches in the Preparatory Department, subject to the general direction of the Faculty.

By hiring a new president at the old salary, and reducing the lady instructor's by twenty-five percent, it only cost the board an additional $500 to increase Merrifield's salary by a third and Montgomery's by twelve percent. As a parting insult to Emma Mott, the board showed her that they considered she had been overpaid.

It is even sadder to know with what high hopes her year at the university began. Emma Mott's letter accepting the appointment is as graphic as her resignation. Had the men in charge included her energy and experience into their deliberations throughout a difficult year, the grave and humorless minutes might not now remind us of a libretto for an academic comic opera, and a brave woman would not have been humiliated for her talents.

Grafton, Walsh Co., D. T.
Aug. 4th, 1884.

F. W. Iddings
Sec. Board of Regents Univ. N. Dak.,
Grand Forks, D. T.

Sir;-

Your letter with remaining credentials at hand. I will place the circulars wherever they may be likely to benefit the University. Next week the Walsh Co. Ins.—teachers—will be held in this town, and I suppose the Univ. will be well represented tho' there can be no harm in mentioning the matter here.

In this I will make a few suggestions, which, however, may not be new to you, at the same time I wish the Board to understand that it is at your invitation. You spoke of a *Matron*. Do I understand a figure-head, or a *working housekeeper*? Even tho' the pupils attend to their own rooms, a *cook* and *dining* room girls may be a necessity. Now in Ripon College, Wis., and Oberlin Coll., Ohio many pupils are glad of an opportunity to pay their way in part, by performing light duties, such as preparing and waiting upon tables. Some such arrangement might tend to augment the number of pupils for the time and could be ruled out in more prosperous times. I had not less than 7 or 8—seven or eight—young ladies and Misses—four of whom are teachers—who worked for their board in order to attend the Minto school last year, and I doubt not that some of them will try to enter the Preparatory Dep't. of the Univ. if *the means* can be found. By a "Working Housekeeper" I mean one capable of ordering the meals and overseeing the work, and doing

whatever occasion demands. The "Help" would then stand thus:—
Janitor and man of all work, combined, house-keeper and cook,
combined,—until increase of numbers demands both—and dining
room assistants. I will here add that if it were necessary, until you could
see a better way, I do not think my dignity as an instructor would be in
any way compromised if *I* were to audit the bills of the commissary
dep't. as often as you deem best. Having cast my lot with the University
for a time, *all my energies* will be exerted to make it a success, whenever
and wherever they are demanded so long as compatible with my position. This I should not offer only under existing circumstances,
wherein "What will it cost per annum?" is the first question. I have
omitted a "laundry woman" but she will be a necessity.

I fear you will make a mistake if you do not furnish the students rooms
with at least, bed-stead, wash-stand, small table and 2 chairs. These may
be *cheap*, and furnished by the quantity, competition will cheapen them.

Hoping that these few suggestions will be taken in the same spirit as
given, and not that of presumptuous interference, I remain

Sincerely Yours
E. S. Mott

Emma Mott was representative of the women of her generation,
the grandmothers and great-grandmothers of those of us now passing our "middle years." In their thirties and forties when the American suffrage movement was gaining in strength and notoriety, these
women were confronted both with increased opportunities and in-
tensified resistance if they chose professional careers. The reform
movements such women joined at the turn of the century have been
so denigrated by popular legend with help from school history
books, that it is difficult now to realize how various and ambitious
they were. Voting was one of several issues, and suffragettes one of
several groups, nearly all of them laughed at. Mention WCTU and
people envision Carry Nation swinging an ax. The Emma Mott who
was a charter member of the Women's Christian Temperance Union
in Grafton and "busted up," in her grandson's words, twenty-seven
bars there, wearing their keys to prove it, also was energetic in other
WCTU projects.

One of these was writing a column, "Letter from the Grafton
Union," for *Western Womanhood*, a North Dakota WCTU journal
started in 1895 in Carrington, then moved to Fargo.[6] *Western Womanhood* addressed a variety of topics. There were articles on notable
women in the state (like Emma F. Bates, the first woman in any state
to be elected state superintendent of public instruction), on "Profes-

sional Life for Women" (August '95), "Woman Financiers" (August '96). Articles advocated child care and better health for women, urged women to become informed about sexuality and physiology, and deplored excessive childbearing. The magazine told women they should go to college and it published a series on state colleges in North Dakota. *Western Womanhood* expressed the radical hopes of WCTU reform. Keeping men sober certainly was one intention of the movement (at a saving of both money and domestic violence). It also importantly gave intellectual and social meaning to women's lives. Then as now, large meetings stimulated women to persevere in the cause, and *Western Womanhood* encouraged its readers to attend the WCTU convention in Fargo on September 15, 1897: "Do not forget to bring your bicycles. It is a long way from one end of Fargo to the other. Remember Fargo has a law-enforcing mayor, so do not forget your lamps and bells" (some anti-feminists claimed women chiefly rode in order to masturbate, and in some areas women bicyclists were harrassed by police for minor traffic violations). Emma Mott's articles in *Western Womanhood* promoted in particular the WCTU "Temple" in Chicago, a central office and educational building, by taking charge of fund-raising in North Dakota.

Henry Mott's four-volume diary, written between 1899 and 1908, gives some glimpses of Emma's private life, though we cannot know it very well. His lamentation about the failure of "equality before the law" betrays strong sympathies for feminism, and nothing in the diary contradicts the impression that he held Emma in high esteem, although he seldom wrote in an emotional or even descriptive manner. Most of the entries are matter of fact, about small events. Even Christmas received a scant attention:

> December 25, 1905. Day about like preceding. An exceptional fine Christmas. Went down at 11 o'clock to Commanday Meeting to partici-pate in Christmas greetings. Bought 15 cents worth candy at Jourgrows (pd). Attended Christmas exercises in Baptist Church in eve. Let Vallie have 20 cts for Christmas.

Henry Mott kept track of the weather and sent reports to the newspaper, he noted money earned and spent and added each month's tally in red in the margins; he told of Masonic and other meetings, of his knighting, of the building of the Baptist Church under his supervision. He described his surveying projects and re-lated trips to Larimore, Grand Forks, and other towns. He wrote down milk sales and their cows' breedings, abortions and births: "The Old Cow died with many regrets on the part of us all" (2–24–02). Now and then, though not often, there was some excitement:

> March 31, 1907. Day raw and chilly, wind SE. An Eventful day all round. Daisy had her calf night preceding. Went to Church in the forenoon. In the afternoon conducted a review of post quarters lessons. Not long after close of Sunday School the Baptist boiler blew up and partially wrecked the interior of the church making havoc generally. Services for the evening had to be called off. Boiler went end first through floor and ceiling and practically through the roof. Collection 10 cts.

Henry Mott's entries about Emma sound as though he considered her her own person: "Wife had Encyclopedias delivered to her and she paid 9.75 therefor" (8–7–02). Much about her he did not feel he had to put into words:

> April 25, 1906. Anniversary of my marriage. How swiftly the years have flown. These have composed the best years of my life. Whatever I have accomplished worth while is embraced here. I realize that I am on the down hill side of life. The day was spent for the most part in bed fearfully sick with stomach and bowel trouble. Let Vallie have 15 cts.

Henry Mott made a practice of noting his birthdays on August 7; these occasions and symptoms of bad health reminded him of his mortality. In 1899: "My birth day. . . . Bought 5 cts worth of salts to physic my blood for oak leaf poison which has grown more aggravated. Went to bed about midnight." In 1902: "My Birthday Anniversary. One half Century." In 1904: "Went to Sunday School. Gave 52 cents for my Birthday." In 1908:

> 56 times. The day was delightful. In the forenoon cloudy. In the afternoon clear. Mrs. Peppard was here all afternoon. Dr. Sutton came in the eve and gave me my usual "dope." Wifie made quite a little birthday spread in the eve to which Mr. and Mrs. Baldes was invited. Gus Baer sent me a bottle of beer by Dr. Suter. 55 today for Gus.

Henry Mott lived only nine months after his fifty-sixth birthday. Although dying had been on his mind for years, his death stirred terrible sadness in Emma. She wrote at least as fiercely about his dying as she had about being fired from the university, with a novelist's outside eye for scene at the very moment she protests her own anguish.

May 15, 1909. Dr. Sutton came, and while they sat talking, Dr. beside the bed, the Death Angel came also. I had been leaning on the foot of the bed, after giving him two tiny pills by order of Dr. who had also given him a hypo injection at 9:15 PM. I sat down in front room with the stove obstructing sight of them. Almost immediately Dr. went out without stopping to say "Good Night." The door hardly closed when a gasp reached my ear. One step and I was in sight of my loved one, but too late. He had entered in. I started to rub his hands but I knew that were futile, then I ran to the door and called "Dr.! Dr.! Come right back." He had gotten only in front of the next neighbor's door—it all happened so quickly—and instantly returned. I plead, "Do something for him, you must." He said, "No use Mrs. Mott." I, with a single stroke composed his face and it took on a look which I shall ever remember, an expression so familiar to me when he had been thinking on some life problems, a sort of quizzical smile that expected me to ask of him "What is it Harry?" And I asked it of him over and over but no response ever came. And I still am asking "What would you say Harry if you could speak."

Emma Mott arranged an elaborate Masonic funeral, conducted by a long-time friend and pastor in Chicago, and she saw to the construction of a vault and took previously agreed-to precautions against her husband's being buried alive, letting several weeks go by before placing the body in the crypt, and leaving the coffin unclosed and a south window also open. She wrote like a practical mystic:

These precautions were unnecessary, but I kept my promise to the letter. Many times I went to the vault and lifting the cover saw and talked to him, but alas. No response came. The weather turning cold we thought best to enter his body into its crypt in order to have the cement harden before freezing.

To describe these funerary events she used journal pages immediately following Henry Mott's last entries. Painful as was her honest skepticism, she spelled it out anyway:

If I could only say and think "The Lord gave and the Lord taketh away," but I cannot. Over work and over worry did it, and so I have no refuge, no one on whom to cast my grief. "The Lord's will"? Never. He receives but does not *take*. He permits, he does not compel. We are poor moral agents and pay for our transgression of *natural laws* as well as of Divine laws. Bronchitis, rupture, heart-failure, liver, all got in their work, and Vallie and I are *alone*. May God guide us to the right and to see and feel and know and do acceptably in his sight. God make my boy a man good in sight. Help him to turn from evil and be worthy of thy counsel. Amen. Emma S. Mott.

That prayer closes Henry Mott's diaries.

Valentine was nineteen years old when his father died. He lived all his life in Grafton, and became a surveyor like his father (and so did his son, the present Henry Mott). From the time Emma Mott's house burned, she lived with Valentine and his family (two daughters and a son), and she died in Grafton on October 4, 1941.

Emma Mott used language as a weapon—against a thieving student, against a mismanaged university administration, and, when she could not resign herself to "the Lord's will," against herself as an ineffectual agent of destructive natural laws, the overwork and overworry that got the better of her husband's heart, liver, and lungs. She was as ruthless to herself as to anyone she thought had done her injury, and she was not kind in her manner of calling attention to an unjust or foolish act. She sounds proud of her own integrity and unwilling to protect other people's self-regard from her scorn.

Like Julia Carpenter, Emma Mott had more ambitious intellectual and social interests than were required where she found herself. Both women were angry at the disparity between what each might have made of herself, and what her circumstances allowed, but only Emma expressed that anger, to her cost. Both women wrote in concretely objective words, and both also were able to evaluate experiences to a degree that none of the Goodwater or Mosher correspondents, for instance, ever did. Yet Julia Carpenter tried hard to keep her anger to herself. Only the manner of her language, not the words, relieved her: the lists, the numbers she repeated to refer to the homestead, her very reportorial energy. She did not want anyone to know, and so she wrote, or fell ill, or went to bed and cried, and wrote about that.

Emma Mott, to some, gave the appearance of being crazed, and her writing may represent the only decisive alternative to Julia Carpenter's strategy. To refuse to be agreeable is to seem a little mad. Emma Mott's dilemma dramatizes women's traditional exhausting devising of strategies not to be mute, forbidden to make known "wants and recommendations," yet expected to perform professionally. Emma Mott virtually acted out a female morality nightmare. Henry Mott's diary and Emma's pages after he died reveal strong affection and respect between them. For many years in Grafton she gave piano lessons and participated in WCTU. But neither the support of a sympathetic husband nor her own talents could allay the shambles of her one university year. Everything she wrote then was accurate and true—no one ever said otherwise, and that was precisely her fault. She and Julia Carpenter both were intelligent, capable middle class women of earnest good will, yet critically limited in the language they were permitted to use, and there appears little to be said that can be hopeful about prospects for women like them in their time and place. The much-touted "sphere" allotted to them was very small: a few friends, some worried family, and most of the abilities gone to waste.

VII

Words of Love
and Hunger

This book began with Henry Adams's observation that "The woman who is known only through a man is known wrong, and excepting one or two like Mme. de Sevigné, no woman has pictured herself." To what extent would we know women differently and better were women to picture themselves? I think we might at least know more of them. The rueful joke about a 51-percent minority is, unfortunately, too accurate to evoke outrage: women remain a hazy, ill-defined anonymous mass out there somewhere. That is not to say, however, that if we knew women better, some charismatic female heroes or "lost" works of genius necessarily would appear to balance the forceful public influence of men. But we would learn better to appreciate and take seriously some of the traditional women's arts—their writing, for example, and handicrafts such as quilting and dressmaking, and even recipes—and learn the names of their creators, recognizing and being sensitive to differences among their works rather than have all blur together.

Certain popular impressions of women might alter if we knew women better. Women's friendships with other women, for instance, have never been taken seriously, by men or even by women themselves. Friendship among men has been idealized from the time of the Greek philosophers, and been institutionalized in the form of armies. athletic teams, and priesthoods, to say nothing of chambers of commerce and professional, business, and social clubs, and secret societies. Women even have been told that they were incapable of forming true friendships. But the writings we have been looking at in this book show that women always have been important to each

225

other, that women in need of companionship, regardless of their relationships with men, seek out other women, and that these relationships have tenaciously been cherished and nurtured through time, sometimes at great cost. Yet women have taken these friendships for granted, and men have been mystified by them, if they noticed them at all.

My observations about what these women have written include a rather striking absence of commentary about place and landscape. Or rather, I notice what I want to call class differences in the way women think about themselves in relation to environment. The very close, concrete, and object-focused writing of working class women contains little of measured distances, politics, business, social issues, or any of the other quadrants by which literature usually informs a reader about place. But the more estranged from place a woman feels (an estrangement among these writers that is parallel with social aspiration), the more she is apt graphically to inform others of her whereabouts. As for the professional woman writer, she is almost always an outsider. Rosellen Brown, as an example, in explaining why she did not write a novel about courageous Mary Kingsley challenging Queen Victoria's policies in Africa (she did not write it, she says, because she found too little of the mysterious in what is already known about Mary Kingsley), tells of the importance of place in her fiction:

> Yet if there has been a constant in all my work, that has been an obsession with place, with the specific of where my characters are. I have gone from Mississippi to Brooklyn to New Hampshire in my writing. I was going to have to know one hell of a lot about London, Cambridge, Libreville and a series of villages called M'fetta, Egage, and N'dorko to be satisfied.[1]

The social separations implied in nineteenth-century grammar books have nowhere been proven more true than in women's experiences: women who write are obliged to study their regions, and those who know the country at first hand have not written. The thinking of such women as Rosellen Brown and Willa Cather is substantially different, I think, from that of such writers as Eliza Keyes or Gwendoline Kinkaid, because their placing is so different. However much professional writers desire to reach the inner consciousness of their characters by accomplishing research that will get the details right, they write from the outside. Virtually no woman has written descriptively and remained where she was.

Women's writings generally also have little to say about the activities of the men around them, even though in most cases major circumstances of their lives—where and how they were living—had been decided by men. Julia Carpenter said almost nothing about Frank's work; most of the time one does not know from her diary what he was doing. The published diary of Mary Dodge Woodward illustrates a woman's separation from men (here by a writer conscious of the gap) and also her feeling of apartness from landscape and topography. Mary Dodge Woodward was a widow, with two sons and a daughter in their late teens and early twenties. Her elder son managed a large farm six miles from Fargo, North Dakota, that was owned by a cousin of Mrs. Woodward's. The scheme lasted eight years, when the farm was sold and she returned to her previous home in Kingston, Wisconsin, and died there on Christmas Day, 1890.

Mary Woodward's diary was edited for publication by a granddaughter, Mary Boyston Cowdrew, who unfortunately gives no information about how much, if anything, she omitted, or the whereabouts of the original manuscript.[2] One must assume that Mrs. Woodward wrote almost daily and that the entries in the published version are fairly representative. Like Julia Carpenter, Mary Woodward enjoys writing and is able to detail a rather coherent account of the family's daily situation, though with little emotional color. The household consisted of Walter, Nellie, and Fred, her children; Daniel Dodge, the owner, who made long visits and constructed outbuildings to improve the farm; two dogs; a cat; and numerous houseplants. With her spyglass Mrs. Woodward could see buildings in Fargo eight miles away, and she says, one hundred farm houses, although in eight years she made the acquaintance of only two or three families, and for three of those years she never went to Fargo at all. Reading matter was important to her; trips to town meant new supplies of books and magazines. She kept a vegetable garden and reports the progress of wildflowers and native plants. She said she was 58 years old in 1884. She had more to say than most women writing privately, about landscape and vegetation:

> The sloughs are pink and white and purple with daisies; and there are yellow marigolds, great quantities of them, just in front of our door. Some of our men went down to the Cheyenne and brought back nearly a bushel of plums, very nice ones too, large and red and sweet. They are sold in Fargo for one dollar a bushel, while wheat is sixty cents. There is a perfect tangle of brush, vines, and trees to the water's edge

where the fires have not destroyed them. Everything that can stand the cold grows luxuriantly in Dakota. Walter sowed turnips on the breaking which were the nicest ones I ever saw, just as smooth, and weighed four or five pounds on the average. Potatoes, beets, cabbages, carrots—all vegetables grow large and smooth. (8–22–84)

Later we went over to the Hayes place and gathered flowers, a great basket full. We stopped the horses on the way back to watch the sunset. Nowhere except in Dakota have I seen anything so beautiful. One can see for miles and miles in one long, unbroken stretch. The prairies are dotted with farm houses, the windows gleaming in the setting sun. I sometimes long for my trees and hills at home, yet nothing can excel this enchanting endless view. The sun flattens on the prairie until it looks like a sea of fire as it disappears from the horizon. (6–16–86)

Dakota is different in many ways from the country down east. Nobody keeps track of his neighbors here. People come and go; families move in and out, and nobody asks whence they came nor whither they go. Walter went down to see if he could get water from a flowing well a mile and a half from here, and found that the owner of the farm had died last winter. I have lived here six years and I do not know who occupies half of the surrounding farms although they are in full view. (8–28–88)

Besides sensitive observations upon the natural scene, Mary Woodward's diary reflects some of her social attitudes, especially on suitable behavior of women. The passages published include relatively few references to people (in comparison to so many unpublished letters and diaries of that place and period), although it is of course not possible to know, without reading the actual diaries, whether this is her editor's doing or Mrs. Woodward's. At any rate, when she does have something to say it seems the more worth noting. What little human contact she describes is mostly with other women, and that always with diffidence. "Miss Phelps called here today. She and her sister came to the territory three years ago, almost without means. They have been trading city lots and taking up claims and are now worth a great deal of money. They think that any energetic, self-reliant young lady could find no place where she could do so well as in this territory" (11–4–84). Whether Mary Woodward agreed with the sisters is not known.

She mentions most often a neighboring German family, the Lessings, whose manner of running their affairs awed her but also drew her disapproval. She sympathizes with a rebellious son, but the women are, she says, beyond her comprehension, particularly, one supposes, because from all appearances, they thrived.

Elsie Lessing was here for awhile. Walter hitched up Cripes so that she and Katie could to go Moran's after butter. Elsie is plowing for her father, a stingy old German who makes the women work out of doors. He thinks an hour long enough for them to prepare a meal, and affords them only the necessities of life, though he owns a half section of land with live stock and machinery. There are eight children who, with their mother, do all the work. Last spring, Fritz, the oldest boy, ran away from home, thinking he had gotten too big to be whipped— he was six feet tall. He went off, out of the vicinity for awhile, and then returned to work at Green's, three miles from home, where he has been all the fall, plowing. His family have not found him yet. He works in sight of home, and can see his sister plowing, and she can see him, but she doesn't dream who he is. I think that's fun! (10–25–85)

Walter let the hens out around the door. They are of every color and breed, which is what I like to see. The Lessing girls went by, hauling wood to Canfield. Such young, slender German girls, how they can work like men is beyond my comprehension. They drive four-horse teams standing up like any teamster. (2–16–88)

Our men are in the hay field. There is a large amount of hay down which must be put into the barns before harvest. Elsie cut all the forenoon, down in their big hay field alone. What would people think in Kingston, I wonder, if a girl should go to Marquette with a mower to cut hay all day! Sometimes her sister, Lena, rakes. They have hauled home five loads apiece from the hay field, making thirty-five miles each. Elsie weighs 104 pounds. They have a man to pitch the hay on, and the girls build the load, haul it home, and pitch it off onto the stack which their father and mother build. Such people can make a living in Dakota. They had only eighteen dollars in the world to start on. They took up land here, and now own two quarter-sections; have horses, cattle, sheep, trees, shrubs, a flower garden, and eight young ones. Most of the settlers spread around and rode in their carriages while wheat was $1.50 a bushel, and when it went down, mortgaged their farms. (7–14–88)

Mrs. Woodward, baffled by women so athletic, places the Lessing girls in the category, "such people."

For her part, Mrs. Woodward did not participate in the heavy farm work that she reports the men did, though she worked very hard at feeding scores of threshers at a time. What she writes of most fondly is plants; they comforted and gave continuity to periods of her life.

A bright, beautiful day after a nice, still rain which was unlike Dakota. I went out around the prairie and gathered a bouquet of many colors and varieties of flowers. People say the wild flowers are rapidly disappearing from the prairie, as they would, for nearly the whole country is sowed to wheat or mowed for hay. The rose bushes which grow among the trees are very large. On the open prairies they die down winters and come up again beautifully in the fallows. A letter from sister, Isabinda. Dear Isabinda, her heart is in her husband's grave. She has not the nerve to get any enjoyment out of life without him, and she says she only wishes to go to him. (6–12–87)

She writes so sympathetically about plants, I think, because they were apart from the purely economic scramble that she saw the whole Dakota settlement becoming. Whereas she was trying to evolve a reasonably humane way of living in even these inhospitable surroundings, her cousin Daniel Dodge was interested only in making money, and when, in spite of his building and improving, the farm no longer prospered, he sold it and she was forced once more to move. For Mrs. Woodward and women like her, the entire settlement experience had something subversive about it, or at least against the grain, for they were for the most part out of phase with immediate profit making. What is published of her diary contains little that could be called complaint, but she does remark upon the prevailing desire for riches: "If wheat were a dollar a bushel, sure thing, year after year, a man might endure this country for the sake of gain. But he would then lose his own soul, so what would it profit him?" (5–23–88). None of the physical arrangements of the farm were made with her needs or interests in mind. She writes of chickens scratching up her plants, and dogs and other animals eating the chickens—no pens or fences to protect either, though she says that one could make a good deal of money selling eggs. Not even her vegetable garden was convenient: "We still make a garden on the corner of the wheatfield which is all right except that it is too far for me to run to in leisure moments, as I so love to do" (6–15–85). Neither a productive flock of chickens nor a thriving and nearby garden was thought, by the men, deserving of their effort in a prevailing profit economy, even though both eggs and vegetables would have considerably improved everyone's way of living.

Mary Woodward writes fondly of all three children on the farm, and of two others who came with families to visit. But she knew she was not included in the center of things. On a shopping expedition when Fred bought himself quite a lot of fashionable clothing, Walter tried for the third time to buy his mother a cloak.

Fred and Walter went to Fargo this afternoon. Fred bought a suit of clothes, shirt, collar, cravat, two suits of underwear, box of socks, and still had money left, so he did not come home with Walter but stayed to spend the rest at the theatre. Walter brought me a very nice looking cloak which, of course, doesn't fit; nothing does. Walter will take it back. This is the third one he has brought, all too tight for me. I have not been to Fargo for three years, nor off the farm. I have been home so long that I dread to go anywhere, but I suppose I shall have to go to buy myself a cloak or go without one. I know the children are provoked because I am not like other people. (11–8–87)

Being thought mildly eccentric distressed her less than being ignored, and she felt disengaged from decisions made around her by the likes of Cousin Daniel and her sons. "He thinks farming does not pay." That was Daniel Dodge's opinion, the world view that determined her life for the last several years, but it was not hers.

Cousin Daniel writes that he is thinking of selling the farm in the spring if a good offer is made. It was not, and he rented for several years. He thinks farming does not pay at the present price of wheat and with no prospect of a rise. He has made so many improvements here, which the average farmer does not take into account and will not pay for, that the place will have to be sold at a great sacrifice. We have been here so long that leaving the farm will seem like again leaving home. Except for the cold winters, I should like this place very much indeed. I like a farm better than a home in town; however, for the rest of my days I do not expect to be considered nor consulted as to where I should rather live. But I'll keep up with the procession as long as I am able. (1–24–88)

Mary Woodward's manner of writing, in what selections are available, is so dispassionate that one reads for the unsaid. She was only 64 years old when she died, which seems early when there were no reports during the Dakota years of her having been severely ill. But her manner of living may well have taken more toll than she was willing to admit:

Katie and I have one drift of snow left and we have melted some of it and washed. The wind blew me down when I went out, but I came in and took a dose of laudanum. Ha! We are neither of us strong enough for the task we have undertaken; but many a weakling before us has performed a job which was too hard for him. Walter bought ten volumes of Chamber's Encyclopedia. Fred is reading Waverley or 'Tis Sixty Years Since. (12–6–85)

Taken altogether, Mary Woodward writes of the eight years in Dakota as having been more satisfying than not, even though expectations for herself were limited: "I suppose this is my last summer on this farm, and no doubt it is the last summer that I shall have anyone who needs or wants me. I had hoped never to see that time, but I have come to it. Had it not been for Cousin Daniel's farm, the time would have come sooner than this, I mean the time of breaking up of the family" (7–28–88). Seen in this context, as an extension for a few more years of her useful life, Mary Woodward's reportings take on special interest. Approaching old age had some compensations: she was not obliged to worry whether the farm made money or not, and the freedom of not being responsible allowed her to explore a more interesting landscape, if a more private and eccentric one than that of her companions. Her detachment was not always a bad thing.

> Two years ago today we arrived at the Dodge farm. They have been short years to me for I have had plenty to do. I have enjoyed my life here very much and have never wished to leave. The girls are sewing, crocheting, ironing, and visiting, and so passing the time, which is very pleasant to me. Evenings they make molasses candy and invite in the farm hands. The boys are gentlemanly and nice. We are never troubled with them for they never stop a minute in the house unless invited. (10–18–84)

> My red, old-fashioned peonies have stuck their pink noses out of the ground. I covered them up last night. I have watched them ever since I was a little girl: in Vermont, in Wisconsin, and now in Dakota Territory where they still thrive. Anything that can live in this cold country should be reverenced. The rose-colored one and the white one are not up yet. I shall see them later. (4–28–88)

> The fall has been so long and warm and dry that the farmers will have no excuse if their fall plowing is not done. The country looks black and dreary now that so much soil is turned over. Prairie fires are growing few in spite of the fact that the sloughs are full of dried grass, weeds, daisies, sunflowers, and othe coarse vegetation which makes a terrific fire. The fire follows the course of the sloughs for miles and miles and lights up the whole country. I love to watch it. (12–1–88)

Separateness and detachment are a common theme in private writings of rural working women, even among those, like Mary Woodward, who participated fairly actively in, and were knowledgeable about, the daily working of a farm or other agricultural or business endeavor.

There is little doubt that settlement traditionally has meant the active involvement of women in a way that all-male enterprises have not. The whaling industry, gold rushes to California and Alaska, fur trapping, exploring, and lumbering are examples of single purpose exploitive occupations that men have engaged in that involved them in a minimum of community settlement. Shepherds and cowboys before ranches were fenced led a nomadic, bunkhouse life. Settlement on homesteads, farms, ranches and towns, the permanence of "home" and supporting institutions, meant that women were involved as well as men.

Women's crucial participation in settlement has also, traditionally, remained nearly anonymous, at best acknowledged honorifically in naming towns for wives of postmasters or railway executives. Part of the reason for such anonymity can be explained by the essential cooperative and unindividualized nature of most agricultural projects. In spite of the mythology of rugged individualism that inspires western folklore, the management of family-centered farms, ranches, and even businesses usually does not allow for much individual style. Successful cattle raising depends more on a careful reading of soil and climate conditions and of the cattle market than, say, an individual rancher's style of horseback riding or roping. Milking, raising chickens, gardening, sewing, the traditional ancillary tasks of agricultural women, likewise give little room for what one might recognize as individualized expression. Within this relatively unindividualized culture men have made names for themselves by amassing great wealth and by involving themselves in politics, both opportunities generally not available to women in their own right. Men are also remembered for singular, non-settlement exploits: mountains, rivers, and towns have been named for explorers, fur trappers, army officers, and the like.

But the unindividualized character of agriculture is only part of the reason, I think, for women being as unknown as they are, especially in the Midwest. And the Midwest, including the Plains States, it is worth noting, is a particularly apt region in which to study the problem of how to reach the story of women's experiences because an agricultural economy and ways of thinking still prevail there. A tradition of singling out notable women has not taken hold or been nourished by such institutions as women's colleges, or women's labor and social organizations that serve women specifically rather than as auxiliaries to men's interests. Women outlaws are popular Midwestern figures (Carry Nation and Calamity Jane), but

even the names of women who have achieved positions of leadership
in politics or the professions are hardly known. Knowing women
well in the Midwest also is hampered by an obliterating mythology:
the many striding "Pioneer Mother" statues in town squares, little
children emerging from behind skirt folds. Pioneer fathers are not,
that I know of, so memorialized. This mythology, sustained by town
and county histories, family histories, displays in historical museums,
asserts that pioneer mothers were strong, long-suffering, resourceful, continually confronted by adversity, and nearly always cheerful
and cheering. They never said No. But the myth hardly pauses to
inquire what women themselves might have said and thought.

The effort of the present study has been to attempt to do so, to
read as examples the writings that happen to have survived of a few
women in order to try to understand, from their point of view, how
they regarded their experiences. Such reading, however, can be
disquieting, and the organizing disciplines of literary or historical
analysis not always reassuring. There are few beginnings and ends; it
is all "middle," and one tries to read forward and back at the same
time, groping through the baffling, too-great intimacies of private
writings which Thomas McGrath describes in some lines in his book-
length autobiographical poem, *Letter to an Imaginary Friend.*[3]

> And the attic night trembles
> For its terrible treasures
>   its secret histories like deadmen's bones
> Unburied in the gapthroated oldfashioned trunks' dark fathoms.
> Here, furbearing bibles, inlaid with fake gemstones,
> Like sand covered drift-fences of tallies of a winter count,
> Record, before Genesis, the early departures and the first begots—
> Writ by hand . . .
>   and the letters, packaged in rotting twine,
> Talk all dark in a language of leaving and loss
>   forgotten
> Tongues
>   foreign
>   sounding
>   —words of love and hunger . . .

The "words of love and hunger" we remember, whether we think
we understand them or not, for these words often leave little else to
go on, and that little takes patience. Our national Calvinist upbring-
ing urges us toward the exceptional, the out-of-the-ordinary, the

individual and unique, equating difference with achievement. And yet we are bound to miss important threads in our experience if we think only with the progressive frame of mind, and if we emphasize always the separateness, the apartness of others, as traditionally most men have thought of women. Yet paradoxically, the unknown also is all too well known. The women who died too young, worked too hard, bore too many children, and never complained (but sometimes went mad)—it becomes harder and harder to extoll them as "pioneers" without wondering, aghast, why we knew so little about them.

Notes

Abbreviations:
> HDP: Historical Data Project, State Historical Society of North Dakota, Bismarck.
>
> NDIRS: North Dakota Institute for Regional Studies, North Dakota State University, Fargo.
>
> OGL: Orin G. Libby Manuscript Collection, North Dakota Room, University of North Dakota, Grand Forks.
>
> SHSND: State Historical Society of North Dakota, Bismarck.

Preface: Pen in Hand

1. Nancy F. Cott, *The Bonds of Womanhood: "Woman's Sphere" in New England, 1780–1835* (New Haven: Yale Univ. Press, 1977); Carroll Smith-Rosenberg, "The Female World of Love and Ritual: Relations between Women in Nineteenth-Century America," *Signs,* I (Autumn 1975), 1–30; *The Mamie Papers,* ed. Ruth Rosen and Sue Davidson (Feminist Press, 1977). Diaries by women listed in *American Diaries in Manuscript, 1580–1945: A Descriptive Bibliography,* by William Matthews (Athens: Univ. of Georgia Press, 1974), tend also to be written by women of the upper class.

2. Leroy Goodwater Papers, OGL 368.

3. Mosher Family Papers, OGL 463.

4. Goodwater, OGL 368.

5. The major history of the state is Elwyn B. Robinson's *History of North Dakota* (Lincoln: Univ. of Nebraska Press, 1966). For more general and high school readers there are D. Jerome Tweton and Theodore B. Jelliff, *North Dakota: The Heritage of a People,* North Dakota American Revolution Bicentennial Commission (Fargo: NDIRS 1976), and Robert P. Wilkins and Wynona Huchette Wilkins, *North Dakota, Bicentennial History* (New York, 1977). *North Dakota: A Guide to the Northern Prairie State* (Fargo: Knight Printing Co., 1938) and Mary Ann Barnes Williams, *Origins of North Dakota Place Names* (Washburn, N.D. 1966) identify places, especially towns no longer on the map. An M.A. thesis, "To Make a Prairie," by Vonda Kay Somerville (Grand Forks: Univ. of North Dakota, 1980), describes lives of settler women as revealed in letters, diaries, and particularly interviews in the Historical Data Project. For extended bibliographies of historical and literary works relating to North Dakota, see *Reference Guide to North Dakota History,* compiled by Dan Rylance, and *North Dakota Literature,* compiled by J.F.S. Smeall (Chester Fritz Library, Univ. of North Dakota, Fall 1979).

I. Introduction: This Is Christmas Eve and I Am in Tintah

1. Henry Adams, *The Education of Henry Adams,* ed. Ernest Samuels (Boston: Houghton Mifflin Co., 1974), p. 353.

2. Some scholars are exploring women's haunts and interests; for instance, two articles analyze Harlequin romances and their readers: Ann Barr Snitow, "Mass Market Romance: Pornography for Women is Different,"

Radical History Review, vol. 19 (Spring/Summer 1979), and Tania Modleski, "The Disappearing Act: A Study of Harlequin Romances," *Signs*, 5 (Spring 1980). Nevertheless, Meredith Gould's review essay, "The New Sociology," in the same issue of *Signs*, emphasizes the discipline's continuing conservatism in regard to examinations of women's lives, in spite of numerous critiques by feminists that she lists. The most searching work on women, she finds, has been interdisciplinary, not exclusively the work of sociologists: "The failure to acknowledge and infuse what women know and who women are into sociological inquiry has rendered static the substantive areas of formal sociology" (p. 459).

3. John D. Unruh, *The Plains Across: The Overland Emigrants and the Trans-Mississippi West, 1840–60* (Urbana: Univ. of Ill. Press, 1979).

4. John Mack Faragher, *Women and Men on the Overland Trail* (New Haven: Yale Univ. Press, 1979).

5. Julie Roy Jeffrey, *Frontier Women: The Trans-Mississippi West, 1840–1880* (New York: Hill & Wang, 1979). The photograph on the cover of *Frontier Women* appears to be taken from the right-hand third of the same photograph of the traveling family in Unruh's book. On Jeffrey's cover, the woman sitting upon the wagon tongue dominates the frame. We see only the man's torso at her feet, and a single child on his lap.

6. Carroll Smith-Rosenberg, "The Female World of Love and Ritual: Relations between Women in Nineteenth Century America," *Signs*, I (Autumn 1975), 1–29.

7. Nancy F. Cott, *The Bonds of Womanhood: "Woman's Sphere" in New England, 1780–1835* (New Haven, Yale Univ. Press, 1977) p. 9.

8. Annette Kolodny, *The Lay of the Land: Metaphor as Experience and History in American Life and Letters* (Chapel Hill: Univ. of North Carolina Press, 1975).

9. Annette Kolodny, "'To Render Home a Paradise': Women on the New World Landscapes," *Women's Language and Style*, ed. Douglas Butturff and Edmund L. Epstein, *Studies in Contemporary Language #1* (Akron, Ohio: I & S Books, 1978), pp. 36–46.

10. The journals of Amy Sylvia Cory are in the possession of Phillip Cory, Grand Forks.

11. The Historical Data Project (HDP), an effort of the Works Progress Administration of the 1930s, consists of about 1500 interviews with early residents, and is on file at the North Dakota State Historical Society in Bismarck. Arranged alphabetically by the last name of each "principal pioneer," these interviews are in two parts: 1) a questionnaire listing immediate family and occupational history; housing conditions; information about schools, churches, and their equipment; a map of the immediate environs; and 2) a narrative written either by the interviewer or by the subject telling about that person's coming to North Dakota and subsequent experiences.

12. Ann Douglas, *The Feminization of American Culture* (New York: Avon Books, 1977).

13. Siebert Family Papers, OGL, 211. The diary runs from December 23, 1903, to March 13, 1904, and May 18 to May 21, 1904.

14. Robert A. Fothergill, *Private Chronicles: A Study of English Diaries* (London: Oxford Univ. Press, 1974).

II. Little Houses on the Prairie

1. Donald Davies, *Southern Writers in the Modern World* (Athens: Univ. of Georgia Press, 1958).

2. By John Hanson and Robert Nisson, produced by Cine Manifest and funded in part through the North Dakota Commitee for the Humanities and Public Issues. For a feminist critique of the film, see Ann Markusen, "Who Were Your Grandmothers, John Hanson?" *Quest,* (vol. V, no. 2).

3. Annette Kolodny, *The Lay of the Land: Metaphor as Experience and History in American Life and Letters* (Chapel Hill: Univ. of North Carolina Press, 1975). "I purposefully omitted women's materials from *The Lay of the Land* on the grounds that insofar as the masculine appears to have taken power in the New World, it seemed necessary to understand its relationship to the landscape first," Kolodny wrote in a footnote to the subsequent essay, "'To Render Home a Paradise': Women on the New World Landscape," in *Women's Language and Style,* ed. E. L. Epstein (University of Akron, Akron, Ohio, 1978). In this essay, Kolodny offers examples of "how, even as early as the eighteenth century, in their private musings and correspondence, women were engaged in a tentative rejection of certain aspects of the popular male imaginings and, with them, the landscape they implied" (p. 44).

4. Diary of Lulah Cavileer, SHSND.

5. Willa Cather, *My Antonia* (Boston: Houghton Mifflin, 1954). Page references following quotations in my text are to this edition.

6. Translated from Norwegian by Marianne Mathies, student in English 398, Rural Women, University of North Dakota, Spring 1979. A photocopy of the original text of the letter was provided by P. V. Thorson, History Department, University of North Dakota, from Norsk Historisk Kjeldeskrift-Institut, Oslo (Norwegian Historical Institute for Primary Source Material).

7. Tillie Olsen, *Yonnondio from the Thirties* (New York: Dell Publishing Co., 1975). Page references following quotations in my text are to this edition.

8. Laura Ingalls Wilder, *By the Shores of Silver Lake* (New York: Harper & Row, 1939).

9. HDP.

10. HDP.

11. HDP.

12. Mrs. W. K. Williams, "Interesting Facts of the Pioneer," Contest, March 1933, sponsored by the Mandan Creamery and Produce Company, Mandan, North Dakota, SHSND A8.

13. Erma Norton, HDP.

14. Angus Neil, "Interesting Facts of the Pioneer," SHSND A8.

15. Charles Rowe, op. cit.

16. DeCou Family Papers, OGL 483.

17. Mosher Family Papers, OGL 463.

III. "Not to Use Correct and Elegant English Is to Plod"

1. Newspaper clipping included in Leroy Goodwater Family Correspondence 1850–1904, 1926, OGL 368.

2. Flannery O'Connor, *Everything That Rises Must Converge* (New York: Farrar, Straus & Giroux, 1965), pp. 195–96.

3. Nancy F. Cott, *The Bonds of Womanhood: "Woman's Sphere" in New England 1780–1835* (New Haven: Yale Univ. Press, 1977), p. 62.

4. *History of the Red River Valley Past and Present by Various Writers,* 2 vols. (Grand Forks: Herald Printing Co., 1909).

5. SHSND A23.

6. N. Johanna Kildahl Papers, OGL 73. The text of her essay "Selfhelp" is printed in *Plainswoman,* IV, no. 4 (June 1981), pp. 8–9.

7. DeCou Family Papers, OGL 483.

8. Bowbells is in the northwestern corner of North Dakota near the Canadian border. Settled by cockneys, the town was named for the bells of the Church of Saint Mary Le Bow in London. Citations are to Adah Bickford Papers, OGL 466.

9. The original copy of Mattie Lampman's diary for 1898 is in Epping, North Dakota, at the Buffalo Trails Museum, whose director, Elmer Halvorson, acquired and transcribed it. Citations are to that transcription.

10. Ella Abbott's letter and the letters of Jane Freeland which follow are in Mosher Family Papers, OGL 463.

11. Cavileer, SHSND.

12. Mosher, OGL 463. The first settlers arrived at the present site of Lisbon, on the banks of the Cheyenne River, in 1878 and platted the town in 1880, naming it for the home cities of two of them: Lisbon, New York, and Lisbon, Illinois.

IV. "Don't Read Aloud"

1. Mosher, OGL 463. All references to Keyes, Pierce, and Mosher letters are to this collection.

2. John S. Haller and Robin M. Haller, *The Physician and Sexuality in Victorian America* (New York: W.W. Norton & Co., Inc., 1974), describe medical-social conditions for women in nineteenth-century America, emphasizing the medically fashionable "neurasthenic" diagnoses and treatments, the teachings of love and marriage manuals, and other lore that confronted women. Studies of women's health issues, particularly in the nineteenth century, include: Richard A. Cloward and Frances Fox Piven, "Hidden Protest: The Channeling of Female Innovation and Resistance" (*Signs,* 4, no. 4, pp. 651–69); Lorna Duffin, "The Conspicuous Consumptive: Woman as an Invalid," *The Nineteenth-Century Woman, Her Cultural and Physical World,* ed. Sara Delamont and Lorna Duffin (New York: Barnes & Noble, 1978); Carroll Smith-Rosenberg, "The Hysterical Woman: Sex Roles and Role Conflict in Nineteenth Century America," *Social Research* (1972), 39, pp. 552–78); Sheila Ryan Johansson, "Sex and Death in Victorian England," in Martha Vicinus, ed., *A Widening Sphere* (Bloomington: Indiana Univ. Press, 1977); Carl N. Degler, *At Odds: Women and the Family in America from*

the Revolution to the Present (New York: Oxford Univ. Press, 1980); and David J. Pivar, *Purity Crusade, Sexual Morality and Social Control 1868–1900* (Westport, Conn.: Greenwood Press, Inc., 1973).

3. This discussion is summarized from *Essays in the History of Medicine* (Chicago: Davis Lecture Committee, 1965), particularly Paul M. Angel, "The Hardy Pioneer: How He Lived in the Early Middle West," and Erwin Ackerknecht, "Diseases in the Middle West," from whom the quotation is taken.

4. Goodwater, OGL 368. All references to Goodwater and Kinkaid letters are to this collection.

5. On March 3, 1873, Congress passed "An Act for the Suppression of Trade in the Circulation of Obscene Literature and Articles of Immoral Use," which forbade sending through the mails "any drug or medicine or any article whatever for the prevention of conception," as well as importing, manufacturing, selling, possessing, or advertising such items through the mails. Many states passed similar laws, whose name honored the secretary of the New York Society for the Suppression of Vice, the Protestant reformer Anthony Comstock (1844–1915). For legislative history, see Peter Smith, "The History and Future of the Legal Battle over Birth Control," *Cornell Law Quarterly*, 49 (1963), 275–77; for state legislation see Robert William Haney, *Comstockery in America* (Boston, 1960). For a history of contraception, including the information summarized here, see John T. Noonan, Jr., *Contraception, A History of Its Treatment by the Catholic Theologians and Canonists* (Harvard Univ. Press, 1966), p. 412. It was not until 1965, in *Griswold* vs. *Connecticut* (381 US 479), that the Supreme Court said that it was unconstitutional to prohibit the use of contraception.

6. Alice B. Stockham, M.D., *Tokology, A Book for Every Woman* (Chicago: Sanitary Publishing Co., 1886).

7. *The People's Home Library, A Library of Three Practical Books: The People's Home Medical Book, The People's Home Recipe Book, the People's Home Stock Book,* compiled by R. C. Barnum (Cleveland, Ohio: R. C. Barnum Co., 1911). For the loan of this volume and of *Tokology* I am indebted to R. Joseph Adams, who, when a student at the University of North Dakota in 1979, brought these books to me from the library of his grandmother, Mary Adams, of Oakes, North Dakota.

8. John Engstad, M.D. 1858–1937. Medical Records, 1885–1890. SHSND B168.

9. Ann Douglas, *The Feminization of American Culture* (New York: Avon Books, 1977).

10. Elsie Hadley White's correspondence and diary are among the Frank White Papers, OGL 30, Box 2.

11. Sandra Gilbert and Susan Gubar, *The Madwoman in the Attic* (New Haven: Yale Univ. Press, 1979).

12. *War Diary of Luman Harris Tenney, 1861–1865,* Printed for Private Circulation by Frances Andrews Tenney (Cleveland, Ohio: Evangelical Publishing House, 1914). The letter-book is at the North Dakota Institute for Regional Studies, North Dakota State University, Fargo, Small Collections 240.

13. John Turner and C. K. Semling, *History of Clay and Norman Counties, Minnesota,* Vol. II (Indianapolis: 1918).

14. Paul E. Steiner has summarized these deaths and other casualties in *Disease in the Civil War, Natural Biological Warfare in 1861–1865* (Springfield, Ill.: Charles C. Thomas, 1968).

15. William Caldwell, "An Enquiry into the Condition of the Health of the Ex-Soldiers of the War of the Rebellion as a Class, and to what Extent the Vicissitudes of the War Contributed to Stamp upon Them a More or Less Permanent Disability," *Cleveland Medical Gazette* IV (1888–1889) pp. 140–51.

16. See Edward T. Devine and Lillian Brandte, *Disabled Soldiers and Sailors, Pensions and Training* (New York: Oxford Univ. Press, 1919) and William H. Glasson, *Federal Military Pensions in the United States* (New York: Oxford Univ. Press, 1918).

17. Haller and Haller, *The Physician and Sexuality in Victorian America,* and Barbara Ehrenreit and Dierdre English, *For Her Own Good, 150 Years of the Experts' Advice to Women* (New York: Doubleday, 1979).

18. Stephen Marcus, *The Other Victorians, A Study of Sexuality and Pornography in Mid-Nineteenth-Century England* (New York: 1974), pp. 1–33.

19. SHSND B168.

20. Leal Edmunds Papers, OGL 548, Box I, Folder 13.

V.   Viola Pierce, 1845–1919.

1. All references in this chapter are to Mosher Family Correspondence, OGL, 463.

VI.   Two Lives

1. Diary of Julia Gage Carpenter 1882–1904, OGL 520.

2. Bonanza farms were characteristically large, single-crop, mechanized, and run as businesses for profit. They did not combine home with livelihood, as do so-called family farms. Two events sparked the sudden development of bonanza farms in North Dakota: the bankruptcy of the Northern Pacific Railroad in 1873, and consequent eagerness to exchange land for securities, and the development of a new milling process for spring wheat in 1870, making Minneapolis a major grain market. By 1885 there were 90 bonanza farms in the Red River Valley of between 3,000 and 12,000 acres, and several cattle ranches in the west, all run by professional managers with a small permanent crew and seasonal migrant labor—precursors of agribusiness a hundred years later. Bonanza farming did not last long. By the late 1890s the weather turned drier, the price of wheat dropped, and an increasing immigrant population wanted small plots of farmland. See D. Jerome Tweton and Theodore B. Jelliff, *North Dakota, The Heritage of a People* (Fargo: North Dakota Institute for Regional Studies, 1976), pp. 82–88, and Hiram M. Drache, *The Day of the Bonanza: A History of Bonanza Farming in the Red River Valley of the North* (Fargo: 1964).

3. Ann Douglas, *The Feminization of American Culture* (New York: Avon Books, 1977).

4. Henry Mott Family Papers, OGL 521, includes four volumes of Henry

V. Mott's diary. Emma Mott's letter to Mrs. Thorpe that follows—presumably a draft copy—is in pencil on two sheets of lined paper inside one of the diary volumes.

5. For information about the history of the University of North Dakota, see Louis G. Geiger, *University of the Northern Plains, A History of the University of North Dakota 1883–1958* (Grand Forks: Univ. of North Dakota Press, 1958), and minute books of the State Board of Higher Education and *University Faculty Minutes* August 31, 1884 to June 9, 1906, in the University Archives.

6. *Western Womanhood,* vols. 1–5, July 1894, to December 1898, OGL 538. Xerox. Original SHSND.

VII.   Words of Love and Hunger

1. Rosellen Brown, "On Not Writing a Novel," *The American Poetry Review* (November/December 1979) p. 19.

2. Mary Dodge Woodward, *The Checkered Years* (Caldwell, Idaho: 1937); republished (Fargo, North Dakota: Cass County Historical Society, 1980).

3. Thomas McGrath, *Letter to an Imaginary Friend,* Parts I and II (New York: The Swallow Press, 1962, 1970) p. 194.